Words
of *Hope*
in Troubled Times

Romney Müller-Westernhagen

Mother Courage Natalina
with endless love from all of us...
your children and grandchildren.

Words of *Hope*
in Troubled Times

SELECTED SPEECHES AND WRITINGS

OF JOSÉ RAMOS-HORTA

LONGUEVILLE
MEDIA

First published by Longueville Media for
José Ramos-Horta 2018

Longueville Media
PO Box 205
Haberfield NSW 2045
www.longuevillemedia.com.au
T. +61 410 519 685

A CIP catalogue record for this book is available from the National Library of
Australia website: www.nla.gov.au

ISBN: 978-0-9876213-9-9

The lessons of the Jewish Holocaust

In 1939, a few months before the outbreak of World War II, Harry Truman read a passionate message from President Roosevelt to the National Meeting for Moral Rearmament, held in Washington [DC].

The same time as the conference delegates were listening and applauding President Roosevelt's moral speech, 900 Jewish refugees on a boat from Germany, anchored off Florida, were waiting for a decision from Washington as to whether they should find sanctuary in the United States or be sent back.

Finally, word came that their application for refugee status had been denied. The desperate refugees had not convinced the morally courageous delegates to the National Meeting for Moral Rearmament that they had a valid fear of persecution.

More than half a century after the Jewish Holocaust, and centuries after the genocide of the indigenous peoples of Australia and the Americas, the same attitude that has allowed these crimes to take place persists today.

- José Ramos-Horta, Nobel Lecture, Oslo 10 December 1996

Contents

My family in 1960, from left: me, baby Nuno, my mother Natalina, my eldest
sister Romana, brother Chico, sister Rosa, and brother Arsenio.

Biography

A clarification

This is not an autobiography. Maybe one day I will write one. However, I am acutely aware that human beings impaired by vanity and ego are too often tempted to polish details of their personal and professional lives, leaving out aspects which they are too ashamed to share with the public, while inflating their meager accomplishments. To date, this is a road I have chosen not to travel.

These introductory notes are meant only for those readers who might like a little more guidance through the maze of Timor-Leste's history, the multiple twenty-first century challenges faced by the international community, and the eternal unresolved dichotomy of war and peace, extreme poverty and scandalous opulence, compassion and avarice, courage and cowardice, justice and crime, and love and hate.

Humble beginnings in a forgotten European colonial outpost

A small force of hardened Portuguese seamen entrenched in this swamp, swarming with legions of malaria-carrying mosquitoes, and protected by coral walls and massive cannons pointing to the narrow entry, could easily sink any intruding Dutch ship. With this, in the mid-eighteenth century, my enterprising Portuguese ancestors decided to put down anchor and set up the capital of their new colony, Portuguese Timor. It was in this capital, Díli, that I was born a few years after World War II.

The Dutch had a habit of ambushing and stealing Portuguese possessions, spices, and territory. Latecomers to the maritime adventures, the Dutch didn't bother with braving the seas to connect with the Far East peoples and their exotic markets. They preferred instead to intercept Portuguese fleets that had braved the storms and were now coming home exhausted and famished, and overpower them.

Knowing that the opportunistic Dutch would attempt to take over the area, the Portuguese had shifted from the original capital, Lifau, in what is today's Oe-Cussi, in the Western half of Timor, to Díli, on the Eastern side.

The people of Portuguese Timor had just emerged, impoverished and traumatized, from World War II when Mother delivered me to the world. The first sounds and lights I saw were in Díli, then a village that we proudly called the capital city of Portuguese Timor. It had one or two cars. By the mid-'60s, when I first went to Díli, I counted 60–80 vehicles, including a few Bedford and Chevrolet trucks owned by local Chinese traders. I was in awe. In Laklubar, my own village, we celebrated the yearly arrival of a truck coming from Manatuto or Díli, bringing few supplies to the only Chinese shop in town. We would look at the Chinese driver with respect. No less respect was shown to his "ajudante", an extremely poorly paid Timorese who, the moment the truck stopped, would jump out to put a safe stop at the wheels, and later start the motor up again with few twists of the "manivela" (crank handle). I was amazed and impressed that this Timorese gentleman had such an important job and could travel to faraway places.

I grew up in isolated villages like Laklubar, Barike, Bualaka, Soibada, Atsabe, and Laga, as remote and impoverished as any of the poorest villages anywhere in Asia. In 1964, having completed elementary school with "distinction" in the oldest Catholic Mission School of Soibada, I was sent to Díli to further my studies.

Malaria was a fact of life then. Few families escaped the loss of at least a child to it. It took independence in 2002 for the disease to begin to be seriously tackled. It is now almost completely eradicated. This is what I would call one of our many "freedom dividends" since 2002.

Back then, Díli and the rest of the country would go dark when the God Sun set on the distant horizon. Now we have 24-hour electricity in more than 80 percent of the country, another "freedom dividend". Solar panels are freely distributed to the remotest households not connected to the main grid.

Like most of my many sisters and brothers, my mother did not deliver me with the help of a trained midwife. There was one hospital in the whole country and a handful of dedicated Portuguese doctors with few tools and medicine. Assisted by our dedicated and tireless nurses, they produced miracles and saved many lives. I dare to say that Portuguese doctors are among the best in the world. To this day I always feel very comfortable with them. Thanks to our Cuban friends, we now have close to 1000 doctors and several hospitals around the country – another "freedom dividend", thanks to generous help of the European Union.

We were 13 brothers and sisters with distinct personalities, always quarreling but loving each other; we drove our mother insane with our daily kids' fights. We had an older brother, Mano Antonio, and an older sister, Beatriz, from another mother. Both passed away; Antonio in 1992. Beatriz saw freedom in 1999 but died of heart attack a few years later. Brother Chico died in 2014 of a bacterial infection caught in Díli; stubborn as always, he went to see the doctor only when it was too late. We managed to have him flown to Darwin but he died at the operating table.

Today we are only six. It pains me profoundly when I think of those who departed, particularly how much they must have suffered and how they died.

My sister Mariazinha was the first to leave this world at 21 years old. It happened in the remote mountain village of Atabai on 18 December 1978, when an Indonesian Air Force OV10 Bronco aircraft strafed the location where she and many people were sheltered. This type of plane was marketed as the "work horse" of Rockwell Corp., an effective low-flying counterinsurgency plane commonly used in Vietnam.

The invasion of East Timor was either a poorly planned operation or the Indonesian army was ill prepared for a sustained operation miles from home, fighting a determined adversary. To the surprise of everyone, Timorese who had been trained by the Portuguese offered effective resistance, causing mounting casualties to the invading Indonesian forces. By 1977 deep concerns were developing in Washington that the invasion was becoming a military fiasco.

It was then that the Bronco aircraft and other lethal equipment, including napalm, were rushed to the Suharto regime by the U.S., at a time when violence was at its worst in faraway East Timor. Our beloved sister Mariazinha was probably the first casualty resulting directly from their actions. There were to be tens of thousands more as the air campaign intensified throughout 1977–79 with cluster bombs and napalm.

Mariazinha was buried by the humble people of Anon, Lolotoi, who looked after her gravesite until we recovered her well-preserved remains and reburied her in Díli next to other family members in 2003.

Our younger brothers Nuno and Gui were not so lucky, if luck includes being properly buried after one is killed, and the location marked for future identification and proper reburial. Caught and killed by the Indonesian military, Nuno and Gui's bodies were discarded somewhere, left to rot, or to be eaten by famished wild animals. All attempts to recover their remains have been fruitless.

My mother, Natalina, knew something about war. As a small girl, she lived through the Japanese occupation of the then Portuguese Timor, from 1942–45. Sadly, she lost her mother, a lady from the Remexio area, and all other family members except for a younger sister, Noemia.

When Indonesian forces invaded, she followed FRETILIN (Revolutionary Front for an Independent East Timor) fighters into the protective sacred rugged mountains, taking my brothers and sisters Nuno, Arsenio, Gui, Licinia, and Aida, and nephew Artur, with her. Arsenio was an innocent FRETILIN prisoner; Nuno became a brave FRETILIN unit commander.

After four years in FRETILIN-held areas, my mother, Arsenio, Aida, Licinia, and nephew Artur fell into an ambush by Indonesian forces and were taken to Díli. Once in Díli they were not bothered, despite my mother's inability to stay quiet, and her habit of openly badmouthing the Indonesian military at every opportunity. I would say to her: "Please, Mom, not every truth has to be spoken. Sometimes truth offends and upsets people, in which case don't say it, at least in public." Her preferred refrain was, and still is, "The truth is to be told".

To protect her from possible reprisals, family members would tell the Indonesians not to pay attention to Mrs. Natalina because she was always critical of everybody – the Portuguese, FRETILIN, of anyone in power. In short, "she is crazy, so please forgive her". Finally, after years of efforts on my part, and with the help of the U.S. State Department and U.S. Embassy in Jakarta, in 1988, my mother, Licinia, and an adopted child, Lindalva, were allowed to depart for Portugal.

Invasion, annexation, genocide, freedom

Under Portuguese colonization, Portuguese Timor was a quiet, undeveloped, forgotten colonial backwater, largely peaceful, except for few periods in its long history under Portugal. This all changed rapidly when the Carnation Revolution unfolded in Lisbon, bringing down the 50-year regime of Salazar, and with it, the Portuguese make-believe Overseas Empire. The new Portugal recognized the right to self-determination of

My brother Nuno (left), me second on right, and Ken
White a writer with Australia's *Northern Territory News*,
in September 1975. Nuno was killed by Indonesian troops
sometime in 1978, his remains still to be found.

Three of my siblings (L-R):
Aida, Gui, Licinia.

With beloved brother Gui, killed by
Indonesian troops sometime in 1978,
his remains still to be found.

all the colonized peoples and began to dismantle its vast colonial domain, including East Timor.

As far back as I can remember, I wanted to be a journalist, and I began a career in journalism, self-taught, in 1969, writing irrelevant news stories for a local weekly paper. I also did some radio. I ventured slightly into film, working with a Bolex Paillard camera, doing short news stories for Portuguese TV in faraway Lisbon.

Instead of pursuing journalism and cinema, on 20 May 1974, I, along with a small band of friends, founded the *Associação Social Democrata Timorense*, or ASDT. The word "Association" was an imposition of Portuguese authorities overseeing the registration of our brand new political parties, the first in our centuries-old country. It was not clear what was the difference between a *party* and an *association*, and I asked a Portuguese military officer why we couldn't just use the word "party". He gave me an unconvincing answer. Still finding our way, we simply went along with their demands.

In September 1974, Francisco Xavier do Amaral, Nicolau Lobato, Mari Alkatiri, Justino Mota and I, among others, decided to rename the ASDT, and rechristened it the *Revolutionary Front for an Independent East Timor* (FRETILIN), intended as a grassroots movement encompassing all Timorese, but retaining the founding principles of social democracy. We were naïve and romantic, with outsized dreams of a free and independent East Timor. One of the group, Nicolau Lobato, was a few years older, much smarter, and a natural charismatic leader. As children we had always deferred to Nicolau. Now again, he inspired awe in us with his mere presence.

Long before the Portuguese Carnation Revolution had opened the political landscape and debate in East Timor, I developed a keen interest in Indonesia, spending many hours reading about their struggle for independence against the Dutch, and the life and speeches of the great charismatic Sukarno. I befriended the Indonesian Consular staff in Díli, particularly the older Consul Pak Elias M. Tomodok. I even took Bahasa Indonesia lessons. Though naïve and inexperienced, it occurred to me as soon as we launched the ASDT that we should meet with Indonesian officials to explain our independence plans.

So, in June 1974, I began my journey to Jakarta, traveling via Kupang in Indonesian West Timor for a meeting with the then Governor, Brigadier General El Tari, whom I had known in a previous visit to Kupang, when I felt we had struck a good rapport. From Kupang I traveled to Bali and Jakarta, with very little money in my pocket.

In Jakarta I stayed in some cheap but comfortable lodging, cruised the city in *becaks*, Indonesian rickshaws, and a scooter with my friend Harry Kawilarang, a writer with the daily newspaper *Sinar Harapang*.

Somehow I managed to meet with Foreign Affairs Minister Adam Malik, a well-known figure in the international diplomatic circuit. I arrived at his official residence on the back of Kawilarang's scooter; not exactly a conventional vehicle for diplomats. Malik was warm and friendly. After one more meeting, without much effort, I managed to get from Pak Malik a very important letter where he stated Indonesia's official position *vis-à-vis* the question of Portuguese Timor. The letter stated Indonesia's recognition of the right of the people of Timor to self-determination, and assuring us that "whoever will govern in Timor after independence may rest assured that Indonesia will always strive to develop [a] strong relationship between the two countries".

Membership in ASEAN was also discussed with Pak Malik, who said he would welcome Timorese into his Foreign Ministry for training in diplomacy.

Back home, we engaged the other major party, the Timorese Democratic Union (UDT in its Portuguese acronym), aiming toward a coalition. By the end of January 1975, we had agreed to the coalition.

Sadly, this coalition did not last; by the end of May the UDT unilaterally abrogated the agreement. From then on, tensions between the leaders and followers of the two parties deepened, culminating in a brief civil war in August 1975.

FRETILIN gained the upper hand by the end of August and many thousands of UDT supporters and common people fled to Indonesian West Timor. The situation quickly calmed down throughout the country as FRETILIN imposed law and order and began to reestablish some semblance of a functioning administration.

However, our fate had long been sealed by Jakarta, as the Suharto regime never really entertained the possibility of an independent Timor-Leste. The formal assurances made by Pak Malik had been entirely false. Indonesian special forces were already positioned deep inside the territory as early as December 1974.

I walked down a dirt road in Balibo on the 12th October 1975, a dangerous undertaking as there were Indonesian forces and snipers nearby. Four days later five Australian journalists from Channels 7 and 9 were murdered.

Me with FRETILIN fighters in October 1975 in Balibo.

On 16 October 1975, five newsmen were working for Australian channels 7 and 9 in the small town of Balibo, several miles deep inside East Timor. While the men were aware that Indonesian troops were to mount an attack on the town of Balibo, they believed that, as journalists, they would not be considered military targets. Instead, they were brutally murdered. To this day, Jakarta refuses to acknowledge and apologize for the needless and cruel murder of these young journalists.

The group comprised two Australians, reporter Greg Shackleton, 29, and sound recordist Tony Stewart, 21; a New Zealander, Gary Cunningham, 27, cameraman for HSV-7 (Seven Network) in Melbourne; and two Britons, cameraman Brian Peters, 24, and reporter Malcolm Rennie, 29, both working for TCN-9 (Nine Network) in Sydney.

A sixth newsman, independent journalist from Darwin, Roger East, was murdered at Díli Harbour on 7 December 1975, his body dumped into the sea. His heroic and tragic story is ably portrayed by Anthony La Paglia in the film *Balibo*.

In 2006, the International Press Institute sent a letter to United Nations Secretary-General Kofi Annan to express concern that UN investigators had failed to fully investigate the deaths of the Balibo Five, as well as three other journalists killed in Timor-Leste in 1975 and 1999, and to request that the UN reopen their investigations. Robert Connolly, director of the 2009 film, said, "It's quite clear the journalists were murdered. The current Indonesian and Australian (government) point of view, that they were killed in crossfire, is quite frankly absurd. We seek out war criminals from World War II, so to dismiss calls for justice for the Balibo Five is crazy."

On 28 November 1975, we proclaimed the independent Democratic Republic of East Timor, in the hope that Indonesia would not invade a sovereign country.

I was appointed Minister for External Relations and Information. My first major diplomatic assignment was to travel to the United Nations in New York and other capitals to gain international support for our country. On 4 December 1975, we left for Darwin, and this being a small Australian outpost as isolated as Díli from the rest of the world, we had to fly down to Sydney and from there take the long route to Lisbon and New York.

Our departure from Díli was not simple. Australian authorities had banned flights into and out of East Timor. Thankfully, some Australian friends, Ken Fry MHR and David Scott (who have both since passed away), influenced the then Australian Foreign Minister Andrew Peacock to authorize a small chartered plane to fly into Dili and take us out. The group was Mari Alkatiri as Head of Mission, Rogério Lobato, and me. I was asked by the International Committee of the Red Cross to take along a young Portuguese called António José Coelho, whose father was in detention by FRETILIN, and I did.

Our cherished independence lasted nine days. U.S. President Gerald Ford and Secretary of State Henry Kissinger were in Jakarta on 6 December and gave the nod for the takeover of Timor-Leste.

Life in exile

Three days after we left for New York, Indonesian warships arrived on our shores. It was the beginning of a 24-year reign of terror. Indonesian soldiers began rounding up FRETILIN and non-FRETILIN members, and executed them on the docks of Dili. Women and children were not spared.

Little did I realize that my arrival in New York would mark the beginning of a 24-year exile. I was one of a handful of FRETILIN members who would not perish in the course of the occupation; with Mari Alkatiri, Roque Rodrigues, Rogério Lobato, Abilio Araujo, and the many FRETILIN activists already studying abroad, each in our varied activities we began the long, lonely mission of speaking for those fighting back home. We pleaded our right to self-determination at every international forum that I and/or my comrades could attend, invited or uninvited.

At 25 years of age, sporting a thick Afro hairdo, I was the youngest person ever to address the UN Security Council, convened at the request of Portugal, as the legally recognized Administering power of Timor-Leste. In response to the invasion, the Security Council adopted a unanimous resolution demanding the "withdrawal without delay" of Indonesian forces from East Timor.

The resolution gave me the naïve hope that soon we would be back in East Timor. It was to be my first lesson in international hypocrisy, in the empty talk and inaction that sadly still characterizes the UN in many aspects.

In the words of a diplomat referring to the Bosnia situation in the 1990's, the UN General Assembly and Security Council adopted "truckloads of resolutions" that were never meant to be implemented on the ground.

Nicolau Lobato and Xavier Amaral, 1975.

Representing Fretilin before the Decolonization Committee on the question of East Timor, 20 August, 1982, United Nations, New York.

From 1975 to 1999 my country was hell on Earth. One third of the population perished under the Indonesian occupation – executed, "disappeared", or starved by forcible displacement. Torture centers arose in towns. Countless women were raped.

With a ban on foreign journalists, few in the world knew what was happening on our small island. Yet at home, the Timorese were looking to us as their last hope.

We had no friends in the power centers in the West; they all sided with Indonesia. This was the norm during the Cold War era. The law of might prevailed over principles. Portugal, not a major player, was a lonely voice, a noble exception. Angola, Brazil, Cape Verde, Guinea-Bissau, Mozambique, and São Tome and Príncipe championed our cause for 24 years, even when our struggle was labeled a "lost cause".

Starting with no allies, the mistaken perception that FRETILIN were a communist threat, and with the West aligned behind Indonesia, I traveled constantly – lobbying governments, creating networks of human rights supporters, and telling the story of our people to anyone who would listen.

With little, and at times, no financial support, I often slept on the couches of Timor activists, and had many free meals from friends around the world. I was often touched and overwhelmed by the dedication of Timor-Leste supporters in many countries who devoted decades of hard campaigning for our cause; their cause as well.

Nobel Peace Prize, referendum and freedom

In December 1996 Bishop Carlos Belo and I were awarded the Nobel Peace Prize for our work "towards a just and peaceful solution to the conflict in East Timor".

The Santa Cruz massacre of hundreds of young protesters on 12 November 1991, and subsequent international media coverage of this carnage, coverage that was possible thanks to the enormous courage of three journalists – Max Stahl, Amy Goodman, and Allan Nairn – the Nobel Peace Prize and the Southeast Asia financial crisis of 1997–98 that toppled the Suharto regime were decisive contributing elements to our freedom.

More than 20 years of hard work paid off when, following protracted dialogue mediated by the United Nations, an agreement on a referendum on self-determination was reached in New York between the UN, Indonesia, and Portugal.

Apart from the factors mentioned earlier, UN Secretary-General Kofi Annan's determined pursuit of a resolution of the conflict as he took office in 1997 was also decisive. Here is a lesson of what the UN can potentially do to prevent conflicts and to resolve them when there is a determined and respected leadership at UNHQ.

The UN has not prevented, and cannot and will not be able prevent, every conflict from erupting into full-scale war, or to successfully mediate between factions in every war, but a visionary and credible Secretary-General, supported by dedicated staff and Member States, may at times produce results and meet our expectations.

Timor-Leste is a case study in failures and success. It is interesting to note that current UN Secretary-General António Guterres was Prime Minister of Portugal during the critical year of 1999 when the fate of Timor-Leste was being decided. Bill Clinton told me in 1999 that one leader who most touched and convinced him that the U.S. must act was Prime Minister António Guterres. But it would be unfair to ignore the role played by Portuguese President Jorge Sampaio, a man of equally great intellect, moral values, and political courage who, for years, championed the cause of Timor-Leste.

Despite the very narrow and precarious window of opportunity that existed in 1999, the UN managed in an extremely tight timeframe of three months to undertake a referendum across the whole of East Timor and in many cities overseas, enabling a vast majority of eligible Timorese to cast a vote. When the vote came in with more than 80 percent in favor of independence, armed militia gangs trained by the Indonesian military were unleashed.

Eighty-five percent of our buildings and homes were burned down; every shop, bank, and school. Hundreds of thousands of Timorese were forcibly displaced internally, and many forcibly displaced to Indonesia. In a systematic effort to bring the country to its knees, the buffalo used to work the fields were slaughtered or stolen, trucks stolen or disabled, and fishing nets burned.

During that crucial week I was shuttling back and forth between New York and Washington, spending endless hours and sleepless nights on the phone, traveling, and pleading the cause of our people. One night, a phone call came – from the White House, telling me President Bill Clinton wanted to see me.

Never in 24 years of our lonely struggle had I received a call from even an assistant at the State Department. A call from the White House? The President of United States wanted to see me? This phone call meant that the U.S. would support a UN Security Council-mandated international security force to be immediately deployed to Timor-Leste.

For this to happen, Indonesia's acquiescence had to be obtained. Kofi Annan, the Thai Foreign Minister Surin Pitsuwan for ASEAN, the late South Korean President Kim Dae-Jung, working closely with Bill Clinton and Prime Minister Keizō Obuchi of Japan, were able to persuade Indonesia to agree to a UN Security Council-authorized force to be deployed to Timor-Leste, and for Indonesian forces to withdraw.

For all the international support, it was in Jakarta that critical decisions had to be made. The extremely difficult decisions from a domestic perspective cannot be underestimated. Indonesia's interim President B.J. Habibie was not the "strongman" of Indonesia that Suharto had been. He was presiding over a country in social and political turmoil, with daily street demonstrations, and ethnic and religious violence. In this environment, after thousands of Indonesian military deaths in the 24-year-long conflict in East Timor, could the proud and notoriously ruthless Indonesian army simply be told that they must vacate the island?

The answer was, yes. Regional and international diplomacy succeeded and Indonesia began to disengage from East Timor. Shortly afterwards, a multinational force led by Australia began to arrive on the island's shores with units from around the world, to end the rampage and prevent a genocide. The 1994 Rwanda genocide and the UN's failure to prevent it was very much on Bill Clinton and Kofi Annan's minds.

Timorese men, women, and children who had been in hiding began to emerge, coming down from the mountains. There was singing, dancing, and praying in the streets. Our people were finally free. At least 200,000 people who had been forcibly displaced to Indonesia during the post-referendum rampage were coming home.

In December 1999, I returned home for the first time in 24 years. I was extremely humbled to be welcomed as a hero by tens of thousands of fellow Timorese from towns and villages across the country.

A UN Administration was set to run the country with full powers, executive, legislative, and judiciary. It was led by one of UN's most experienced diplomats, Sérgio Vieira De Mello. The UN had an extremely tight timeframe of just two years, from October 1999 to May 2002, imposed by the Security Council, to build a nation and a democracy from the ashes of conflict.

The UN was the subject of much criticism from many quarters during its mission in East Timor. In fairness, neither the UN nor any manmade institution could have done more in such a tight timeframe. It did what it was mandated to do, and did it well.

At the stroke of midnight on 20 May 2002, Secretary-General Kofi Annan, with Sérgio Vieira De Mello at his side, lowered the UN flag and turned the reins of the country over to the newly elected President and Parliament of our nation, now named Timor-Leste. We became the world's newest democracy.

An estimated 100,000 people were at the celebration, including Bill Clinton and other leaders from around the world. Indonesia's new President, Megawati Sukarnoputri, attended the event. When I announced her presence there was an extraordinary emotional applause.

Sérgio Vieira De Mello left Timor-Leste on 21 May 2002. I intended to be at the airport to bid him farewell. I kept asking one of my non-Timorese Personal Assistants about Sérgio's departure time. I was inaugurating a local school when I asked again and was told Sérgio was already in the plane. I was mortified for not being at the airport to bid him farewell. It was a complete failure on our side. We should have organized a full military and protocol honors at his departure.

Sérgio had been appointed High Commissioner for Human Rights when we met one Saturday morning in early March 2003 in the charming "Vieille Ville" of Geneva, and over some renversé (the Geneva version of white coffee), we conversed about Timor-Leste, his new mission as High Commissioner for Human Rights and his fateful assignment to Iraq, meant to be "temporary" – a six-month assignment after which he would return to Geneva.

Sérgio was very ambivalent about his assignment to Iraq, but as he told me, "A request by the Secretary-General is an order" that he would not decline. But Sérgio wanted to finally quietly settle after three decades on overseas deployments.

Sérgio and more than 20 UN staff were killed on 20th August in a terrorist attack in Baghdad.*

I was appointed Minister for Foreign Affairs and Cooperation and I began the arduous process of setting up the Foreign Ministry and starting a diplomatic agenda to begin the process of building formal relationships with governments around the world. It forced me to be absent from my country up to nine months of the year.

A riddle circulating in the country aptly described my peripatetic life: "What is the difference between God and Ramos-Horta? God is everywhere, including in East Timor. Ramos-Horta is everywhere, except in Timor-Leste." A less kind joke said: "There is a mistake in Ramos-Horta's title: He is not the Minister of Foreign Affairs; he is the Minister of many affairs in foreign countries".

On 10 July 2006, following the resignation of then Prime Minister Mari Alkatiri amid civil protest, I was sworn in as Prime Minister of Timor-Leste. I stepped into the post following weeks of tensions and violence that had culminated in Alkatiri's resignation.

The main cause of the 2006 crisis was the firing of newly recruited 600 soldiers, all from the Western districts of Timor-Leste. They were fired by the then Head of the Armed Forces, Mr. Taur Matan Ruak. Dr. Alkatiri was blamed for their dismissal, but in reality, he had been against this decision by the Head of the Armed Forces. The 600, who were unarmed, were joined by another group of soldiers and had broken away from the army, taken to the mountains with arms, and begun to mobilize gangs to burn homes and create havoc.

On assuming the position of Prime Minister, and working with then President and former guerrilla leader Xanana Gusmão, we began to restore peace and return the displaced to their homes. We worked to end the conflict, and to put our country back on the path to its hard-won peace.

Healing the wounds of the heart

In 2007 I was elected President of the country by a 70 percent margin. I was sworn in as the second President of Timor-Leste on 20 May 2007. On 11 February 2008, I found that standing up against violence comes at a price, when I was critically injured in an assassination attempt by a group of renegade soldiers.

While painful for me, the event proved fortuitous for my country, acting as a catalyst for the last of the rebels to come down out of the mountains and turn in their arms. The renegade soldiers waited until my return from Darwin hospital in order to lay down their arms in my presence.

The country has since remained at peace.

At the service of the United Nations

At the stroke of midnight of 19 May 2012, I formally ended my term as President.

A few months later I accepted an invitation by Secretary-General Ban Ki-moon to head the United Nations Integrated Peace-Building Office in Guinea-Bissau, a country so unstable that since independence in 1974, no President had finished his term. On 12 April 2012, democratic elections had been violently interrupted by a military coup, one of many that had set back the country again and again since its independence in 1974.

In partnership with ECOWAS, the Economic Community of West African States, the African Union, the European Union, and with strong support from Timor-Leste, in cash, in kind, and with election experts, we oversaw fair, democratic, and transparent elections that returned Guinea-Bissau to Constitutional order.

On 31 October 2014, I was appointed Chair of HIPPO, the High-Level Independent Panel on UN Peace Operations. On 16 June 2015 I presented the panel's report containing detailed recommendations on the reform of the UN Peace Operations to Secretary-General Ban Ki-moon.

On 13 September 2017, the Secretary-General announced the establishment of a High-Level Advisory Board on Mediation. I was pleased to be invited to sit on this Board, which provides the Secretary-General with advice on mediation initiatives and backs specific mediation efforts around the world. Most recently, on 26 September 2017, I was invited by Mr. Miroslav Lajčák, the President of the General Assembly of the United Nations, to be on a new team of external advisors to advise him on how best to advance his priorities for the General Assembly's 72nd Session.

My life has taken many turns since I departed my beloved Timor in December 1975. The honor of being able to serve my people, the UN, and the world, even in a very limited way, has sincerely been a privilege.

I have crisscrossed the globe countless times, speaking on war and peace, poverty and sustainable development, and climate change, to inspire young people and those struggling for peace and justice, sometimes meeting with individuals or small groups of people eager to listen and seeking advice and endorsement. Many thank me for my messages of hope where there is despair. Some have told me that my words changed their lives. Not all agree with some of my assertions, but I always try to be frank and honest.

I refuse to pretend that I can offer answers to every question and solutions to every problem in the world. Greater minds than I, with far more power at their disposal, have not been able to resolve many of world's crying tragedies.

So, who am I, and what can I do? So many travels and speeches, and to what end? To what good, I often ask myself. The world seems to be getting worse, not better.

When many in my country or in Guinea-Bissau thank me for having positively influenced their lives, I am consoled that while I might not have solved all the world's great problems, I have inspired and made a few people happier. Maybe that's what really matters – that we do make a difference in the lives of real people through our words and deeds.

Preface: The State of Our World

A reflection on the State of the World saddens and worries me deeply. Yet, the Twenty-first Century offers us all a unique opportunity to coalesce around common global interests. We cannot give up hope.

Anywhere we turn, any day of the week, we read about violence and death, immense suffering of the innocent, of children and youth, of countries imploding violently along ethnic and religious lines, or successful model multilateral bodies such as the European Union rather than consolidating regional partnership risk unraveling.

Home to half of humanity, Asia remains a very promising continent; however, I also believe that our region is the most dangerous of all, with the most intractable maritime and land border disputes and the largest number of nuclear-armed countries.

Serious security challenges are piling up: nuclear proliferation, the volatile Korean Peninsula, South China Sea disputes, the India-Pakistan standoff over Kashmir, China and India territorial disputes, continuing wars ravaging Afghanistan and Pakistan, escalating ethnic and religious conflict in Myanmar threatening to spread and invite extremist external involvement, unresolved insurgencies in Southern Thailand and the Philippines, and the ever present threat of ISIS-inspired sympathizers and militants across Asia are some of the more silent challenges our region faces.

In addition, we must not forget the environmental cost of the weight of half of humanity on Asian soil; every day, more than four billion people extract the most precious of all Earth's resources – water. Water is becoming a scarce commodity; industrial waste is poisoning our rivers, lakes, and seas; firewood consumption and unscrupulous commercial logging have reduced our forests to alarming levels; the Himalayan glaciers are melting. A complete list of challenges could still go on and on. How can we remain optimistic about Asia's future?

At 50, ASEAN leaders and peoples should rightly celebrate the impressive progress achieved so far in our region, made possible only by the stabilizing role of its regional association which has been successfully promoting peace, economic development, and regional integration. But, at 50, they must also show concern and resolve in addressing the security challenges that may severely undermine ASEAN unity and progress.

While I have the fullest admiration for Kofi Annan, a true world's Statesman who has produced a comprehensive and balanced report on the situation in the Rakhine region, I would have thought that Myanmar would have sought assistance from ASEAN to help resolve the conflict. Unfortunately, there have been some unusual public and acrimonious exchanges between Myanmar and some fellow ASEAN officials and this surely must have cancelled out ASEAN as mediator.

ASEAN does have outstanding former – and serving – leaders and diplomats with deep knowledge of the problems facing Myanmar and the region as a whole, with a solid track record in the mediation of conflicts in the region.

Extremist Islamic-inspired insurgencies in Myanmar, Southern Thailand, and Southern Philippines should worry all. Deep divisions in Thai society continue, unresolved, exposing lack of national wisdom and resolve; and it also exposes the weaknesses in ASEAN institutional mechanisms on conflict prevention and mediation.

The BRICS (Brazil, Russia, India, China, and South Africa), once a formidable political and economic bloc, is gasping for air, at least temporarily moribund.

The euphoria of the Arab Spring that began in Tunisia has been drowned in the seas of violence in the streets of Egypt, Libya, and Syria. Turkey, once considered an example of how modern Islam can absorb and live with democratic political pluralism, has descended towards dictatorship.

World leaders cannot be proud of their failure to end the barbarities in Syria and South Sudan, the two most deadly conflicts raging in the world. They are by no means the only two conflicts ravaging entire countries and peoples.

South Sudan is being torn apart by tribal warfare in a shocking scale approaching genocide, and there is real risk of renewed conflict in the Democratic Republic of Congo. There is no end in sight to the conflicts in Mali, Darfur, Burundi, CAR, Nigeria, Afghanistan, and to tensions between the two regional rivals, India and Pakistan.

A nuclear-armed North Korea seems inevitable. I believe that the other nuclear powers must begin to get used to the idea that they will have to share this 'privilege' with the other guy in the block. Who is to blame? China? It is an absurdity to suggest that it is in the interest of a major regional power to share nuclear status with a neighbor; this is as much an absurdity as to suggest that China has real influence on the North Korean regime. The real culprits are all the nuclear powers, who have not had the statesmanship to de-escalate nuclear arsenals and dismantle them all.

In my view, the powers that be, must continue to strive for dialogue with North Korea, being an unassailable fact that dialogue is the only means available to deescalate tensions and prevent a war.

Wherever and whenever possible we must explore every opportunity to expand technical, scientific, medical, cultural, and trade cooperation with the North Korea, as much as we all abhor the horrendous nature of the regime and its total suppression of freedom.

The three major East Asian economies, China, Japan and the Republic of Korea, must engage in dialogue to resolve the painful legacies of the past and enhance cooperation at all levels. They must not continue to be hostage to the past.

Japan must do more to show 'deep remorse' about the pain and destruction the Japanese Imperial Army caused to the peoples of Korea, China, and much of Asia. If Japan wishes the people of China and Korea to believe in its sincerity, it should tell the full truth about the crimes perpetrated by the Japanese army without obfuscation or adulteration.

A strong partnership between the three Northeast Asian countries and common approach in managing the security challenges in the region, patient and sustained dialogue may induce North Korea to feel less threatened and thus more open to compromise on its nuclear programs.

I believe that the Silk Road Economic Belt and the Twenty-first Century Maritime Silk Road supported by the Asian Infrastructure Investment Bank are visionary concepts that may promote Asia and world's prosperity and peace. It is, in fact, a Chinese Twenty-first Century version of the Marshal the Plan in a much grander scale.

In view of the historical and deep-seated mutual suspicions and rivalries, these ambitious and visionary concepts articulated by China are viewed with suspicion by many in Asia. It is incumbent upon China as an aspiring benign global power, to reassure the skeptics that there is no ingrained hegemonic agenda in this strategy that aims to connect peoples and nations through trade, and in the process promotes world solidarity and peace.

My humble advice to the Republic of Korea, Japan, and other regional powers: there are more than enough nuclear devices in Asia to decimate hundreds of millions of people and send Asia back to the Stone Age. Hence, I do not counsel anyone in the region to bet on the nuclear option in response to the near certainty that North Korea will be a nuclear power in the very foreseeable future.

As the two largest economies and mightiest military powers of the world, the US and China should cooperate to enhance dialogue and cooperation in the Northeast Asia region and in Asia in general. The US should not seek opportunistic alliances to *contain* China, but rather, the two countries should pursue dialogue and explore partnership mechanisms to contribute to lessen tensions in the Korean Peninsula, South China Sea, and in the whole of Asia.

Barack Obama is a great orator but for this he didn't win the prestigious Booker Literary Prize. He won instead something better, a Nobel Peace Prize, literally for two major speeches, one delivered in Prague, where he promised to work towards nuclear disarmament, and the other in Cairo, where he extended a hand of friendship to Arabs and Muslims.

On the promise to de-escalate the nuclear arms race, Obama did exactly the opposite. He presided over the beginning of a 30-year program of modernizing the US nuclear arsenal. On relations with the Arabs and Muslims, one cannot blame him for the debacle of the Arab Spring and rising extremism. On Cuba, Obama did what he could: a historic visit to Cuba while Fidel Castro was still alive. But the most unfair draconian sanctions ever imposed on a relatively poor country by the most powerful and greediest of all continues.

Only a few years ago we read about 'Africa on the move', as Africa's potential for growth is real and is still possible, as the continent of one billion people, young and increasingly educated, holds the riches of the world, from agricultural potential to valuable strategic minerals. But powerhouses like South Africa, Nigeria, and Angola are facing serious challenges to their growth and stability. Depressed commodity prices have benefited importing countries, like China and India, and all other non-oil-producing countries, but have caused havoc in the ministries of planning and financing of the commodity-producing countries.

The rich and powerful continue nonchalantly to manufacture and export weapons of mass destruction and profit from the wars they fuel. Not surprisingly, one industry that has not suffered the effects of the US-led 2008–2009 economic and financial crisis is the weapons industry.

We see these weapons being indiscriminately used by States and non-State entities in the wars in Syria, Iraq, Libya, Yemen, Mali, Central African Republic, Congo (DRC), South Sudan, Sudan, Afghanistan, and so on.

Who are the 'international community'? Leaders of nations, bloated and often self-serving bureaucracies of the international bodies like the UN and its many agencies, funds, and programs, the World Bank, regional and national banks, the corporate sector, the opulent Churches of the world, the billionaires of the Americas, Europe, Asia, and Africa who possess scandalous fortunes obtained mostly fraudulently. We are this amorphous international community who have mostly failed to root out systemic poverty, and failed the people of Syria and South Sudan, among others.

We have witnessed the holding of expensive Summits on Poverty, the Millennium Development Goals (MDGs) and now the Sustainable Development Goals (SDGs); we know of the unfulfilled pledges by the rich industrialized countries in increasing contributions to overseas development assistance (ODA). Commendable exceptions: the UK, Norway, Sweden.

Overseas development assistance has been literally obliterated since 2009; emergency humanitarian needs are not being met. But yet hundreds of billions of dollars were – and are still – easily found to rescue exposed European banks whose CEOs pay themselves scandalously high salaries and bonuses.

Portuguese, Spanish, Greek, and Irish workers and middle classes were force-fed draconian austerity through higher taxes and social services cuts to pay for the debt incurred by the banks of the few scandalously rich

CEOs, the same cabal of people who, through greed and incompetence, mismanaged these same financial institutions in the first place.

A sclerotic generation still harboring illusions of a *Great* Britain, led by a secondhand car salesman, a certain Mr. Farage, led the 'leave the EU' charge. The older English men put all the blame of the problems of their once mighty Empire on the EU and voted for Brexit. The young and educated, exposed to the vibrant cultural diversity of Europe and the world, the Irish and the Scottish, wanted to stay in a stronger EU.

I have long been an admirer of the EU. It has shown genuine solidarity and has invested more in the developing world than any group of countries, received more immigrants and refugees, and allocated more generously for global humanitarian efforts.

Maybe it expanded and pursued political and economic integration too fast, particularly after the end of the Cold War.

The EU and the US pushed their luck too far in their relations with their giant Eastern neighbor, Russia. For many years, observing Europe-Russia relations from afar and up close, I could not understand why NATO saw the need to expand its borders right to Russia's gates. And I don't understand what additional US troops and hardware deployed close to Russia's borders may achieve.

In the US, someone not a fan of multilateralism, the UN, EU, and NATO, who disdains immigrants, refugees, Mexicans, Arabs, and Muslims, now holds the nuclear button and began to wreck international treaties (TPP, Climate Change, NAFTA), encourages the breakup of the European Union, and dismisses both the United Nations and NATO, the North Atlantic Treaty Organization, which has been providing the key framework arrangements for security in Europe and with North America.

The cauldron of the Middle East wars and the endemic poverty plaguing much of the African Continent have uprooted more than 60 million people, and of these, many have sought, and are seeking, shelter and a new life in the *old* Continent – Europe.

Some European leaders and people have shown great heart in welcoming their fellow human beings fleeing wars and deprivation, but, understandably, other European leaders and communities have been less generous, reacting often out of ignorance and fear. Let me clarify that while I use the word *understandably*, I am not condoning the xenophobic mindset of many in Europe; I am simply saying that in any given society, different people act or react differently in similar circumstances.

The US, Canada, the Latin American States, Australia, and New Zealand are very much a product of the religious wars and extreme poverty in Europe that prompted the greatest movement of people ever, in previous centuries. Now, we are living witnesses to an ongoing and irreversible demographic transformation of Europe, a continuation or repetition of the massive movements of people caused by wars and poverty in Europe that, in previous centuries, prompted millions of Europeans to flee to the Americas.

No matter how high and thick our national walls may be, there will be no fortress Europe or fortress US that can stem the tide of people fleeing wars and poverty. The demographic transformation of Europe from a predominately aging Judeo-Christian continent to a vibrant and younger, multiethnic, multi-religious, and multi-culture Europe is unstoppable. These phenomena are not always entirely peaceful, and, sadly, many will suffer immensely, but with wisdom, determination, and compassion, Europe would emerge rejuvenated and stronger in the long run.

The social, economic and political scenarios for Europe do not look promising. We can only pray that Turkey will not cause a refugee and political Armageddon by unleashing the refugees it is hosting into Europe.

The Austrians, Dutch, French, and Germans have stopped what seemed to be an inexorable political takeover of Europe by extreme right-wing demagogues who nevertheless continue to stoke fears and racial hatred. Racially motivated incidents and violence have also risen dramatically in the UK after the Brexit referendum.

Will there be wisdom and realization that Europe is staring at an abyss and there is an urgent need for all to step back and engage in a grand dialogue on the challenges Europe and the world face?

Not all is bleak in the world, though. While there is gang violence and deaths in some Latin American cities and towns, by and large Latin America is free from the extreme ideologies, religions, and ethno-nationalism that plague much of the Middle East, parts of Asia, and parts of Africa.

Timor-Leste is a country of only a little more than one million. We survived and prevailed through centuries of colonial rule, occupation by the Japanese Imperial Army, recolonization by Portugal, and occupation by Indonesia.

In victory, in 2002, we celebrated our freedom and honored our former adversaries; we forgave our captors and tormentors without demanding or waiting for an apology; we rejected an international tribunal to try those who committed war crimes and crimes against humanity.

Those who tortured and killed did not apologize for their crimes, and they continue in denial, unable to summon enough courage and accept their part of guilt. But this is now their problem; they live with their crimes on their conscience, the screams and faces of their victims still haunting them, every day, every night.

We are now free and refuse to be hostage to a tortured past, hostage to anger and hatred.

I had the unique privilege of chairing the High Level Independent Panel on the United Nations Peace Operations (2014–2015), appointed by the Secretary-General Ban Ki-moon, endeavoring to deliver a better, more effective, and credible multilateral system anchored on the UN.

My colleagues and I, a 15-member panel, produced a comprehensive report with more than 100 recommendations on how to improve overall the UN's role in conflict prevention and mediation, more agile and effective deployment of peace-enforcers, and on sustaining peace.

We also made far-reaching recommendations on improving leadership and coordination at the UN Secretariat.

I am not a romantic pacifist who believes that force must never be used. Sometimes, the use of force is necessary when it is the only option available to prevent genocide. Bosnia, Rwanda, the Cambodian Killing Fields are just some reminders that non-use of force to prevent genocide and mass atrocities is the moral equivalent to complicity.

However, the preferred option should always be prevention of conflicts, dialogue and mediation to settle disputes; and when these are actively, creatively, and patiently exercised in a timely fashion, they often produce results.

National actors, rather than external, are best placed to engage in conflict prevention processes at every level, from community to national levels. External actors are not the best substitute, and should not be the first responders; however, in some situations, credible threat of sanctions, including use of force, may help domestic actors to engage in meaningful dialogue and resolve their differences peacefully.

Take the tragic example of Syria. I sum up in few words three main obstacles: overestimating one's own power, underestimating the adversary's, and miscalculation.

In my view all have erred: the Assad regime erred for not making real efforts in reaching out to those wanting more freedom; the opposition erred in overestimating their own power, refusing to negotiate with the regime, demanding instead its resignation; and underestimating the staying power of the Assad regime and failing to understand the fears of the Allawite minority in power that inspire its actions; Europeans and Americans who underestimated the Assad regime, misread the complexities of the so-called Arab Spring, and, euphoric with their pyrrhic air campaign against Muhamar Ghadafi of Libya, believed they could arrange another regime change. All miscalculated, and we all know the consequences of this miscalculation.

Europe and Russia cannot continue to drift apart. This vast region with endless resources and highly motivated and educated people, working in honest and innovative partnership for peace and progress, can transform the world; there is more in common between Europe and Russia than what divides them.

The US should also rethink its relationship with Russia and China, treating them as equals and not as second-class powers.

Whether the US like it or not, China is inexorably emerging as a Twenty-first Century global power. This inevitably leads to fears among China's neighbors, and this being the case, it is China, an aspiring world power, that must behave in a responsible manner, and thus reassure its neighbors that it does not promote hegemony and domination.

The world should not fear China, but China should fear itself: it has overwhelming challenges on its hands, a social time bomb in a population living longer, potentially with tens of millions on wheelchairs and with no social network to care for them.

And Chinese are fast becoming a heartless society towards the elderly; stories abound of aged parents and grandparents abandoned in towns and villages across the vast countryside and of doors shut in their faces as they come to the megacities and knock at the door of a son or a daughter.

The US replenishes its population with tens of millions of people from across the globe who then provide the children and youth that are necessary for a superpower to remain a superpower. But China (and, for that matter, Japan and Korea) has the lowest population growth in the world. They remain obsessed with 'racial purity' and are not able to produce enough new citizens for their economy.

China can be a new global power that does not have to possess an awesome military machine like the US. It can be a smart, benign superpower, relying more on soft diplomacy than on military hardware to convince, not to coerce. But China is still very far off being a global soft power. China's government has polished pro-Third-World speeches but the legions of Chinese trade officials and workers who descend on mineral- or forest-rich countries are not engendering much admiration and loyalty.

Chinese traders dump hundreds of millions of dollars of junk products all over the world and are killing local small businesses in poorer countries.

If China wishes to be a truly benign global power that conquers hearts and mind – and win friends and allies – it has to seriously rethink its development aid policies and action, trade, and loan practices, improve the quality of the aid, and restrain its voracious merchants from looting the rich seas, forests, and rare minerals from peoples across the world.

For too many in China and Russia, and indeed in many other countries, the US is the real evil. Its actions are always suspect of being inspired by strategic hegemonic goals and selfish economic interests. This is an exaggeration, although it is understandable as they view the US through the prism of past policies of invasions and support for countless corrupt dictators.

In Latin America, many remember decades of US imperialism, with marine landings, CIA operations, embargoes, and sanctions against Latin American popular regimes and interventions on the side of the most corrupt and oppressive oligarchs.

I have a balanced, rational view of the US. American society has produced thousands of great achievers, scientists, and millionaires whose roots can be traced back to impoverished towns, ghettos, and villages around the world.

The US was a force for good when it lost hundreds of thousands of young men and women to save Europe from Nazism. The reconstruction and prosperity of Europe after World War II owed much to the US. Without the mighty US deterrence, the Soviet Union would have marched into Western Europe and elsewhere in the world, as it did try –

Somalia, Ethiopia, Southern Africa, Central America are some examples of Soviet attempts at gaining influence and footprint.

The Soviet Union was not a benevolent power and it was determined to expand its doctrine and spheres of influence, but its empire building collapsed under its own rot: tyranny, corruption, falsehoods, incompetence.

The US Army is the only army in the world that, at a moment's notice, can deploy engineers, medics, nurses, sniffing dogs, heavy equipment, water treatment facilities, and so on to assist peoples' suffering from cyclones, tsunamis, earthquakes, whether in nearby Haiti or in faraway shores like Pakistan and Indonesia. US military have done so countless times.

The Twenty-first Century offers us a chance, a unique chance, to coalesce around common global interests – to reverse the nefarious consequences of climate change, manage clean water reserves that are becoming a rare commodity, save our polluted rivers, lakes, and seas, replenish the depleted fish stock, eliminate extreme poverty and hunger, and de-escalate tensions on the Korean Peninsula and South China Sea, and between India and Pakistan, India and China. If we were to spend less on armament, we would be able to spend more on education, health, and food security for all.

These are matters of survival for all and yet there hasn't been enough understanding of the urgency of addressing these challenges. Only when they are understood and felt by all will there be concerted global action.

Jose Ramos-Horta
Díli, 16 November 2017

Early Proposals for Peace in East Timor

A Peace Plan to Resolve the Conflict in Occupied East Timor

Brussels, 23 April 1992

Addressing the Human Rights Subcommittee of the European Parliament, in Brussels, in April 1992, I outlined a three-phase Peace Plan that would peacefully and relatively smoothly resolve the festering violent conflict in East Timor.

Phase One (one to two years to be implemented)

The CNRM does not pretend that this plan is the only blueprint for a peaceful resolution of the East Timor conflict. However, it believes that it at least can be the basis for discussion by all parties.

This phase of the talks must focus on achieving:

- Immediate end to all armed activities in East Timor
- Reduction of Indonesian troop presence to a maximum of 1000 within a six-month period
- Removal of all heavy weapons, tanks, helicopters, combat aircraft, long-range artillery
- Immediate and unconditional release of all political prisoners
- Reduction by 50% of Indonesian civil servants in East Timor
- Stationing in the territory of UN specialized agencies, such as UNICEF, UNDP, WHO, FAO
- A comprehensive census of the population
- Establishment of an independent Human Rights Commission under the Catholic bishop

- Lifting of all media control by the army
- Freedom of political activities
- Removal of restrictions on the teaching of Portuguese – a Portuguese Cultural Institute is set up
- Appointment of a resident representative of the UN Secretary-General

Phase Two – Autonomy phase (five to ten years)

Full implementation of phase one is a pre-requisite for the successful implementation of phase two. Elections for a Territorial Assembly will be free and fair only if they are conducted after the full implementation of phase one.

The following must be implemented in the second phase:

- Political parties, including those advocating independence for East Timor, are legalized
- The EU sets up a legation in East Timor, headed by a senior Portuguese official
- Elections are held for a Territorial Assembly; the UN to provide technical support and supervision of the entire process
- Only Timorese identified as such may vote and be eligible
- The Assembly elects a Governor of the Territory
- The Assembly and the Governor have a five-year mandate
- The Territory may enter into trade relations with foreign countries, promulgate its own laws affecting investment, land ownership, property, immigration, etc.
- Remaining Indonesian troops are withdrawn within three months
- The Territory will have no army; a police force is trained by the UN and is placed under the elected governor
- Further reduction of Indonesian civil servants
- Portugal and Indonesia normalize relations

The second phase can be extended only if a two-thirds majority of the Assembly deputies vote for such an extension, and this recommendation has to be put to a referendum.

This referendum is a safeguard for the people, since there is no guarantee that the Territorial Assembly members will reflect the true sentiments of the people on such a crucial issue.

It is obvious that if the result of this referendum results in a majority rejection of the extension of the autonomy status, the implication will be that the people will reject integration in Indonesia.

Phase Three (Referendum on self-determination)

If the Territorial Assembly rejects an extension of the autonomy phase, or if the Assembly votes in support of an extension but this vote is rejected in a referendum, then the final status of the territory is resolved.

A UN-supervised referendum is held on the three options provided for in the UN General Assembly Resolution 1514 (XV) of 15 December 1960: independence, free association (with the colonial power Portugal), or integration with another independent state (Indonesia).

A referendum must be held within one year of the end of phase two.

Nobel Lecture[1]

Building Bridges of Dialogue: Timor-Leste Will Not be Based on Revenge

Oslo, 10 December 1996

Those who pretend to be objective and neutral in the face of racism and discrimination, the rape of a small nation by a larger power, the persecution of a weaker people by a ruthless army, must share the guilt. No amount of intellectual argument will suffice to erase their responsibility.

My eternal gratitude to those who nominated me. I am forever morally indebted, and I can assure them that God's modest gifts of health and wisdom to me will always be put to the service of peace and justice, not only for my country and people but also for the cause of peace, freedom, and democracy everywhere where my faint voice can be heard.

My deepest appreciation goes to the Nobel Committee for having chosen us for the 1996 Nobel Peace Prize. Your generosity in thinking of the wretched of the earth, and your courage in standing up to the might of states, the cynicism and indifference of too many, and betrayal by some, tells also a lot about the soul and history of courage of this great country of yours that fought bravely during World War II.

In recent years Norway has played a central role in fostering dialogue and peace among historical enemies. In the Middle East and Central America, your discreet nature, determination, and creativity have proven that some of the world's seemingly intractable conflicts can be resolved

---

1   Address delivered on the occasion of the acceptance of the Nobel Peace Prize. Copyright © The Nobel Foundation 1996.

when there is an honest mediator and when the parties in the conflict are willing to end the war.

Small countries, like Norway, Costa Rica, Portugal, and others, can succeed in mediating conflicts when mighty powers failed. Diplomacy and mediation are not prerogatives of the major powers. The small and medium-size countries without ambitions to a neo-imperial role and whose strength is their moral integrity are best placed to open dialogue among the parties in a conflict.

The East Timorese Church
The people of East Timor owe almost everything to their Church. Hence, the 1996 Nobel Peace Prize is a tribute to the whole Church, the courageous priests, nuns, and lay workers, and the people of East Timor.

∾

This speech belongs to someone else who should be here today. He is an outstanding man of courage, tolerance, and statesmanship. Yet, this man is in prison for no crime other than his ideas and vision of peace, freedom, and dignity of his people.

Xanana Gusmão, leader of the people of East Timor, remains incommunicado in a prison thousands of miles away from his country. His trial in 1993 was universally condemned as a charade and was no more valid than the Dutch imprisonment and trial of the late President Sukarno, founding father of the Indonesian Republic.

I bow to Xanana, and through him to my good friends Nino Konis Santana, David Alex, Taur Matan Ruak, Fernando Araújo and all East Timorese prisoners of conscience in jails in East Timor and Indonesia, to the thousands of victims of torture, and the widows and orphans. I bow to the memory of Sabalae and the thousands of our dead.

Through Xanana I bow to my people with profound respect, loyalty, and humility, because they are the martyrs, the real heroes and peacemakers.

The New Order regime and the Indonesian people
The East Timorese are not the exclusive victims of the Indonesian New Order [Orde Baru] regime installed in 1965. For more than 30 years, the

Indonesian people have known massacres, imprisonment, torture, bans on writers, journalists, academics, and labor leaders. Muslims, Catholics, Buddhists, and Hindus have all known their share of repression. The only non-discriminatory policy of the New Order regime is when it comes to repression.

I pay tribute to the many tens of thousands of Indonesians who died in their own struggle for freedom and democracy, who languished in the jails of the New Order, or were forced into exile in China, Albania, the USSR, and Western Europe. I met many of them over the years and shared long hours of conversation about our people's suffering and dreams.

The lessons of the Jewish Holocaust

In 1939, a few months before the outbreak of World War II, Harry Truman read a passionate message from President Roosevelt to the National Meeting for Moral Rearmament, held in Washington [DC].

The same time as the conference delegates were listening and applauding President Roosevelt's moral speech, 900 Jewish refugees on a boat from Germany, anchored off Florida, were waiting for a decision from Washington as to whether they should find sanctuary in the United States or be sent back.

Finally, word came that their application for refugee status had been denied. The desperate refugees had not convinced the morally courageous delegates to the National Meeting for Moral Rearmament that they had a valid fear of persecution.

More than half a century after the Jewish Holocaust, and centuries after the genocide of the indigenous peoples of Australia and the Americas, the same attitude that has allowed these crimes to take place persists today.

Opinion-makers and leaders, academics, writers, and journalists who pretend to be objective and neutral in the face of racism and discrimination, the rape of a small nation by a larger power, the persecution of a weaker people by a ruthless army, must share the guilt. No amount of intellectual argument will suffice to erase their responsibility.

Synagogues are still being desecrated. Gypsies are still discriminated against. Indigenous peoples continue to see their ancestral land taken over by developers, their culture and beliefs and their very existence reduced to a tourist commodity.

Cold War footnote

The conflict in East Timor can be traced back to the political context of the Cold War.

You might recall a picture that made headlines in the spring of 1975. I refer to the picture of an American helicopter landing on the rooftop of the US Embassy in Saigon to rescue remaining diplomats, CIA operatives, and a few privileged South Vietnamese stooges, as Saigon fell to the Vietcong. Cambodia and Laos followed. This picture illustrates better than a thousand words the ignominious American retreat from Indochina.

In another continent, in the Horn of Africa, the longest reigning US ally, Emperor Haile Selassie, of Ethiopia, had been overthrown a year earlier by radical army officers. Further south, the Portuguese empire had collapsed. These events seemed to confirm Lyndon B. Johnson's domino theory, which was the rationale for US intervention in Indochina.

It was in this geopolitical context that President Gerald Ford and his Secretary of State, Henry Kissinger, visited Jakarta in early December 1975 as part of an Asian tour to reassure leaders of the region that the US would continue to honor its security commitments in Asia.

The invasion of East Timor which took place within hours of Ford's departure from Jakarta was a mere footnote in the Cold War events of 1975. Thousands of East Timorese who died in the days, weeks, months, and years that followed were mere footnotes in the post-Vietnam era and the Cold War.

Inviolability of colonial boundaries

One and a half years before these events, in June 1974, I visited Jakarta in my capacity as Secretary for Foreign Affairs of the Timorese Social Democratic Association that had just been created less than a month earlier. I had the privilege of meeting with the then Foreign Minister of Indonesia, Mr Adam Malik. After our third round of talks, Mr Malik addressed to me a letter, which read in part:

> *The independence of every country is the right of every nation, with no exception for the people of (East) Timor … whoever will govern in Timor in the future after independence can be assured that the government of Indonesia will always strive to maintain good relations, friendship and co-operation for the benefit of both countries.*

The following year, in April 1975, I again visited Indonesia and met with President Suharto's senior adviser, General Ali Murtopo, to whom I reiterated our collective desire to develop friendly relations with Indonesia. General Murtopo reassured me that Indonesia harbored no territorial ambitions over East Timor. However, we soon learned that the word of an Indonesian general or diplomat can be broken as easily as it is spoken.

Some simple but fundamental issues need to be addressed. Does Indonesia have a valid historical claim to East Timor?

The current boundary of the Republic of Indonesia is a product of the Dutch East Indies administration. West New Guinea was absorbed by the Republic not because of a reasonable historical, cultural, ethnic kinship, or geographic continuity. The only link that justified the annexation was West New Guinea's brief colonization by the Dutch.

The arbitrary carving up of Africa at the Berlin Conference can be blamed for some of Africa's problems today, but respect for the colonial boundaries, as unfair as most might be, has provided some peace and stability and kept most of Africa, Latin America, and Asia from disintegrating.

Saddam Hussein, of Iraq, attempted to redraw the map, and rectify what he perceived to be an unfair colonial legacy, by invading Kuwait. Iran has longstanding claims over Bahrain. In Latin America, there are some inter-state territorial disputes resulting from perceived unfair border delimitation.

The right of peoples to self-determination

Millions of peoples (around the world) seek to assert their most fundamental rights, and if we attempt to find a common denominator for the problems I have just listed, there is one: the right of peoples to self-determination.

In most cases the demands are not for secession. They are about their survival as a people with a language and a culture, with their land and environment protected from rapacious multinationals. Only when these basic demands are not met has there been recourse to other forms of struggle with an escalation in their demands.

While self-determination in the decolonization process of the non-self-governing territories almost always led to independence, this is not the case in most of the conflicts of today.

The preservation of the territorial integrity of a country can be achieved only if those in power are sensitive to the basic demands and aspirations of the many indigenous peoples and nationalities that make up the country.

Brute force might silence and keep dormant the dreams and aspirations of a people, but the anger simmering for decades will inevitably resurface and break up the country.

The right of the people of East Timor to self-determination

The right of the people of East Timor to self-determination is widely recognized. Apart from the former Spanish territory of Western Sahara, East Timor is the largest non-self-governing territory in the UN General Assembly decolonization list, which dates back to 1960.

The UN General Assembly and Security Council have adopted a total of 10 resolutions on the question of East Timor, all reaffirming this right.

In its ruling of 30 June 1995, on the Case Concerning East Timor (Portugal v. Australia), the International Court of Justice stated that the right of self-determination has an *erga omnes* ["toward everyone"] character and that the people of East Timor are entitled to it.

Dialogue without pre-conditions and the CNRM[2] Peace Plan

The Israeli-Palestinian peace talks and South Africa's transition to democracy give us renewed hope in that they demonstrate that seemingly intractable problems can be resolved if there is political will and vision by all involved.

In this room today there are East Timorese leaders of every persuasion – some have come all the way from East Timor, Portugal, and Australia – and I can speak for all when I say that we are ready to enter into a process of dialogue with the Indonesian authorities, under the auspices of the United

---

2   Portuguese acronym for the National Council of Maubere Resistance. This umbrella organization included the Timorese guerrilla fighters and all political parties and outstanding Timorese personalities, calling for dialogue towards a peaceful settlement to the violent occupation of East Timor.

Nations, without pre-conditions, to explore all possible ideas towards a comprehensive settlement of the conflict.

In 1992, after thorough consultation with our people in the country, Xanana Gusmão gave his seal of authority to what is now known as the CNRM Peace Plan, which was formally presented to a meeting of the European Parliament in Brussels on 22 April 1992.

The CNRM proposal remains valid as a modest contribution towards finding a solution to the conflict.

Phase One – Humanitarian phase

This phase, which should take up to two years to be fully implemented, would involve all three parties working with the UN to implement a wide range of "confidence building measures" (CBMs) but would not deal with the core of the problem which is the issue of self-determination.

These CBMs must include release of all prisoners, the end of torture and summary executions, and a drastic reduction in Indonesia troop presence in the territory.

These are some of the ideas which I believe could be implemented immediately without loss of face for Indonesia. Its international standing would improve significantly, and its presence in the territory would be less resented, thus relieving a very tense situation.

In view of the time constraints, the full text of this plan is attached to this speech.

Phase Two – Autonomy, five years

Phase two, lasting between five and ten years, would be a period of genuine political autonomy based on ample powers vested in a local, democratically elected Territorial Peoples' Assembly.

At the end of the second phase, the autonomous status of the territory could be extended by mutual accord.

The East Timorese people, having enjoyed a period of peace and freedom without the presence of the most hated symbol of the occupation, the army, might accept to continue this form of association.

Conversely, the changing generation, attitudes, and perception in Indonesia might result in Indonesia accepting as natural that East Timor becomes independent.

Phase Three – Self-determination

If all parties agree that phase three should enter into effect immediately, then the UN would begin to prepare a referendum on self-determination to determine the final status of the territory.

If, God willing, East Timor becomes independent, ladies and gentlemen, allow me to share with you our vision for our country's future and role in the region.

Our vision for the future

East Timor is at the crossroads of three major cultures: Melanesian, which binds us to our brothers and sisters of the South Pacific region; Malay-Polynesian, binding us to Southeast Asia; and the Latin Catholic influence, a legacy of almost 500 years of Portuguese colonization. This rich historical and cultural existence places us in a unique position to build bridges of dialogue and cooperation between the peoples of the region.

Portugal

East Timor will maintain close ties with Portugal, a country which colonized us for almost half a millennium, and has shown an abiding commitment to our right to self-determination. Portugal and East Timor will be most valuable partners for ASEAN in its relations with the EU, Africa, and Latin America.

Australia and the South Pacific

The majority of the East Timorese residents outside the country are in Australia. In spite of our sadness over Australia's role on East Timor, I wish to state here our deepest appreciation to Australia for the shelter, hospitality, and generosity shown to the thousands of East Timorese refugees on Australian soil.

We appreciate the many representations the previous and current governments of Australia have made to impress upon the government of Indonesia regarding the human rights situation in East Timor. No other Western country has been more persistent in this regard.

We fought together during World War II, and many East Timorese gave their lives for our common cause. Now, and in the future, we look up to Australia for help.

ASEAN and APEC

We are conscious of our geography, which compels us to co-exist with our neighbors in that part of the world. We will seek membership in ASEAN and APEC within days of our independence.

Rule of law

We will endeavor to build a strong democratic state based on the rule of law that must emanate from the will of the people expressed through free and democratic elections.

Human rights and international obligations

All international human rights treaties will be submitted to the parliament for ratification. We believe that human rights transcend boundaries and must prevail over state sovereignty.

We will introduce into the school curriculum at an early stage, starting in the kindergarten, the subject of human rights.

We will actively work with like-minded countries, NGOs, and the media to strengthen the UN human rights machinery.

Amnesty and national reconciliation

East Timorese now serving in the Indonesian administration in East Timor, the security forces, and police should not fear an independent East Timor. They will be invited to stay on. Their full and active involvement in running the country will be necessary to insure a smooth transition.

Our society will not be based on revenge. Because of its credibility and standing, the Catholic Church will be expected to play a major role in the healing process of our society.

In August 1975, too many East Timorese died in brief but violent civil strife. Many more died even after the invasion because some in the leadership of the movement I belonged to took upon themselves the role of judges and executioners.

National reconstruction and development

East Timor is a relatively small country. But with an area of 18,889 square kilometers and a total population of 700,000 (1974 figures), it is at least equal to, if not larger in size and population, some 40 independent states.

It is potentially self-sufficient in most agricultural goods, meat, and fish. It has large reserves of oil, natural gas, marble, and manganese.

The invasion uprooted thousands of people. Properties were abandoned, destroyed, or sold at unfair prices. This situation will be redressed. A voluntary resettlement plan will be effected to allow the many tens of thousands of displaced East Timorese to return to their ancestral lands.

We believe in free education and health care for our people.

Indonesian migrants
It is estimated that over 100,000 Indonesians are now living in East Timor. Most are poor Indonesians who came to our country looking for a better life. Indonesian migrants in East Timor will be welcome to stay.

The Suharto regime, its achievements and what it should do
No one can honestly suggest that the 30-year regime of General Suharto has not done good for Indonesia. The record of the past 20 years has been impressive. The Suharto regime lifted the Indonesian economy from extreme poverty to the status of an economic tiger. Living standards, literacy, health care, and food production increased to impressive levels.

President Suharto can show leadership by releasing all prisoners and meeting Indonesia's greatest living author, Pramoedya Ananta Toer; Megawati Sukarnoputri, leader of the PDI [Indonesian Democratic Party of Struggle] and daughter of Indonesia's founding father, the late Bung Karno [Sukarno]; Muchtar Pakpahan, Indonesia's Lech Wałęsa; Sri Bintang; and George Aditjondro, Indonesia's most decorated environmentalist.

The leaders and militants of the PRD [People's Democratic Party] are among the best children of Indonesia. Instead of hunting them, he should invite them to his palace for a dialogue about the future.

Fostering a democratic and peaceful transition in Indonesia
No country, no matter how rich and endowed with natural resources, is an island unto itself. In an increasingly small world and competitive age, where modern electronic communications break the barriers of silence erected by dictators, Indonesia cannot continue to flout the right of the people of East Timor to self-determination and the rule of law in Indonesia.

The next two to three years will witness a transition in Indonesia. Australia, New Zealand, the US, Canada, and the EU can encourage a peaceful, evolutionary transition with a discreet yet firm policy of pushing for democratic reforms and rule of law in Indonesia, and for a genuine act of self-determination in East Timor.

The role of the international community

We are as determined as we are optimistic about our future. To Indonesia and our other neighbors in the ASEAN we are offering a hand of friendship and appealing to them to help us bring peace and freedom to East Timor.

The EU, working with the US, Canada, Australia, New Zealand, Japan, and Indonesia's partners in ASEAN, can accelerate the ongoing dialogue under the auspices of the UN Secretary-General, and give it some impetus and real substance.

The US Administration is the only major power that has adopted some concrete measures to encourage changes in Indonesia and East Timor. I express here our sincere appreciation to President Clinton for his actions on East Timor and I appeal to him to lend his youthful energy and compassion towards a permanent resolution of the conflict, which he once described as "unconscionable."

The West and arms sales

We are not asking that Indonesia be punished with comprehensive economic sanctions. We believe that economic engagement with a country can at times foster positive changes through the development of a democratically conscious class.

However, we find it repulsive that the Western countries that more loudly make rhetorical speeches about human rights are the ones that manufacture most weapons that have killed more than 20 million people in the developing world since World War II.

Land mines, torture equipment, cluster bombs, and chemical weapons are weapons designed to inflict pain and death on human beings. Most victims are civilians, women, and children. How can arms manufacturers, weapons designers, plant managers, politicians, who have families of their own whom they love, be so insensitive when it comes to the suffering of other human beings?

Human rights and "Asian values"

The peoples of Burma, Thailand, the Philippines, South Korea, and Indonesia are telling the rest of the world that democracy and human rights are not an invention of the West.

The thousands of Asians who died in the streets of Manila, Bangkok, Jakarta, Rangoon, Beijing did not die for so-called "Asian values" that deny the people of Asia the basic and fundamental freedoms enjoyed in Europe, Latin America, and in an increasing number of countries in Africa.

South Korea

The brave people of Korea who endured decades of dictatorship and occupation won the struggle for democracy not with guns but with their tenacity in fighting the troops in the streets of Seoul and Gwangju.

The South Korean people can also show greater courage by being magnanimous and forgiving those who have done wrong. Sometimes in history individuals in power are driven to commit wanton crimes, but those who survive and are in power today should resist the temptation to exact revenge in the name of justice.

The death sentence must be abolished, and the brave people of Korea should set the example by commuting the death sentence on former President Chun Doo-hwan. From here I appeal to my Korean friends not to exact revenge against those who have been defeated. In victory, be magnanimous.

Burma

I extend our most heartfelt solidarity to the brave people of Burma and their elected leader, Nobel Peace laureate Daw Aung San Suu Kyi, in their struggle for democracy, rule of law, and human rights.

I also fully endorse the recommendations on Burma adopted by the Forum of Democratic Leaders in the Asia Pacific, led by Kim Dae-jung and Cory Aquino, in their recent meeting in Manila.

Cyprus

Cyprus, a shining example of democracy and tolerance, remains divided and occupied by a NATO ally whose history of aggression and violence is well known.

Recently I received a letter signed by the students of Classes C11 and C22 of Kykkos B' Lyceum, in Nicosia, who wrote:

Your homeland is an occupied country at the far end of the ocean. Our homeland lies partly occupied at the far end of the Mediterranean. We live in a divided city and we cannot cross the dividing line...

To the students of Kykkos B' Lyceum I can only say that, like ancient Armenia, you, too, will recover your lost land.

The prophets of doom

The world has changed dramatically over the last few years and the theorists of irreversibility and status quo have been discredited by the collapse of the USSR.

Who would have thought it possible that the great Armenian people, persecuted for hundreds of years, would regain a country called Armenia? The entire world conspired against the Eritrean people. Americans, Russians, and Cubans all connived against that small nation. Two great nations, the Israelis and Palestinians, who swore eternal hatred, have shown courage and wisdom and begun a painful process of dialogue. In South Africa, former enemies are trying to rebuild their common home.

Last, but not least, for the prophets of doom, for those in government who counsel us "realism," allow me to remind them of a news item in the ever-reliable BBC a few years ago.

It was sometime in early 1991, and I was driving from the small Swiss town of Nyon to the Palais des Nations, in Geneva, for yet another round of futility in a place where some diplomats pretend to be too busy to listen to real problems of real peoples.

The BBC was telling us the story of a Soviet cosmonaut who had gone into space a few months earlier on a record-breaking mission in space. When he was blasted off from somewhere in the Soviet Union, he carried a passport and a nationality granted to him by the most feared military empire in the world.

Once he completed his tour of duty for the pride of the socialist motherland, he prepared the spacecraft for its return voyage to Earth. But he no longer had a country to return to. The mighty empire had ceased to exist. He was forced to circle the Earth a few days longer until people of good will on Earth decided which country he should go to.

With this note, I will end with renewed hope that no matter the level of brute force used against us, our dreams will never die.

God bless you all. Thank you.

Nobel Peace Prize Ceremony, Oslo Norway, 10 December 1996.
D. Ximenes Belo, Bishop of Dili (Left), and José Ramos-Horta (right),
Special Representative of CNRM Abroad.

Previous page and above: Addressing the general debate of
the sixty-fifth session of the United Nations General Assembly,
September 25, 2010, New York.

Exchanging gifts with Pope Benedict XVI at the Vatican
January 21, 2008.

With United Nations Secretary-General, Kofi Annan, 1997.

With eighth United Nations Secretary-General, Ban Ki-moon, 2008.

With Governor-General of Australia, His Excellency General
the Honourable Sir Peter Cosgrove AK, MC. I was honoured to
be invested as a Companion of the Order of Australia,
Sydney, 2015.

With President Bill Clinton in New York, after he had left office.

With President Barack Obama and First Lady Michelle Obama during a reception at the Metropolitan Museum in New York, September 23, 2009.

With two great of friends of Timor-Leste in the US senate:
the late Senator Ted Kennedy (L) and Senator Tom Harkin, 2010.

Meeting with the late President Fidel Castro in 2011, soon after he had undergone surgery following a prolonged illness.

Some of my less political meetings, with (L to R) Sydney Pollack,
Harrison Ford, Jennifer Lopez, and Antonio Banderas.

Speaking with President Harmid Karzai of Afghanistan in 2007.

Signing the Comprehensive Nuclear-Test-Ban Treaty
in September 2008.

The 2008 Timor-Leste–Indonesia dialogue on reconciliation and
normalisation of relations. Xanana Gusmão and Susilo Bambang
Yudhoyono were the chief architects of the exceptional relationship
our countries have today.

In 2006, with Infantry Major Michael Stone (L) and Brigadier General
Mick Slater DSC, AM, CSC, Commander of the International Stabilisation Force.

< With Portuguese Prime Minister
Antonio Guterres, June 1998.

< Kofi Annan with Sergio Vieira De Mello murdered with 20 other UN staff in a terrorist attack on the UNHQ in Bagdad August 2003.

With my favorite people, the innocent of the world. In Guinea-Bissau visiting a school, 2013. >

< With the Emperor of Japan.

Shoe polisher and friend, in Lisbon. We went to lunch nearby. >

< These secluded nuns were allowed out of the Convent walls to have a picture taken with me.

With the longest-serving leader in Asia, Prime Minister Hung Seng of Cambodia – a staunch supporter of Timor-Leste. >

< The 2009 World Oceans Conference in Manado, Indonesia.

Top left: Me with Xanana Gusmão, and Mari Alkatiri (R).

Top right: The Prime Minister of Japan, Junichiro Koizumi, Xanana Gusmão, and the late Sergio Vieira De Mello in 2002.

Centre right: Me with the sacred Mount Ramelau as backdrop.

Lower left: Xanana Gusmão cheering General Peter Cosgrove as he departs a free Timor-Leste in 2000.

Lower right: Xanana Gusmão with Kofi Annan.

President Francisco Lu'olo, in Timorese headdress, campaiging in 2017.

In emergency care following
assassination attempt in 2008. >

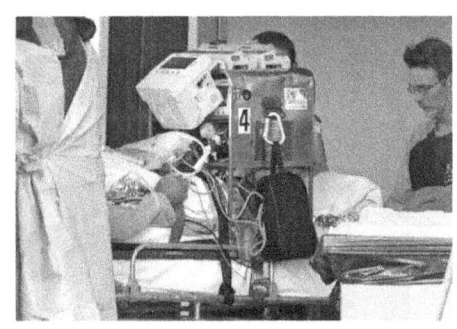

With actor Oscar Isaac who played
me in the film Balibo, 2011. >

Visiting Santa Cruz Cemetary, Dili, site of the November 12, 1991
massacre of at least 250 Timorese during the years of
Indonesian occupation.

An initiative that I cherish is tree planting for the reforestation of Timor-Leste.

Welcomed by local dancers and the Timorese community at some of my countless reconciliation visits and dialogue excercises to listen to communities: Bobonaro (above and right), Baucau (top right)

Below: At the Tour de Timor bike ride.

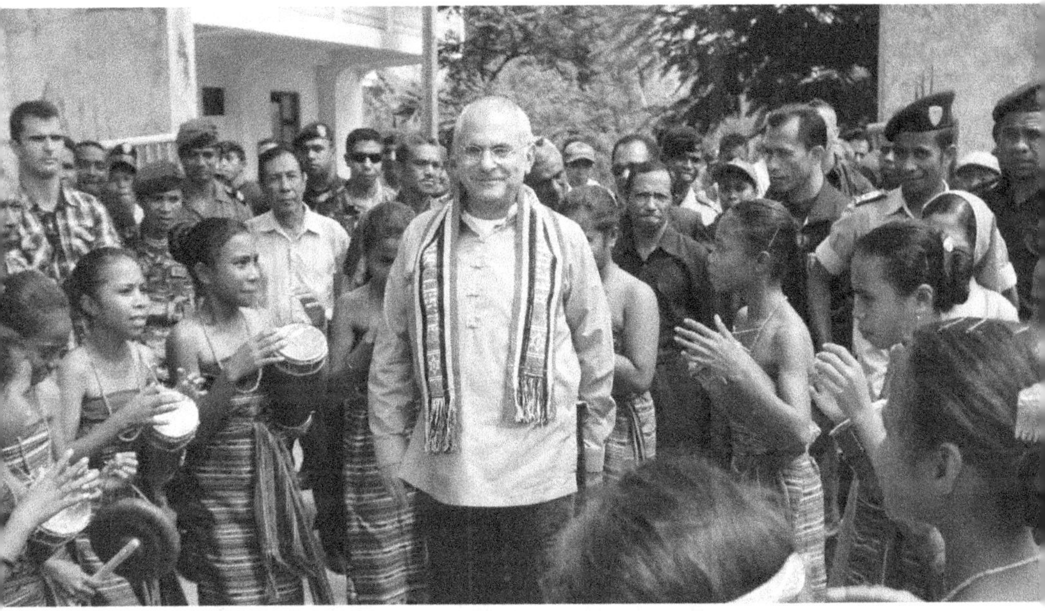

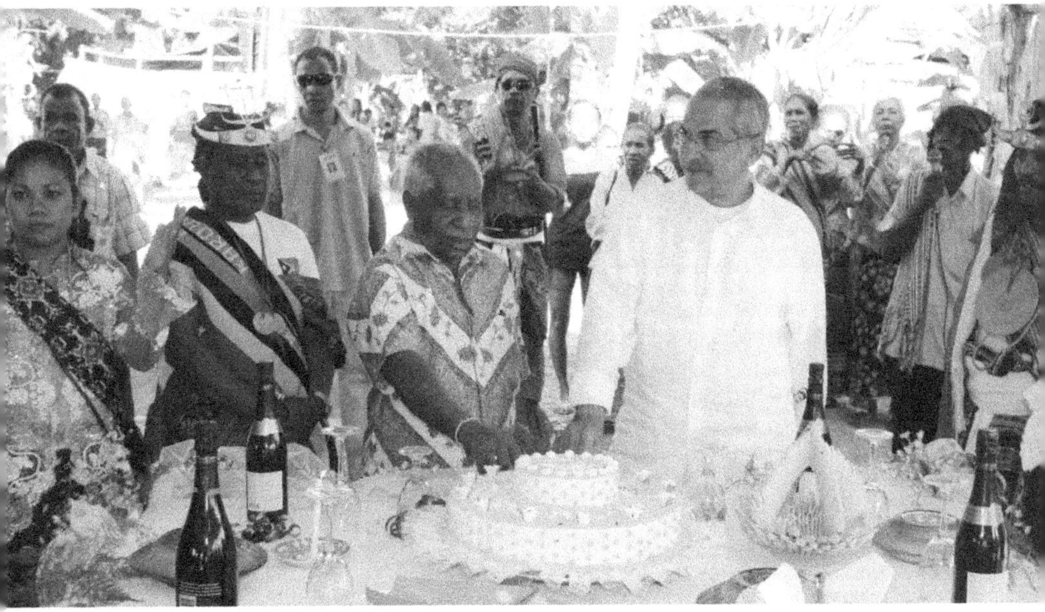

(From left) Me, Francisco Guterres Lu Olo, General Taur Matan Ruak, Xanana Gusmão and Mari Alkatiri.

Above: Delivering an address to a full house at the University of New South Wales, 'The Grand Challenge: Protecting the Rights of Refugees and Migrants'.

Meeting with a new generation of Timorese students, studying in Australia.

Lunch in 2016, from left: mum, me, a neighbour,
local fruit vendor, and fisherman.

My grandson, Bruno, 2014.

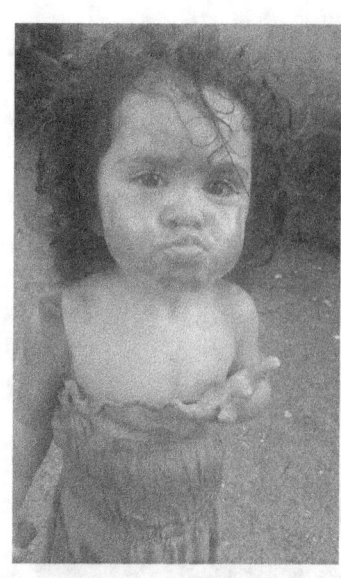

My great grandniece, Kyana,
3 years old, trying on lipstick,
2015.

On
World Affairs

On Human Rights, Conflict and Reconciliation

Charlottesville, 5-6 November 1998

A conference promoted by the University of Virginia and the Washington, D.C.-based Institute for Asian Democracy on 5 and 6 November, 1998,[3] heard presentations from and debated with nine Nobel Peace laureates on peace and human rights.

This morning, as I was sitting next to my good friend, Oscar Arias, in the bus coming here, I asked him, "Do you have a written speech?" He said he did. And that's when I got nervous, because if Oscar Arias, such a brilliant, wonderful statesman, brings a written speech, and I don't have a written speech… He literally spoiled my morning. And so, I have to apologize to you if my speech is going to be a rambling one.

Let me start by sharing with you a story. A few years ago, I was in Sweden, and paid a courtesy call to the Cuban ambassador in Stockholm. A colleague of mine accompanied me to the meeting. After the meeting, my colleague told me, "If your intention was to tell the Cuban ambassador how the situation in East Timor was very confused, you did a very good job, because the man was totally confused. You mixed three languages throughout the discussion. Why the hell didn't you just speak in Portuguese?" So, please, my apologies if my English is not clear enough,

---

3   The two-day conference was held in Old Cabell Hall Auditorium, at the heart of Thomas Jefferson's academic village, and is now available in a variety of broadcast, cable, and web-video formats. The conference was structured to engage students and faculty from a variety of disciplines in an open forum with these great hearts and minds. Later, a book presenting the key points of the conference was published by the University Press of Virginia (*The Art of Peace: Nobel Laureates Discuss Human Rights, Conflict and Reconciliation*, Snow Lion, New York, 2000).

eloquent enough, to convey to you what the people of East Timor feel, and what I feel.

You might recall – to situate the question of East Timor and the region in its historical and geopolitical context – you might recall a picture that made headlines in 1975. It was a picture of an American helicopter trying to land on the rooftop of the US Embassy in Saigon to rescue American diplomats, CIA officials, South Vietnamese collaborators. Soon after the collapse of the US presence in South Vietnam followed Cambodia, Laos. Better than a thousand words, that picture illustrated the humiliating retreat of one of the two superpowers from a peasant war in Asia. In another continent the same year, the Portuguese empire had collapsed and Cuban–Soviet forces entered the battleground for influence in Angola. Mozambique became independent under a Marxist movement. The battle between East and West for influence in Southern Africa rages on. In the Horn of Africa, Haile Selassie of Ethiopia had been overthrown, again shifting the balance of power to the Soviet side. The Soviet Union was already in control, so to speak, in Somalia: with the collapse of Haile Selassie, a Marxist regime took over. It seemed as if the "domino theory", first articulated by Lyndon Johnson, and which served as a strategic rationale for US intervention in Indochina,[4] was being confirmed.

It was against this background that then President Gerald Ford and Secretary of State Kissinger visited Indonesia, on 6 December 1975. Within hours of their departure, East Timor was invaded by Indonesia. East Timor, a country with 700,000 inhabitants then, 95 percent subsistence farmers, peasants, squeezed into an area of only 19,000 square kilometers, were to experience in the following years one of the worst massacres – amounting to genocide – since the end of World War II. The tens of thousands of people who died in East Timor in the following days, weeks, and months and years were, in fact, just a footnote to the Cold War, a casualty of Realpolitik and the pragmatism of states.

Twenty-three years ago, no one thought the East Timorese could survive the onslaught. Every major country in the world provided weapons to Indonesia. Countries that preach democracy and Human Rights provided the most weapons, not only to Indonesia but to many dictators around the world. All kinds of weapons were unleashed

---

4   Mainland Southeast Asia.

on the people of East Timor. Twenty-three years later, we are there, kicking and surviving, and it is the Indonesian empire that is collapsing around us. The Suharto dictatorship is gone. There is a dynamic, lively democracy movement taking shape in Indonesia. And Indonesian people are beginning to ask, "What have we done to this small nation of East Timor?" Who is going to explain to the Indonesian people the loss of their own people – thousands of Indonesian soldiers, young people, who lost their lives in the fields of East Timor? Who is going to explain to the Indonesian people the hundreds of millions of dollars wasted in weapons purchases instead of channeling them to education, health care, clean water, housing for their people?

The West has something to answer for as well. With the end of the Cold War we thought there would be fewer conflicts, but as Europe could no longer find a market in Europe itself for its weapons since the end of the Cold War, it actively promoted weapon sales to the poorest countries of the south. We became the dumping ground, the market for the excess weapons produced by the democracies of the north. I will not elaborate much on this topic because our good friend Oscar will address this issue. But the collapse of the East Asian myth, of the East Asian tiger economies – Malaysia, Indonesia, Thailand, South Korea – as painful as they are, these economic collapses, for the millions of people in the region, they opened extraordinary opportunities for democracy and the rule of law to finally triumph and prevail in the region. And they have destroyed the so-called "Asian values" that supposedly are unique and stand against the Universal Declaration of Human Rights. The millions of people pouring into the streets of Rangoon, Bangkok, Manila, Indonesia, and South Korea are telling their leaders that human rights, democracy, rule of law are also our aspirations, are also our rights. That is the extraordinary opportunity offered by this economic and financial collapse in the region. And, as I speak here today, I must say thanks, President Clinton, for the US leadership in this current crisis in the region. Sometimes I think back on the criticism that people addressed at the US, but the reality is when the need comes, it has been the US, particularly under this administration, that has offered leadership for economic recovery in East Asia, for peace in the Middle East, in Bosnia, Kosovo, Northern Ireland. And again, after many, many years of Africa being ignored, being off the agenda, being off the radar screen of the US administration, it was Clinton that put Africa back on the map. And I say, "Thank you, Mr President." And thank you for the modest things you are doing on East Timor; and I hope that in the last two years of his administration, he will forcefully support the emerging democracy in Indonesia, support the economic recovery, and use his abilities, his extraordinary energy and creativity, to bring peace about, finally, in East Timor.

And last but not least, let me share with you a story. A few years ago, in Switzerland, I was driving from Nyon to Geneva to attend yet one more of those almost futile exercises at the UN Commission on Human Rights. I tuned in to the BBC, the only good thing the British ever invented. I know it is a wild exaggeration, and my sincere apologies to any British subject in the room, but it is my favorite radio station, the best anywhere in the world. I tuned in to the BBC at eight in the morning, and I heard this extraordinary news of a Soviet cosmonaut who had gone into space a few months earlier when the Soviet Union was the Soviet Union. And as he prepared his spacecraft to return to Earth, the startling news came from Moscow: do not come back. Your country no longer exists. Just imagine someone out of Houston, Texas, telling John Glenn, "Don't come back." If it were with other US politicians, I would like to hear someone telling them not to come back. But John Glenn, please come back. The Soviet Union had ceased to exist. The mighty empire had ceased to exist. Someone, in a second thought from Moscow, told him, "Circle the Earth a few more times." And he diligently did. Because there was disarray in Moscow. No one knew what to do with him. Finally, after many hours, they brought him back to Earth. The empire had ceased to exist. Armenia became independent; the Baltic States were liberated; Vaclav Havel became President of the new Republic of Czechoslovakia, now Czech Republic; Poland – all the countries in Eastern Europe, Central Europe – became independent, contradicting those who have told us year after year that we must accept the irreversibility of military occupations, the rule of force. We remember this extraordinary lesson and we will survive. We will win.

Lessons Must be Learnt: The Arms Trade Must Stop

12 May 1999

The consequences of the weapons sold to developing countries during the Cold War period helped devastate national economies in South Africa, Central America, East Asia. I also appeal to the West to forgive, to completely delete, the debt of the least-developed countries.

I often remember a true story where a cosmonaut who had gone into space months earlier was told to hang on beyond the scheduled time in orbit as his country, the mighty Soviet Union, no longer existed. While the demise of the Soviet Union felt astonishing, it was just the end of yet another empire in a succession of thousands of years of empires built on tyranny, on myths, on falsehood.

And also built on the might of weapons.

Despite its weapons, the empire couldn't resist the force of the common citizen, of the dreamers, the academics, the students, the intellectuals who demanded freedom. And I ask: why are billions[5] of dollars wasted in weapons systems when they could have been diverted instead to feed the peoples of the world? The weapons trade tells us plenty about the futility, and insanity, of weapons and wars.

And then, as we all know, came the liberation of South Africa, the democratization in Latin America, the liberation of the Baltic States and Central Eastern Europe, as one dictator after another fell during the last ten years.

In our region, Southeast Asia, one dictator after another has fallen. First, Marcos in the Philippines, ten years ago. Democratically elected

---

5   Thousands of millions.

Kim Dae-jung in South Korea took over after 30 years of military dictatorship. Almost precisely a year ago, at about three in the morning, I was woken up by a journalist asking me to comment on the downfall of the Suharto regime in Indonesia. It had been 23 years since my country, that tiny little country of only 700,000 people, was invaded by another of 200 million people, supported by every Western country you can think of that produces weapons. I don't want to be unkind to anyone, but I have to say that the same countries – not all – but those that more 'heroically' have gone to the Balkan region and are bombing Serbia back to the Stone Age are the ones that provided all weapons to the Indonesian regime – enabling it to prosecute the war in East Timor.

East Timor, as are other situations like Indonesia itself or Guatemala, Chile, Argentina, South Africa, Somalia, Sudan, the Great Lakes, and Zaire in particular, is a casualty of the Cold War, sacrificed on the altar of pragmatism and the Realpolitik.

As the Cold War ended, 10 years ago, as we talk about the new millennium – I have some misgivings about the "new millennium" mantra as not only Christians exist; I wonder what the Hindus might think, or the Muslims, or the Buddhists. Still, as I was saying, when everybody talks up the new millennium, I might as well join in and say that the Western countries, which have a tremendous potential to do good with their science, their wealth, and their creativity, should also learn from the tremendous failures, mistakes, and loss of lives of the Cold War period, and have some soul searching to do about the harm done to the rest of the world in the latest 40 years or so.

One lesson to be learnt: do not support dictators and do not sell them weapons.

Beyond the ethical dimension of selling weapons, we have also the security concerns, the strategic nonsense of selling weapons to dictatorships. They say it enhances our security: we learn from the past that weapons sold to unstable regimes, because they are not based on popular will, often end up harming your own interests. And because of the consequences of the weapons you sold to the developing countries during the Cold War period that have devastated the economies of South Africa, Central America, East Asia, I would appeal to Western countries to forgive, to completely cancel, the debt of the least-developed countries. Last, but not least, the case of East Timor.

A few days ago, we signed a historical agreement in New York. I wish to thank first all those who around the world have contributed to make possible this almost-miracle. I say "almost" because we still have a few months ahead that are going to be very challenging and dangerous. First and foremost, I want to thank one man: Kofi Annan, Secretary-General of the UN. His integrity, courage, dedication, resolve facing extraordinary obstacles were key to making it possible for the agreement to be signed. I fully trust the United Nations under his extraordinary leadership, and in our capacity as citizens, we all must give the UN our utmost support in order to guarantee peace and security in the decades to come.

Neighbors and Friends Should be Able to Resolve Differences in an Amicable and Fair Manner

Sydney, 29 November 2004

The vast Timor Sea contains some of the richest proven oil and gas reserves in the region. A fair and equitable share of these resources would quickly lessen Timor-Leste's dependence on external assistance.

I am most grateful to you, Mr Frank Lowy, for your kind invitation to me to address your prestigious Institute. When Alan Dupont and I talked in mid-August or so, we both, and many other people, were hopeful that, as I addressed this body a few weeks after the Australian federal elections, I would be able to share with you some good news about the ongoing negotiations between our two countries in regard to the riches of the Timor Sea. My friend the Hon Alexander Downer said, after our meeting on 11 August, in Canberra, that he wanted to deliver to the people of Timor-Leste a major Christmas present. These were Alexander's words, not mine. But I shared his optimism then.

Today, I am thoroughly disillusioned and do not believe that the two sides, on their own, will be able to show wisdom, statesmanship, and leadership to reach a just and fair resolution of this seemingly intractable dispute over interpretation of international law and practice in regard to our respective maritime boundary claims. But, ladies and gentlemen, I beg you to be patient. I will turn to this issue later in my comments. Allow me first to share with you some information on the situation in my nascent nation and some reflections on the state of the world.

Today we are free and sovereign, slowly building the institutions of the state that we believe best serve our people. It was less than three years ago that the UN Secretary-General, Kofi Annan, handed over power to our elected President. Let me start by saying that, overall, the situation in Timor-Leste is peaceful, politically dynamic, and stable.

We have made real progress in some sectors, like public administration, education, and health, but we are failing in others. The most fragile sector of the administration in Timor-Leste is the judiciary. We have very few trained judges, prosecutors, and lawyers. Most foreign business would not trust our judiciary. Small-time offenders languish in jail without trial. And there are no short-term solutions. We are committed to creating a strong and independent judiciary, but this is many years off.

We are grateful to Australia, the UK, and Malaysia for their generous support in enhancing the operational competence of our security forces. Australia and the UK are jointly supporting the training of our police force, while Malaysia is providing training and logistic support to our Rapid Reaction Unit. We are sensitive to, and welcome, constructive criticisms of our police force. Working with our partners and friends, we are confident that in the end we will have a capable police force that has the trust of our people.

Our economy is limping along, doing much better than anticipated when the UN began, in 2002, to drastically downsize its presence. We are confident that in two to three years we will experience a strong economic growth as a result of revenue from oil and gas; capital investment in public infrastructure such as roads, bridges, ports, and airports; telecommunications; public housing; health; agriculture; fisheries; and tourism. We should be able then to begin to drastically reduce the current unemployment and poverty rates.

The UN and its constituting members have been very generous and remain committed to complete the job of nation-building we started together in 2000. The current UN Mission of Support for East Timor ends in May 2005. By then the UN will have completed five years of an active and successful engagement in Timor-Leste. However, much remains to be done and we believe that the international community should continue to consider providing the government of Timor-Leste assistance with the following:

- International advisers to assist the government in key areas, namely, justice, finance, etc. The needs are being identified through consultations between my government and the United Nations.
- Police advisors, whose role remains necessary to ensure that our various police forces attain a high degree of operational preparedness and are imbued with human rights values. It is not enough that the law and order agencies are operationally effective; their behavior must be beyond reproach. Our people expect no less from us.
- UN military liaison must continue to be deployed (maybe 30 or so should be enough) as long as Timor-Leste and Indonesia do not finalize and sign a formal agreement on our common land border. While the border area has seen real stability in the last two years, our failure to resolve the remaining segments of our border compels us to request that the UN maintains a military liaison group in the country; the UN unarmed observers have proven to be very effective in liaising between our own security forces and Indonesian military. There has been a healthy relationship between them.
- A strong UN Human Rights Unit must continue to be part of the future UN Mission in Timor-Leste after May 2005, in order to monitor the situation on the ground, provide the government agencies, and in particular our law enforcement agencies, with much needed guidance and training, with a view toward consolidating and entrenching the observance and the culture of human rights in my country.

We believe that a visible and credible follow-up UN presence in Timor-Leste, though much smaller than the current one, will be necessary. The price tag for such a mission will be very modest. In our view, such a UN mission comprising a security element should continue to fall under the peacekeeping system and be paid for by the UN-assessed contributions.

While there might be some requirement for a UN extraction force to be deployed, this can be a largely symbolic one, requiring only two or three helicopters. As a backup to this UN extraction force based in Timor-Leste, Australia could make available on a standby basis additional airborne means based in Darwin that could be activated at short notice to assist the UN in Timor-Leste at the joint request of the Timor-Leste government and the Special Representative of the Secretary-General.

We are conscious that we are a small dot in the world and there are competing claims for attention, from the Middle East to our own region, and it might be difficult for the UN to agree to our request. We hope that they see our request as a modest one, that it is a valid one, and that it is fully justified.

We are building solid relations with all our neighbors, in particular with Indonesia. While our side endured 25 years of often brutal occupation that resulted in the loss of an estimated 200,000 lives, we recognize that the other side lost thousands of its soldiers too, and many families mourn their dead, human beings just like us.

I wish to congratulate the Indonesian people for their great experiment in democracy. Few imagined in 1999 that within only a few years, the fourth-largest nation in the world and largest Muslim country would emerge as a vibrant democracy.

However, Indonesia must come to terms with its own past of violence and impunity. Indonesians must summon the courage and humility of the truly great to confront the demons of the past and present and free themselves once and for all from this culture of violence and impunity that has been deeply entrenched throughout the security forces.

Our country was thoroughly destroyed, and the culprits were those who were entrusted with the mission under the May 5th Agreement to ensure law and order before, during, and after the ballot. None of the culprits who masterminded, financed, directed, and took part in the orgy of violence and destruction have been brought to justice.

We have established diplomatic relations with some 100 countries. We have embassies in Jakarta, Kuala Lumpur, Canberra, Brussels, Lisbon, Washington [D.C.], Maputo. We have permanent missions to the UN in New York and in Geneva. We have a Consulate-General in Sydney. In only a matter of weeks we will inaugurate our Embassy in the People's Republic of China.

Early in the New Year we will establish embassies in Bangkok and Tokyo. In the next two years, we will establish additional embassies in Manila, Hanoi, Seoul, and New Delhi, reflecting my government's clear engagement with our region. The existing embassies cover a number of neighboring countries.

Timor-Leste enjoys privileged relations with Japan, and as it is well-known to all, Japan has been by far the largest contributor to the UN and Timor-Leste through its multilateral and bilateral assistance programs. Timor-Leste also enjoys fraternal ties with China and the Republic of Korea.

In the energy sector, PetroChina is already actively engaged in exploration for gas and oil onshore in Timor-Leste. We actively seek further Chinese official and private sector investments in our country.

In January 2005, a group of 70 Thai entrepreneurs will undertake a study tour of Timor-Leste with an eye on possible investments. We hope that in early 2005 my government and the German company MAN Ferrostal will reach an agreement for the development of a modified cassava and sweet potato starch production plant in Timor-Leste.

More than 20 countries and international agencies have full-fledged diplomatic representation in Timor-Leste.

We continue to develop ever closer relations with our neighbors in Asia. We hope that, in 2005, on the occasion of the next ASEAN Regional Forum meeting, Timor-Leste will be admitted as its newest member. We have received formal pledge of support from President Susilo Bambang Yudhoyono and Foreign Minister Hassan Wirajuda. Support has also been received from almost all ASEAN members and non-ASEAN Regional Forum members.

In regard to membership in ASEAN, this, we hope, will occur before the end of this decade, as our country has consolidated its internal order and organization and our economy has experienced a significant growth.

My country enjoys excellent relations with countries of the European Union as well as Norway. On a per capita basis, EU assistance to Timor-Leste remains the highest in Asia, reflecting the solid commitment by all EU members to Timor-Leste's democratic development. Among the European countries, top on the list of our generous friends are Portugal, the UK, Federal Republic of Germany, Republic of Ireland, Norway, Sweden, Finland, Spain, Italy.

Our relations with Portugal have a unique dimension deriving not only from 500 years of colonization but, more significantly, from the courageous and dignified stance of the Portuguese in the unrelenting defense of our right to self-determination. In our darkest years, when most of the world had turned a blind eye, or had given up hope, the

Portuguese stood by us. Today, Portugal remains our steadfast, solid ally in the world and in particular in the European Union. We are forever indebted to such a noble nation.

New Zealand has shown a truly exemplary solidarity with Timor-Leste, treating us with real friendship and deference, without a colonial paternalistic attitude. I have been pleased to hear in many quarters in the region and in the UN high praise for NZ.

Allow me to share with you some reflections on our world. In the last 20 years or so, our world has been the stage of several major conflicts, namely, the invasion of Iran by Saddam Hussein in the 1980s, resulting in the death of over a million people. Chemical and biological weapons were unleashed on civilians and combatants. The West turned a blind eye when Kurdish people and Iranians were gassed to death by the thousands by the butcher of Baghdad.

Soon after the end of the Iraq–Iran war, the same regime in Baghdad unleashed yet another invasion, this time against the State of Kuwait. A coalition of countries intervened and Kuwait was freed, but not without wanton destruction carried out by the retreating forces that set on fire hundreds of oil wells.

In the nineties, Europe believed it had shaken off the demons of war of a recent past, only to wake up instead to the tragic ethnic wars in the Balkan region. The last chapter of the Balkan wars was the war in Kosovo and the simmering ethnic tensions here threaten the fragile peace in the area.

Most of us have now relegated the Cambodian tragedy of the seventies to a footnote in our intellectual library. But let us not forget the genocide unleashed by the Khmer Rouge regime with almost universal indifference or the Taliban rule in Afghanistan in the nineties that took us back to the savagery of the Middle Ages; nor can we forget the 1994 genocide in Rwanda, and the violence in parts of Africa, in particular in West Africa and the Great Lakes region, and parts of Asia, namely in Nepal.

With only few notable exceptions, for the most part the international community has failed to pre-empt the occurrence of violence or to intervene when violence had begun.

More often than not the UN is paralyzed and becomes hostage to the narrow interests of some of its members. We had illusions that the (mis-)use of the veto was a fact of the Cold War and it would be less and less exercised in the New World (Dis-)Order. However, with notable exceptions, national interests endured beyond the Cold War and we have all remained hostage to them.

Many have written and spoken on the world's misfortunes as a result of the current prevailing unipolar system whereby one single world power imposes its will on the rest of us. I will put forward a question: Was the bipolar world that prevailed during much of the 50 years after the end of World War II, up to the implosion of the USSR, a safer and more just world?

During the time of the bipolar world, we were witnesses to numerous intra-state and interstate conflicts, involving directly, or indirectly, the two rival superpowers that dominated the bipolar power system. An estimated 40 million people died in conflicts during these years.

The US and the USSR fought or sponsored wars in Latin America, Africa, and Asia in their attempt to exercise influence and control over strategic areas of the world such as Central America, the Horn of Africa, Southern Africa, Southeast Asia, etc. The US fought a senseless ugly war in Indochina, and the USSR had its own Vietnam in Afghanistan. The nuclear threat was much more real then than today.

The abrupt collapse of the USSR and the end of the Cold War in 1990 ushered in a new era, a more promising "New World Order" free from the nuclear threat and proxy wars sponsored by the two superpowers.

Human rights and the struggles for democracy that were hostage and fell victim of the Cold War gained new life and momentum. Soon after the end of the Cold War we saw the beginning of the end in rapid sequence of the class of military regimes in Latin America, Africa, and Asia. A permanent international tribunal that was a non-realizable dream during the Cold War period is, today, a reality.

Much to the consternation of the enemies and critics of the US, the American Empire emerged triumphant, as there was no doubt that the collapse of the totalitarian communist system and beliefs were a vindication of the western liberal thought and values.

The US can be a force for change and good. It can be a benign power. It can turn the world into a much safer, better-living common home for all of us, as long as it has the humility of the truly great and walks halfway, and to its other half of fellow human beings, acknowledge its own limits and errors, and share with the rest us a more compassionate vision and agenda. The US can use its enormous power in leading the fight against poverty and the debt trap that stunts progress in many parts of the world.

Like many of you and the thousands of peace marchers around the world, I am opposed to violence and wars. But sometimes we must ask ourselves some troubling questions. Should we oppose the use of force, even in situations of genocide and ethnic cleansing?

On the eternal dilemma of war and peace, there are the pacifists, or idealists, who oppose the use of force under any circumstances, and the realists who support the use of force under certain circumstances, namely if they are sanctioned by the UN Security Council.

Those opposing the use of force under any circumstances have not been able to articulate a better strategy to deal with situations of ethnic cleansing and genocide. Patient diplomacy lasts as long as it lasts, and might bear fruit, but might not. But genocide goes on, as in the case of Sudan right now, where thousands of our fellow human beings have died.

Let me offer some examples for reflection, starting with the tragic case of Cambodia in the seventies. The world knew, or at least the US and much of the West, as well as Cambodia's neighbors knew, that an evil regime was deliberately cleansing the nation and causing the death of hundreds of thousands of innocent human beings.

The Security Council did not even discuss the Khmer Rouge genocide. In any case, if anyone had any inclination to bring this matter to the Security Council it would have been vetoed. So, there was no chance the Security Council would act, assuming there was a general political will to intervene. Vietnam finally intervened unilaterally in 1979, putting an end to the Khmer Rouge rule, but rather than being applauded for saving a whole nation, the brave Vietnamese were castigated by the powers that be and by their own neighbors.

In the African continent, in Uganda, genocide was taking place around the same time as the Cambodian tragedy. The Organization of African Unity and the Security Council did not debate, let alone take any action in regards to, the situation in Uganda under Idi Amin for reasons of state sovereignty and the principle of non-interference.

It required the moral courage of a Julius Nyerere to put an end to Idi Amin's genocidal rule.

If there had been a lone world leader with moral courage who had ordered his country's armed forces to intervene unilaterally in Rwanda in 1994, would he have been condemned for this unilateral action?

The UN, and in particular the Secretary-General, were criticized for their alleged failure to act on Rwanda. But it is too convenient to lay blame on the UN, when in fact in most past cases of alleged UN's inaction, real blame should be laid at the door of the powers that be.

In selectively recalling some of the most flagrant cases of our collective failure to prevent wars and genocide, my sole intention is to provoke us into reflecting on the failings and weaknesses of the collective organization, the United Nations, with a view toward exploring avenues to make the organization a more effective custodian of peace in the world.

Allow me to add some thoughts to the ongoing debate, with some ideas, not very new, on how we could see an improved United Nations.

The existing UN collective security mechanism is outdated and undemocratic, a relic of the Cold War that no longer meets the challenges of today's world and does not reflect today's economic, demographic, and strategic realities. There is an obvious need for reform, and I list some ideas.

My government is not among the privileged few that were consulted by the Secretary-General's "High Level Panel on Threats, Challenges and Change." We hope that those entrusted by the Secretary-General to write up recommendations on UN reform will first make a thorough review of past and current UN failures and weaknesses, identify the reasons or root causes of such failures, and then maybe prescribe possible remedies.

First, I must say that I do not believe that a simple expansion of the Security Council membership with more or less permanent members would suffice to strengthen the UN. It would make it more representative, as it would better reflect the current world's demographics and balance of power, but it might not be more effective.

There has to be a review of the workings of the UN General Assembly and of some of its subsidiary bodies, namely, the Environment and Communities Scrutiny Committee and the UN Commission on Human Rights, the Treaty bodies, as well as of the Specialized Agencies, to streamline the bureaucracies, simplify work, reduce duplication and waste, and introduce meritocracy and professionalism in the recruitment and promotion of personnel.

There are too many UN agencies headquartered in two industrialized countries that are notoriously expensive. Agencies such as UNICEF, UNDP, UNHCR and a few others should be relocated to the developing world, to be closer to the people they are supposed to serve and where property costs are much lower.

There is a clear need for an expansion of the membership in the Security Council to include new permanent members that would reflect twenty-first-century realities and challenges, demographic, economic, and strategic balance. In this regard, Timor-Leste fully supports the Franco-German initiative on UN reforms.

We believe that the new expanded Security Council should include countries like Germany, India, Indonesia, Japan, Brazil, and one or two from Africa.

Timor-Leste supports permanent membership status for Indonesia because we believe that due attention has to be paid to the need for a balanced representation in the new Security Council to encompass all major civilizations and faiths. Non-inclusion of Indonesia as a new permanent member would leave the Security Council again with a disproportionate Christian representation.

The veto power should be eliminated and replaced by a two-thirds majority vote for all major decisions. The existing veto power has been used and abused and was responsible for the inaction of the Security Council.

The two-year rotation for non-permanent members should be shortened to one year so as to give better chance for more members to serve in the Security Council. For your information, my government has already received requests for support for a seat in the Security Council for as far away as 2020.

Having said all of the above, we must realize that even a reformed UN system would not resolve all problems. After all, ultimately, in facing up to the challenges, what is required is moral and political leadership, for no amount of structural adjustments of the UN bureaucracy can make up for the moral vacuum and the lack of political leadership.

As a small nation we are baffled by the apparent inability of world leaders to grasp the magnitude of the problems we all face as a human family inhabiting a shrinking planet under pressure from industrialization; pollution; and competition for scarce resources, such as land and water; our ever growing population and voracious appetite that cause the depletion of our fish stock and forests; we poison our river systems, pollute the very air we breathe with an ever increasing level of poisonous emissions that are released into the space every minute of the day.

The world is faced with a growing AIDS pandemic, whose epicenter is now shifting to Asia. Malaria and tuberculosis have been with us for many generations. Yet there seems to be no real commitment in terms of resources to enable our scientists and societies to address this.

The combined Official Development Assistance [ODA] of the rich industrialized countries does not exceed US$50 billion[6] annually. Compare this with the more than US$300 billion in subsidies provided to their obsolete and uncompetitive farmers and industries. We do not wish to sound ungrateful, but we have reasons to be skeptical about an ODA where much of it actually ends up in the hands of donor countries, with only a fraction of such much-publicized aid really benefiting the recipient country.

There has to be a thorough reform of ODA with a view to ensuring that developing countries actually receive what is pledged.

We join with others in urging the rich of the North to allocate 0.7 percent of its national wealth to ODA, thus meeting the target set by the UN. It is perplexing that only four small rich countries have met and/or overtaken this modest target. They are Norway, Denmark, Sweden, and the Netherlands.

Europe and the US should gradually eliminate all agriculture subsidies to farmers in the US and Europe that kill competition and market access for poor countries. It is estimated that at least some $60 billion[7] a year would flow to low- and medium-income countries if agriculture subsidies in US and Europe were to be eliminated.

Weapons-producing countries flood the world with all types of guns that fuel conflicts. There has to be a strict code of conduct on weapons exports aimed at reducing the flow of conventional weapons to poor countries and regions in conflict. Certainly, the control of the spread of weapons is not an easy task, but we could start by having a strict,

---

6   Fifty thousand million US dollars.
7   Sixty thousand million US dollars.

binding code of conduct along the lines of the Anti-Personnel Land Mine Convention.

Timor-Leste is a debt-free country and we are somewhat suspicious of those who are encouraging us to borrow. The more we learn about the burdens of debt, the more we are hesitant.

One issue that concerns my government most is the situation in Myanmar. Some positive signs seem to have emerged out of that country. The release of some prominent dissidents is cause for celebration. We must expect more.

We appeal to our senior Asian leaders, in particular, China, India, Japan, Republic of Korea, and the ASEAN to redouble their efforts to find a peaceful resolution to the conflict in Myanmar. This is an Asian problem and our leaders must be able to show to the rest of the world that Asians can resolve their problems. The impoverished people of Myanmar are enduring a double punishment, one inflicted on them by their own military rulers and the other by the West, through what seems to be "politically correct" sanctions policies, but that in the end cause more harm to the poorest of the poor.

I will turn now to the issue of terrorism. Extremists strive in many cultures and religions. The daily news bulletins are dominated by the extensive coverage of the actions of a few, but their actions have turned Islam into a word almost equal to terrorism.

I believe that the Islamic extremism that is the basis of the current wave of international terrorism is a passing phenomenon. Like other extremist groups before them, namely the European terrorist groups of the sixties, they have no popular support and can be defeated through a multi-pronged strategy.

The terrorists have made good use of modern technology and global funds to enact their war on the West and on all secular Arab and Muslim nations. The key is to subvert, undermine, disrupt their ability to use modern means of communication, cut them off, isolate them, and deny them access to funds.

Prudent but firm security measures are also necessary.

However, those fighting the terrorists should be careful not to descend to their level of inhumanity. There has to be always a careful balance between legitimate use of proportional force against terrorists and their supporters and respect for human rights.

There is deep-seated resentment and anger among Muslims and many nonMuslims around the world over Israeli policies of land grabbing and annexation, denying the Palestinians their right to a dignified existence and a homeland.

The two-state solution agreed upon by all sides has to be rapidly resurrected and implemented as a first step towards a durable peace in the region. The Palestinian Intifada and suicide bombing, as well as Israeli policies of annexation and retaliation, have resulted only in deepening anger and hatred. There has to be a way out. The two sides should agree on an immediate cessation of all acts of violence, accepting a cooling-off period, enabling mediators to work out the details and timetable for the full implementation of the two-state solution.

Now, some words of wisdom on the Iraqi crisis. While there might never be an agreement among the pacifists and the realists over the dilemma of war and peace, there has to be an agreement now that the forces of fanaticism and terrorism cannot prevail in Iraq.

Where there is a chance today for democracy in Iraq, a hasty withdrawal would deliver the Iraqi people and the Kurdish to a Taliban-style rule that would destabilize the entire region. If I were a political leader of any consequence and asked a question regarding the options for Iraq, I would say retreating and conceding victory to the terrorists is not an option, for the consequences are far too high to contemplate.

Hence, we hope that the US, which initiated the war in Iraq and gallantly freed the Iraqi people and the region from a tyrant, will walk halfway and meet those on the other side of the debate. The US and Europe are among the most important pillars of the world's security and economic wellbeing, sharing the same values of democracy and freedom. They fought together against the evils of Nazism, they stood side by side and prevented Soviet domination of Western Europe. Surely, they are wise enough to overcome their differences, however deep, and give the Iraqi people a chance to finally be free and at peace among themselves and with their neighbors.

And finally, I return to an issue that, if not resolved, will soil Australia's international image and do irreparable damage to Australia-East Timor relations.

You all know how I care and respect this country. In my own country, and in a number of international forums, I have stood up for Australia, rebutting some of the harshest criticisms I have heard leveled against this country. Today, again I am speaking as a friend, a pragmatist and realist who believes that Timor-Leste's vital strategic interests must be anchored on a close relationship with our two closest and giant neighbors, Australia and Indonesia.

From day one of the initial talks between UN and Australian officials some four years ago, I held the view that the permanent maritime boundary between Australia and Timor-Leste could be deferred for a number of years to be agreed. I believed that Australia and Timor-Leste should instead work on a Strategic Framework Agreement covering the entire breadth of the Timor Sea on the basis of a fair and equitable share of the resources.

This is what I have conveyed to the Hon Alexander Downer more than three years ago and more recently at the end of June, in Jakarta, and in August, in Canberra.

The Australian side knows too well that its continental shelf claims are not credible and sustainable in international law. Not surprisingly, conscious of such an untenable position, Australia served notice to the International Court of Justice [ICJ] in early 2002 that it would no longer accept ICJ's jurisdiction on maritime boundary disputes. It does not accept international arbitration or a third-party mediation.

Australia is caught in a diplomatic imbroglio of its own creation with the 1972 maritime boundary treaty with Indonesia in which Australia prevailed in imposing on a then weaker Indonesia its continental shelf claims. Till this very day, Indonesians feel they were "taken to the cleaners" in the words of some. Having "charmed" a weaker Indonesia to accept the absurdity of its continental shelf claims, Canberra is understandably irritated that a Lilliputian East Timor should display such audacity in refusing to surrender on the same terms as the giant Indonesia did more than 30 years ago.

Nevertheless, understanding the imbroglio Australia has found itself in, I have argued that we put aside the issue of a permanent maritime boundary for a reasonable number of years and put our minds to work on a pragmatic, creative, fair, and just resource-sharing arrangement without prejudice to the two countries' sovereign claims to a permanent boundary.

Prior to, and during, the federal election in Australia, there seemed to be much determination to intensify talks and reach an agreement by December.

Following the elections, there were two rounds of talks, one in Darwin and one in Díli. However, following the Díli round in October, Mr Dough Chester abruptly ended the talks and seemed in a hurry to return to Canberra. His words amounted to an unacceptable blackmail. Said he: "Take it or leave it", by 5.00 pm of 27 October. Mr Chester wanted the East Timorese side to accept, on Australia's terms, a permanent maritime boundary with a $3 billion[8] compensation spread over 30 years. This figure was much less than the $4.5 billion figure offered by the Australian side during the Darwin talks.

It was agreed in Díli that there would be no comments to the media by either side. However, within minutes of this agreement, accepted by our side on the insistence of Mr Chester, the same Mr Chester was feeding to the media his spin on the talks, alleging that our side had changed its mind, that we had rejected Australia's many "creative" proposals.

Timor-Leste has insisted that a goal for our country is to participate fully in the development of the downstream of the Timor Sea petroleum resources. Industries that can spring from exploration and development, but particularly from the downstream, are an enormous opportunity for the long-term sustainable development of our economy and of our human resources.

So far, our rights to such participation have not been met. Benefits have flowed elsewhere. The Bayu-Undan gas project will see a pipeline to Darwin and the construction of an LNG [liquefied natural gas] plant there. Given that Bayu-Undan is in an area of the Timor Sea Treaty, which Timor-Leste has 90 percent share of, this is, from our point of view, not just. We have been generous to Darwin and the NT [Northern Territory] for this.

The Greater Sunrise field lies in an area of overlapping claims by us. It lies at least two-thirds closer to Timor-Leste than to Darwin. Previously, the companies were saying that a pipeline crossing the Timor Trench was not feasible. Earlier last year, the Joint Venture partners in Greater Sunrise agreed to undertake a study for a pipeline and an LNG plant

---

8   Three thousand million US dollars.

option to Timor-Leste. This option has been the subject of discussions between world-class experts in pipeline and LNG construction, and the Sunrise joint venture partners. It is agreed by both the companies and our experts that the construction of a pipeline to Timor-Leste is feasible. The myth of the Timor Trench has been blown away.

Our experts have also advised us that the construction of a pipeline and LNG plant to Timor-Leste is economically feasible. Our government will continue to discuss the option of a Timor-Leste pipeline and plant with the companies. Discussions on this issue to date have, from our point of view, been useful in establishing for us the viability of a pipeline and LNG onshore in Timor-Leste. We remain open to these discussions.

The Northern Territory continues to insist on a pipeline from Sunrise to Darwin. They already have a pipeline, which should have been built to Timor-Leste. It is somewhat greedy for a territory of a couple of hundred thousand people to have priority over resources which could benefit nearly a million people in our country. But more importantly, we argue it should come to Timor-Leste because we claim the resources and should benefit from their downstream, particularly given the Northern Territory has already benefited from Bayu-Undan, which has lifted its economy.

In conclusion, ladies and gentlemen, the Timor-Leste side shares the view of a majority of the international community that where there are overlapping claims between two coastal states, the principle of equidistance should apply.

Furthermore, according to geologists, Timor-Leste and Australia share the same continental shelf.

Australia and Timor-Leste, neighbors and friends, should be able to resolve our differences in an amicable and fair manner that would do justice to our people. The vast Timor Sea contains some of the richest proven oil and gas reserves in the region and a fair and equitable share of these resources would quickly lessen Timor-Leste dependence on external assistance.

Since it seems that the two friends and neighbors are not able to resolve this dispute, we should go the ICJ. We are prepared to accept an independent, neutral mediator. We are prepared to consider any other form of mediation or arbitration. When the Hon Alexander Downer attempted to explain what was clearly unexplainable, Australia's abrupt withdrawal from ICJ's jurisdiction on maritime boundary disputes, he said the reason was that he believed that Australia and Timor-Leste should be able to resolve their differences without any outside involvement. Well, it seems that we are not able to. So, let's all show good faith, faith in the legal multilateral bodies such as the ICJ, and jointly request mediation or arbitration.

We are poor and are in no hurry to become rich. We can wait. We are a patient, proud people. We are not impressed by pressure or bullying tactics. We have self-respect and a sense of dignity. If Australia wishes to penalize us by cutting off aid, that is fine with us. Others will help. And we will still respect and love our neighbor Australia. In my many trips across this great land, I have come across thousands of generous, loving people. We know they will be with us for a long time to come.

At the Handover Ceremony of the House of Europe Building to President José Manuel Barroso of the European Commission

The European Union Truly Deserves the Nobel Peace Prize

Díli, 24 November 2007[9]

The building of the EU as a multinational, multiethnic, pluralistic, democratic, and solidarity-wielding polity is unparalleled in world history. The EU can play a major role in preserving world stability at a time when the tensions cause widespread concern.

The European Commission has displayed active and generous solidarity towards Timor-Leste and is one of the major development partners of our young democracy.

The statistics of the European Commission's bilateral and multilateral assistance do not fully capture the importance and the impact of its support to Timor-Leste. The quality of the assistance provided and the impact it is having on our communities and institutions have been quite remarkable.

The handover ceremony of the building that is to become the House of Europe reflects our commitment to the EU and our willingness to strengthen the relations between our small country and the large and small nations of Europe.

As you well know, Your Excellency, Timor-Leste is one amongst very few countries in the world that can proudly claim to have ratified

---

9   President José Ramos-Horta did nominate the European Union for the Nobel Peace Prize, which it later received, in 2012.

all human rights treaties, as well as other international treaties and conventions related to justice and aimed at promoting world peace.

Timor-Leste has also subscribed and endorsed all the draft resolutions initiated by the EU on the human rights situation in particular countries. This shows that Timor-Leste and the EU share common values, such as the respect for human rights and fundamental freedoms.

I believe that the EU can play a major role in preserving world stability at a time when the tensions between large powers and emerging powers are causing widespread concern.

I take note of the central part played by the EU, and more specifically by the European Commission that you chair, in seeking and fostering a dialogue between civilizations and cultures. In an increasingly interdependent world, the European Commission can perform a fundamental role in bridging the gap between poor and rich countries and in reducing the tensions that spring from the inequalities and injustice separating the rich Northern Hemisphere from the poorer South, and the few rich nations in the South from their poorer neighbors.

The Nobel Committee in Oslo has presented the Nobel Peace Prize to many individuals and institutions. Since 1901, the Nobel Peace Prize has been awarded to 95 individuals and to 20 organizations, including the United Nations and some their specialist agencies. I would argue with the Nobel Peace Prize Committee that the EU would be worthy a recipient of the Nobel Peace Prize.

The institution over which you preside has promoted dialogue for peace and mutual understanding between civilizations and cultures; by supporting refugees, it has been a major contributor to the UN Peace Force; and the EU has been at the forefront of the fight against poverty through integrated mechanisms such as ACP and the "Everything but Arms" initiative.

Europe was the battleground for many wars fought in the twentieth century. But it was able to heal the wounds of its past, to promote the reconciliation of peoples, to consolidate democracy, rule of law, and human rights. In doing so, it has transformed the Old Continent, once a stage for wars and genocide, into a free, democratic, prosperous, and solidarity-wielding zone for mankind. Now that Central and Eastern Europe have been liberated, Germany is reunited, and the most recent wars in the Balkans have been settled, Europe will extend its boundaries even further and possibly welcome into its midst one of the world's richest civilizations – Turkey. Indeed, Turkey and Indonesia are two countries that refuse credence to certain prophets and adherents of Samuel Huntington's thesis put forward in *The Clash of Civilizations*. Quite the contrary, these two large countries with a mostly Muslim population have completely absorbed the ideals of freedom and democracy for which dozens of millions of Europeans and other peoples sacrificed their lives.

The building of the European Union as a multinational, multiethnic, pluralistic, democratic, and solidarity-wielding polity is unparalleled in world history. That is why I believe that the EU truly deserves the Nobel Peace Prize for the central role that you have played in fostering a Europe that is aware of, and attentive to, the plight and aspirations of poorer peoples. You are definitely my nominees to the Nobel Peace Prize of 2008.

On the Death of the Ex-President of Indonesia

Timor-Leste Bore Witness to Suharto's Era

28 January 2008

President Suharto stabilized and developed his country and reduced poverty, elevating Indonesia's prestige, but corruption, impunity, and the occupation of Timor-Leste took its toll.

The moment that ex-President Suharto left this world, one historical chapter was closed in Indonesia, in Timor-Leste, in our region, and of the Cold War.

Suharto came into power in 1967, in the sequence of major internal unrest in Indonesia in 1965–66. Hundreds of thousands of Indonesian citizens died, and more than one hundred thousand were imprisoned. Millions of innocent Indonesian citizens were imprisoned and executed. Some were executed after more than 20 years spent in jail without trial.

The ideological rivalry started with the Bolshevik revolution in 1917. After World War II, with the Soviet Union becoming a nuclear power, the rivalry between the two major nuclear powers deepened, with negative impacts reaching across the world.

The North American intervention in Vietnam, and its consequent political and military defeat, aggravated the regional and international tension.

General Suharto's regime was established in this political context. Hundreds and thousands of Indonesians citizens died in 1965–66, and the persecution of hundreds of thousands more in the following years should be understood as the consequence of this great ideological struggle where small countries across the world were affected.

In 1975, Timor-Leste turned into another Cold War victim with the Indonesian invasion, adding to the millions of victims all over the world, in Asia, Africa, and Latin America, where human beings were sacrificed at the altar of interest of two superpowers.

The West, in particular the United States, was a great defender of Suharto's regime and were its major beneficiaries, turning a blind eye to the nature of the regime.

Under these circumstances, Timor-Leste bore witness to Suharto's era. He stabilized and developed his country and reduced poverty, elevating Indonesia's prestige in the region and in the world. But corruption, the total impunity of the regime, and the occupation of Timor-Leste allowed the material progress to take its toll on ex-President Suharto.

Today, Indonesia is finally a free nation, democratic and in peace. Timor-Leste is also a free democratic country and in peace.

We, the Timorese, not forgetting the tragedy that knocked on almost all of our families' doors, should show our grandeur as a small nation, having won our freedom, knowing how to forgive the one that has caused us harm.

We have one mission to overcome: to build peace in the present and consolidate peace in the future.

To the family in mourning, please accept my sincere condolences.

An Open Letter in the *Huffington Post*

Iran's War Against Knowledge

From José Ramos-Horta and Archbishop Desmond Tutu[10]

25 September 2011

Freedom of education and freedom of information are integral to freedom of thought. Few advances have been made by humankind which were not preceded by new ways of looking at our world and new schools of thought.

The forward progress of humankind in the last centuries has been fueled, more than any other factor, by increasing access to information, more rapid exchange of ideas, and, in most parts of the world, universal education.

Freedom of education and freedom of information are integral to freedom of thought. Few advances have been made by humankind which were not preceded by new ways of looking at our world and new schools of thought.

So, it is particularly shocking when despots and dictators in the twenty-first century attempt to subjugate their own populations by attempting to deny education or information to their people.

Not only it is futile in the long term; it also makes them appear fearful of the very age they live in and haunted by the new thinkers in their midst.

Perhaps the most glaring example of this fear today is the denial of higher education to the members of the Bahá'í faith in Iran, a peaceful religion with no political agenda which recognizes the unity of all religions.

In 1987, after being barred by their government from Iranian universities because of their faith, the resourceful Bahá'í community

---

10 Anglican Bishop (retired) Desmond Tutu is a South African social activist and Nobel Peace laureate (1984).

in Iran organized the Bahá'í Institute for Higher Learning [BIHE], a decentralized network of teachers delivering college-level classes in kitchens and living rooms across Iran.

Bahá'í professors and administrators who had also been banned from their universities for their faith were joined by courageous Muslim academics who would risk their careers and even imprisonment to support the network and teach the youth.

Taught by accredited professors, the quality of the coursework has been recognized and accepted for credit by more than 50 universities outside of Iran, allowing the BIHE students to continue with graduate work abroad. This creative solution has lifted the lives of thousands of Bahá'í students who would otherwise have been denied meaningful careers.

On 21 May 2011, the BIHE came under attack when Iranian officials raided thirty Bahá'í homes and arrested over a dozen of its teachers and administrators. Those arrested were neither political nor religious leaders. They were lecturers in subjects that included accounting and dentistry, who today face the prospect of decades in prison. The crime with which they are charged: delivering higher education to Bahá'í youth.

The suppression of education in Iran is not limited to those of the Bahá'í faith. Other Iranian youth have been expelled from universities for their beliefs, or for holding viewpoints determined to be counter to the ruling party, including pro-reform views. Iranian officials have forbidden new delivery of, and are in the process of rewriting the course content of, 12 social sciences on the university curricula, including law, philosophy, management, and political science, to make them more closely align with their own interpretation of the Islamic faith. They have stated that up to 70 percent of the course content in the Social Sciences will be rewritten by government officials.

We believe it is important to recognize that these actions are neither the result of, nor dictated by, the Islamic faith. One need only look at the Dark Ages of Europe, or the Spanish Inquisition, to see that Iranian Ayatollahs are certainly not the first to use religion as the cloak to attempt to forcibly suppress ideas and knowledge that they fear could threaten their power. The rich philosophical and artistic Iranian traditions, the contributions of Iranian scholars worldwide, and the actions of the Muslim community members who have aided and supported the BIHE are testament to the fact that the actions of their leaders are no reflection of the Muslim faith or the many good-willed Muslims in Iranian communities.

And while we believe that both historically and in today's "wired" world it is futile to suppress the quest for knowledge, there are many in Iran whose lives are being threatened or damaged by the attempt.

They need our support.

We call on the international academic community to come to the aid of those whose lives are being subjected to these oppressive laws.

Specifically, we, the undersigned, ask that the international academic community:

1. Call on the Government of the Iranian Republic to release unconditionally, and drop charges against, the BIHE educators currently under arrest and facing charges related to their educational activities.

2. As academic leaders, have its administrators and professors register through any possible channels in the Iranian academic community their disagreement with, and disapproval of, any policy which would bar individuals from higher education based on their religious background or political persuasion, or which would remove or corrupt any established fields of study from a university curricula for religious or political reasons.

3. Encourage their own universities to review the educational quality of the BIHE coursework for possible acceptance of its credits, so that those who have had the benefit of its programs can continue at higher levels of study.

4. As possible, offer available online university-level curricula, through scholarships if needed, to students in Iran who would otherwise be deprived of the right to higher education or who, due to government limitation on social sciences, would not have a full array of educational options available to them in their own county.

Thank you for your support.

On the 2012 Rio+20 Summit

Asia Should Lead in Sustainable Development

Huffington Post, 26 June 2012

A green and sustainable development model, based on peaceful cooperation from the local communities up, enables economically viable growth that works hand in hand with environmental sustainability, protecting the inheritance of future generations.

We gathered in Rio from 190 countries, to review what we have done since the historic Earth Summit in Rio in 1992 and what our world should look like in the coming decades. There was no cause for celebration and much to regret and fear as we continue to lack vision and leadership.

I did not travel to Rio with much optimism. Actually, I must have been the only Head of State who did not attend the previous conferences in Copenhagen, Monterey, and Durban which, as I had feared, had not reached a substantial, binding agreement that could meet the challenges of climate change.

We are still in the midst of an unprecedented financial, economic and social crisis that began in the US in 2008, spread into Europe, and is still affecting countless world economies.

Again, as I feared, we emerged from the Rio+20 United Nations Conference on Sustainable Development, June 20–22, with a Declaration entitled "The World We Want," and lacking in substance and solid financial commitments.

We all knew it would be impossible to bring all parties to agree on a binding international agreement entailing deadlines and costs. So, pragmatism and realism cautioned UN Secretary-General Ban Ki-Moon, and President Dilma Rousseff of Brazil, that to avoid abject failure we must lower our expectations to the lowest possible common denominator.

The truth is that the financial, economic, and social crises that affect the US and almost all of Europe have tempered the political willingness of the rich countries of the North regarding substantial contribution to any bold sustainable development program to achieve the Millennium Development Goals.

Even before the 2008 crisis, most rich countries were never able to mobilize the political and human will to allocate 0.7 percent of their GDP for development aid.

Aid pledges made in international conferences have been rarely kept. When they are, the funding has not always been effective in achieving the intended benefit for the receiving countries.

The path taken over the past decades in the relationship between rich and poor countries, between north and south, had ups and downs, with much waste and mismanagement, programs based on wrong concepts, wrong assumptions and wrong policies. The mistakes were not only on one side of the relationship. Donors and recipients shared in the mistakes, and share the responsibility for the lost decades.

So where do we go from here? I believe that rather than attempting to forge the one agreement that will change the course of the world, or being satisfied with one without much substance, it may be more realistic, practical, and effective to think of agreements and plans on a regional level.

For instance, shouldn't Asia consider an Asian road map for 20 to 30 years for an integrated, equitable, sustainable Human Development, targeting eradication of poverty, illiteracy, TB, malaria, HIV/AIDS, etc., and restoration of our forests, rivers, and seas?

Asia, with half the world population, extracts a lot more from our planet to satisfy our needs of survival and development than any other region in the world. For our own survival, and in solidarity with our brothers and sisters from other parts of the world, we must act with vision and determination. We must do more to free our people from extreme poverty and save our common planet.

China, India, Pakistan, Japan, Republic of Korea, Indonesia, Singapore, Malaysia, Thailand, Turkey, Saudi Arabia, and the Gulf countries together have an unparalleled pool of know-how. They have enough financial resources to transform Asia into a prosperous, peaceful, and happy region for our four billion[11] citizens.

Africa, the Middle East and Latin America should and could do the same. Each region in the world should adopt its own road map for sustainable, equitable, integrated development, adapted to the conditions of each region and sub-region, and mobilizing regional resources and seeking additional funding from other partners, if and as needed.

The US and Europe still lead in science and technology and they should invest even more in education, research, and new technologies for the benefit of their own peoples and the world.

The US and Europe should contribute know-how, technology, and financially to the programs in each region or sub-region. But Asia should create its own fund, the Asian Fund for Sustainable Development, that can be managed by an existing institution such as the Asian Development Bank, in partnership with UN Specialized Agencies such as UNDP, UNICEF, WHO, or NGOs with solid regional or international reputation such as Oxfam.

Each country should mandatorily contribute to such a fund, according to its GDP. The leading Asian economies can easily mobilize US$100 billion[12] to be invested during the next decade. Asia's industrialized nations such as Japan, Korea, Singapore, China, India, or natural resource-rich countries, i.e., the oil, gas, gold, and diamond producers, should lead by example and contribute 0.7 percent of their GDP to this fund. The Asian private sector would also be invited to contribute.

Asia's poor, low-income countries with little or no mineral resources, vulnerable to climate change, would qualify to benefit from this fund, to develop programs targeting extreme poverty, illiteracy, TB, malaria, HIV/AIDS, etc., and reforestation, as well as cleaning up their rivers, lakes, and seas.

Asia, the most populous region in the world, represents half of all mankind. The largest, oldest, richest civilizations appeared and met in Asia. Fifty years ago, the region was extremely poor. Today, it is emerging as a center of world power. But the challenges it faces are immense and complex. The region is the most dangerous in the world, the most

---

11   Four thousand million.
12   One hundred thousand million US dollars.

militarized, the most nuclearized, with complex land and maritime border disputes, regional rivalries, and ethnic and religious conflicts that have exploded frequently in and among states.

It cannot, however, continue to demand from the aging and impoverished Europeans and from today's less powerful US to come to our rescue and lead or to continue the blame game.

If it is an established and obvious truth that Europe and the US have contributed the most to the environmental degradation of our planet in the last 100 years, it must also be noted that they also contributed the most towards advances in medicine, science, and technology to the benefit of all humanity.

It is now Asia's turn to unite and act responsibly to correct the mistakes inherited from the past and those of the present, and adopt a road map to build the future we want.

My country, Timor-Leste, although young and with modest resources, has given examples of solidarity. In the past five years, we have contributed a total of about ten million dollars in aid to some countries affected by natural disasters, such as Cuba, Brazil, China, Portugal, Australia, Japan, Indonesia, Myanmar, and to some UN Specialized Agencies.

Our people have shown that we are, and will be, ready to contribute as much as possible to make the Asian road map a reality, through a Fund for Sustainable Development.

Meanwhile, as we have waited with great expectation for a Global Agreement and Plan to come out of Rio+20, or any Regional Agreement and Plan, in Timor-Leste we are already implementing our Strategic Development Plan 2011–30.

We are determined to achieve all of the Millennium Development Goals and become a high-income country in the next 10 to 20 years, with a per capita income of US$10,000.

Since independence in 2002, Timor-Leste has ratified the three Rio Conventions: the United Nations Framework Convention on Climate Change, the United Nations Convention on Biological Diversity, and the United Nations Convention to Combat Desertification.

We have produced three strategies and Action Plans in response to these conventions, namely, the National Adaptation Plan of Action for Climate Change approved by the Council of Ministers in 2011, the National Biodiversity Strategy and Action Plan approved by the

Council of Ministers in February 2012, and the National Action Plan for Sustainable Land Management, currently awaiting the approval of the Council of Ministers.

We have established a new Directorate to support and strengthen the traditional custom of *Tara Bandu* to protect and conserve natural resources in order to achieve environmental sustainability, as well as a means to build trust within communities and resolve conflicts.

A green and sustainable development model, based on peaceful cooperation from the local communities up, enables economically viable growth that works hand in hand with environmental sustainability, protecting the inheritance of future generations.

It is our hope that this young country and new democracy may well become a model for sustainable growth that can be emulated in other parts of our region, and other parts of the world, as we all seek the compassion, wisdom, and courage necessary to face the challenges of the twenty-first century.

Internecine Divisions of the Freedom Fighters Risk Losing International Goodwill

Daily Beast, 18 July 2012

In our own struggle for freedom, the Timorese fighters never abducted, tortured, or killed a single Indonesian civilian. My advice is to fight on with the full strength of your faith, but do not join your adversaries at the bottom of the gutter.

Just four decades ago, at the height of the Cold War, Timor-Leste, known to many as East Timor, was nearly isolated in its struggle for freedom and democracy, like many countries at the time. Every major western and Asian power supported the other side in our struggle, which began with Indonesia's 1975 invasion of our island.

We did not give up our own dreams of freedom. But we died for them for 24 years. The Indonesians, too, endured a dictatorship that did not seem to even stop and think before slaughtering real or perceived enemies en masse.

No one came to our rescue. On the contrary, all regional and world powers consorted with the Suharto regime.

That was then. That was the Cold War. The West has changed. Today, it is wiser and more sensitive to public outcry against gross and systematic abuse of human rights. Today, nearly the whole world backs the Syrian struggle for freedom and democracy. Syria's freedom fighters have reason to be hopeful.

But divisions within the movement are as obvious as they are inevitable, and undermine their own efforts.

These divisions are not going to dissipate any time soon. And it is the actions of the freedom fighters within the country that will prove to be the lynchpin in the conflict.

So, for the Syrians fighting for freedom and democracy, allow some unsolicited advice from a fellow freedom fighter, someone who has been there.

First: fight on, with the full strength of your faith. But do not join your adversaries at the bottom of the gutter. Do not kidnap, torture, humiliate the captured soldiers or civilians who have collaborated with the regime.

In our own struggle for freedom, tens of thousands of our innocent civilians were arrested, tortured, and disposed of. But we never abducted, tortured, or killed a single Indonesian civilian. All captured soldiers were treated humanely and eventually released.

You have won the diplomatic battle. But you risk losing the international goodwill you have gained if you do not overcome your own internecine divisions, and, worse, if you descend to the level of your adversaries, using similar inhumane tactics against captured adversaries.

Second: be patient. It is possibly your best weapon. The regime is running out of options.

What it does still have is enough fire power and loyalty among its army and certain sectors of the society to continue to inflict widening carnage on its citizenry. In the face of the regime's military superiority, to challenge it militarily is to define the battle where they are the strongest.

When you are weak militarily, you try to outfox the other side politically and diplomatically. Use the goodwill you have gained strategically.

Third: be pragmatic and smart. Accept the Annan Plan, and step into the peace and political process. This is where you can outsmart the regime with cunning patience. In this globalized world and Arab Spring fervor, the days of regimes such as the one you face in Syria are numbered. As you play a constructive role within the Annan Plan, you will win over the trust of those still hesitant or entrenched within the al-Assad regime, including the powerful army. You would further consolidate support in your region and in the world.

We know there are serious risks in playing political chess with the regime; your leaders can be assassinated or co-opted. But you have shown us now how capable you are of enduring risk for the ultimate prize.

There are more actions the international community can take that are still short of a sea blockade and air campaign. For instance, in the coming months the Arab League should lead efforts in the United Nations Credentials Committee and the General Assembly to reject the accreditation of the al-Assad's regime delegation.

As it might be premature to recognize any Syrian faction, maybe the more representative Syrian opposition groups should be granted observer status in the General Assembly, with the right to speak but without the right to vote. As soon as the Syrian opposition comes up with a more unified and broadly representative body, it should be accorded full diplomatic recognition.

The Syrian democracy movement and the international community should offer an olive branch to senior officers in the Syrian Army. Say they are given three months to defect, and if they decide to do so, they will be granted full amnesty and the possibility of returning to active duty after liberation. This offer should be extended to civilian leaders as well as business leaders.

Much greater effort must be made by the Syrian opposition and their Arab allies, such as Qatar and Saudi Arabia, to make contact with and entice the Syrian Army to change sides. The Army will eventually arrange for al-Assad's exit, as happened recently in Egypt and in Indonesia in 1989.

The al-Assad family should be offered safe passage to Saudi Arabia. The Kingdom has been a safe haven for dictators – often a valuable element to the resolution of a conflict – over many decades. Idi Amin of Uganda, for one, died in the Kingdom after many years of quiet but apparently comfortable seclusion.

The US and its NATO partners are right in being prudent, and they are doing what is possible in a very complex region. Yet, finding a solution to the unfolding situation in Syria cannot rest solely with the United Nations and the major powers such as the US, Russia, and China. If China and Russia were to change their stance and decide to dump the al-Assad regime, it is certainly not clear that the regime would topple any faster. And those advocating a Libyan-style intervention are wrong. Syria has fought wars with Israel, directly or via proxy forces, and has been in a state of war for decades. Its military preparedness should not be underestimated.

The Annan Plan is the only realistic way forward. Intelligence, cohesiveness, and strategic thinking and execution on the part of the Syrian freedom fighters, with support from its neighbors and the west, could bring it to fruition.

Asia Has to Lead in Tackling Twenty-First Century Challenges

29 November 2012[13]

Asia has resources to alleviate and eradicate poverty; we master the sciences and technology; we have know-how to lead the search for global answers to the challenges of climate change and the need for sustained increase in food production.

We are living in times of great challenges in much of the world, but also of hope and optimism for our peoples and our continent. Japan, the only nation in humanity's history to have directly experienced the effects of atomic bombs, knows too well the costs of wars and the values of peace. I'm a frequent visitor to Japan and have visited several times the historic city of Hiroshima and toured the Museum that so vividly walks one through the corridors and chambers of horror of the devastation caused by the one single atomic bomb dropped on that city one clear day in August 1945, at the end of World War II.

No less heartbreaking have been my visits to the Holocaust Museum in Berlin that reminds us of the systematic cleansing of millions of Jews in Europe by the Third Reich. In both cities we are sadly reminded of human beings' capacity to inflict destruction and pain on fellow human beings. And Japanese people should be honestly and truthfully educated about not only the horrors of the devastation and death caused by the atomic bombs dropped on Hiroshima and Nagasaki but also the suffering

---

13   Lesson on Global Governance and Peacebuilding, by invitation of the academic authorities of the UN University, in Tokyo.

and destruction caused by the Japanese Imperial Army in many parts of Asia during its years of aggression and occupation.

Unfortunately, human beings do not seem to ever learn from history. So soon after the end of World War II we had the Korean War, unleashed by the communist regime in the north of the Korean Peninsula as it attempted, in a lightning surprise attack, to overrun the people and forces of the south. And we had Stalin's maddening policies in Russia, and Mao's in China, the 1965–66 mass killings in Indonesia, the Indo-Pakistani War of 1971, the Vietnam War that lasted 15 years until the fall of Saigon in 1975, the Khmer Rouge Killing Fields in Cambodia in the mid-seventies, the genocide in East Timor beginning in 1975, the Rwanda genocide of 1994, the Balkan wars and ethnic cleansing in the 1990s, the ongoing tragedies in Darfur, Sudan, Congo, Afghanistan, Syria.

Let us not forget the past wars of partition of India, Pakistan, Bangladesh, Biafra, the Iran-Iraq war, the invasion of tiny Kuwait by the Saddam Hussein regime, etc. And let us not forget either the almost forgotten indigenous peoples of the Americas and Australia who had been annihilated by successive "Christian civilizing" invasions, beginning in the fifteenth century till this very day. Yes, ladies and gentlemen, indigenous peoples, the few remaining, are still dying today from humiliation, dispossession, exclusion, drugs, massacres, suicide.

The catalogue of human brutalities is a far too long one and still ongoing that makes me wonder whether we ever learn!

As the US and NATO forces begin their phased withdrawal from Afghanistan, there is growing anxiety and fear among many Afghans about their future – about their hard-won democratic gains. Will these gains survive the American withdrawal in 2014 or will the country and the people be once again overrun by the Taliban? And what will happen in Pakistan, which faces its own internal Taliban and other security challenges?

Rising Asia: Opportunities, challenges and risks

But let's also look at the good news. Let's also look at Asia now. And to the challenges we together have to face. Asia's economic performance has been the single most remarkable development since the end of the Cold War in the early 1990s.

Hundreds of millions of people have embarked upon self-reliant development and freed themselves from poverty, in particular in China, India, Pakistan, Bangladesh, Vietnam, Indonesia, Malaysia, Cambodia, Laos, the Philippines, and Thailand; others – Japan, the Republic of Korea, and Singapore – continue to outshine much of the world in science, technology, and innovation. Asian economies have become the powerhouse of global economy.

China, India, and Indonesia have been growing at annual rates of between six and 10 percent for sustained long periods, indeed, decades. The economies of Japan, China, Korea, and India put together already account for over US$14 trillion[14] of annual GDP. If you add some two trillion dollars of combined annual GDP of another fast-growing economic region, ASEAN, the economy of Asia a whole is equal to or even surpasses the $15 trillion of US economy and the $16 trillion of combined output of EU countries. Every day, the sustained high economic performance of leading Asian countries helps, pulling smaller neighbors into the path of economic growth and human development.

The world has changed, but Asia is changing faster, and in the face of the financial and economic predicaments of the US and Europe, Asia must seek center stage – and lead. I believe that the time has come for Asia to lead and guide the world while navigating the challenges of the twenty-first century.

Asia can, and should, lead on tackling the challenges we face in the twenty-first century: we have resources to alleviate and finally eradicate poverty; we master sciences and technology; we possess know-how to lead the search for global answers to the challenges of climate change and the need for sustained increase in food production. But to lead is to inspire, to be able to forge partnerships, build bridges, and seek common ground. For this to happen, Asia and the world need to set on a road map of priorities and resource allocation to answer our challenges and we also need leadership to establish and implement this road map, strengthening peaceful relations.

As Japan has achieved much, other Asian countries can, and should, lead on reversing environmental damage and ensuring sustained development, while keeping up with the welfare of our peoples. In our globalized world, Asia can lead only in partnership with other

---

14   Fourteen million million US dollars.

stakeholders, even with other emerging countries far away from Asia, like Angola, Mozambique, Nigeria, South Africa, Brazil, Mexico, Venezuela, and other fast-developing economies and societies that are looking for solutions to challenges similar to those we face.

In spite of the remarkable progress in many areas, there are also enormous risks facing Asia as a whole that should not be underestimated. I thoroughly disagree with the optimists, Asian scholars and others elsewhere, who want us to feel good about ourselves and paint too rosy a picture about the emerging twenty-first-century Asia. The challenges facing us are, in fact, overwhelming and daunting. And we can overcome these challenges only by pooling resources, solutions, in partnerships with the US and the EU that remain technological powerhouses that have much still to contribute to global solutions.

Need for a long-term vision

Asian leaders should consider a 30-year Asian road map for integrated, sustainable Human Development that includes not only the goals of eradicating poverty, illiteracy, TB, malaria, etc., but also of restoring our forests, rivers, and seas by harnessing new and unimaginable technical know-how that we can marshal.

We have heard that knowledge is more powerful than the sword. But, remember what Albert Einstein said: "Imagination is more important than knowledge." For our own survival, by solidarity with our brothers and sisters from other parts of the world, we must now act with vision, imagination, and determination.

Asian leaders and elites must rise to the challenges of the twenty-first century, to the dreams and hopes of a peaceful and dignified life for our peoples, and lead with vision and courage.

Today, Asia is the most populous region in the world with its population of four billion,[15] out of a little more than seven billion in the world as a whole. We represent more than half of humanity; the largest, oldest, richest civilizations appeared and met in Asia. Only 50 years ago our region was extremely poor. Today, Asia emerges as a center of world power, and the twenty-first century could be Asia's century; we have the brainpower, advanced technology, and financial means to make this dream come true.

---

15   Four thousand million.

The challenges and risks we face in Asia are immense and complex, though. I daresay that our region is the most dangerous in the world, the most militarized, most nuclearized, with complex land and maritime border disputes, regional rivalries, ethnic and religious conflicts that have exploded frequently in and among states. The sheer size of current standing armies and the weaponry available to each side, ready to unleash devastating wars, is maddening. More maddening still is the mindset of some people who still believe in chauvinism, bellicose patriotism, or in their imagined national superiority and glory. It's a symptom of the nineteenth and early twentieth centuries that lingers on. We must rise to the expectations of the new twenty-first century.

Europe, and even Africa and Latin America, have freed themselves from the legacies of the past century and the world of Westphalia.[16] European countries have transcended past animosity and mistrust and formed a union. Africans and Latin Americans have created regional political bodies. In Asia, smaller countries of Southeast Asia have been trying to come together and move forward, but our big brothers of Northeast Asia look like they are still living in feudal nineteenth century.

Only in Asia there is still a regime like the one in North Korea, as barbaric as the worst of the Stalinist era, although there is a hint of change that may emerge under new leader Kim Jong-un; in some parts of Asia, there are still extremist Stone Age beliefs and practices that deny girls the right to go to school; in some other parts of Asia, acid is thrown on girls for daring to sit in a classroom; girls are shot for daring to walk to school; girls are married off or simply sold off; and a girl is murdered by her own parents. Her sin? Looking at a boy!

---

16 The German city where, in the second half of the seventeenth century, successive landmark peace treaties were signed by several European powers which established peace and a new international order in Europe. Paramount among the principles agreed in Westphalia are the respect for the boundaries of European sovereign states and non-interference in their domestic affairs. The European powers didn't extend the practice of those principles to countries in other continents, but did apply them to colonies under European control. However, many of those principles eventually became central to the world order and still apply today as decolonization progressed, notably after the Second World War. The Westphalian model of international relations has been weakening, though, under the combined pressure of ever-increasing volumes of international trade, the emergence of continental trade blocks, and of a number of unrelated global challenges which know no borders and require global responses, including climate change and the repression of terrorism and other international crime networks.

Only in Asia can a woman be sentenced to death by stoning for committing adultery. I'm sorry to say, as long as all these horror stories occur daily in our region, as long as we have religious fanatics who want half of humanity, the women, to remain enslaved to ignorance and poverty, as long as too many in Asia believe in a God that is NOT MERCIFUL but MERCILESS and VENGEFUL and in killing on His behalf those who disagree with certain interpretations of the holy script; as long as Asia has an anachronistic regime like the Kims' communist dynasty, the twenty-first century will not be ours.

As long as leaders and peoples of Northeast Asia [China, Japan, and Republic of Korea] are not able to free themselves from the past, as long as Japanese officials and educators continue to trivialize the facts of the suffering caused by the Imperial war unleashed on Asians, and as long as leaders and peoples in China do not have the courage to free themselves from this chapter in their history with Japan, this century will be still the American Century or it might be the African Century – either way, an Asian Century will be elusive to us!

Japan and Asia in need of leadership

Asia faces these enormous challenges and risks, yet it has opportunities to become a region of the future. Japan has an opportunity to lead the region if Japan makes another transformation as it did from the feudal Tokugawa era to the Meiji reformation.

I am glad to be visiting Japan at a time when Japanese people are choosing political parties and leaders to rebuild the country. This time, it should be more than just to build a strong nation, physically and militarily.

Japan should exercise leadership in building not only a just society for its own people, but also a just world for everyone. A just society, that Japan is close to achieving, is one in which resources of society are distributed to all in a fair manner, including those most deserving first. As John Stuart Mill advocated such a society a century and half ago, the government attended to the "common good," and all other citizens worked collectively to build communities and programs that would contribute to the good of others. Japan can extend its vision of social welfare to the rapidly globalizing world that needs mutual trust and assistance. Japan, in short, should strengthen more the bond of mutual relationship, or *kizuna* as I understand you call it, between the Japanese and other peoples of Asian countries.

But to do so, Japan first needs to overcome the past. Japan needs to become cognizant of its past brutality, as Germany was of the Jewish people. In dealing with the maritime territorial issue, Japanese Prime Minister Noda rightly stated that it should be resolved based on international law. But international law should be applied not only to defend Japan's position but also to enable fair and impartial settlements of disputes. The principle of international law should indeed be upheld in resolving issues surrounding Takeshima [Japanese] or Dokdo [Korean] islands but also other islands claimed by Japan and other countries.

Malaysia and Singapore did so with regard to Pedra Branca and several other islets located at the eastern entrance to the Singapore Strait. The dispute that began in 1979 was largely resolved by the International Court of Justice [ICJ] in 2008, which opined that Pedra Branca belonged to Singapore and Middle Rocks belonged to Malaysia.

Timor-Leste is also prepared to take the maritime boundary issue to the ICJ. The reason I suggest this approach is not just to have a group of international jurists to render their impartial judgments but, more importantly, to move ourselves from the world of Westphalia created five centuries ago to a world of global democratic governance in which we all can live, based on laws and standards common to all.

Maybe the various claimant States in the South China Sea dispute should agree to turn the whole area into a Zone of Peace and Joint Development, and revenues from the oil, gas, and other wealth extracted from the area should go to a newly created Asian Fund for Sustainable Development to be allocated and invested in the whole of Asia. In few words, rather than engaging in dangerous brinkmanship and saber rattling, the claimant States in the South China Seas should engage in dialogue, build bridges of understanding, and search for common ground beneficial to all in Asia.

As Japan rose above the atomic bombs dropped over Hiroshima and Nagasaki, so should China and Korea move beyond the "Nanking Massacre" and "comfort women." To do so, the three countries should consider establishing a truth and reconciliation commission, as Timor-Leste and Indonesia did. Such an international commission should include outside leaders so that the commission can record in an impartial manner what happened in terms of not only suffering and misery they brought about to countless people but also historical perspectives of what happened in past wars and conflicts.

Then, the Northeast Asia region will be free of the past and can lead the whole of Asia to form a formidable union that can surpass, in its size and power, the European Union and the United States of America.

For these transformations of Japan and Asia as a whole to occur, we need a leader who possesses the true leadership quality of Mahatma Gandhi to inspire and unite us, to have the courage to overcome the shackles of the past and the differences that exist among us. There is a chance if such a new leader emerges in Asia and leads us all, the four billion[17] people of this vast region of great civilizations, religions, and cultures, of great challenges and great possibilities, he or she can then enable us to face the present and adopt a road map to build a future of Peace, Freedom, and Prosperity in not only Asia but also the entire world.

Thank you for listening to me and sharing my vision of the Rising Asia and an analysis of its Challenges, Risks, and Opportunities.

---

17   Four thousand million.

Our Brothers in Guinea-Bissau are Victims of Drug Cartels

10 January 2013

In February, José Ramos-Horta, former President of the Democratic Republic of Timor-Leste, will assume "with serenity" the office of the Special Representative of UN Secretary-General Ban Ki-Moon in Guinea-Bissau. The Nobel Peace Prize laureate wants to help the Portuguese-speaking country out of its "cycle of instability," and says Guinea-Bissau is "not a lost cause."

Q: You have just been chosen by the Secretary-General to lead the United Nations mission in Guinea-Bissau. The United States and many international organizations say that the country is a narco-state. Is your task compromised from the outset?

JRH: The drugs are not being produced in Guinea-Bissau. They are not being consumed in Guinea-Bissau. Our brother Guineans are ultimately victims of the production and marketing of illicit drugs.

Of course, the problem of Guinea-Bissau is not only the issue of drugs; it results in part from the crisis of the state and its democratic institutions. But Guinea-Bissau is not Somalia, Congo, or Syria – fortunately.

I am convinced that, with goodwill, increased support of the European Union and the United States, a better partnership, a greater alignment of political thought and strategy with the African Union, the CPLP,[18] and ECOWAS,[19] the UN may succeed. It will not be an easy mission, obviously.

---

18 Portuguese acronym for the Community of Portuguese Speaking Countries.
19 Economic Community of Western African States.

You know many of the political and military actors in Guinea-Bissau. How do you assess the ongoing conflict in the country? Is it about rivalries, personal ambitions, ethnic issues? And what will your mandate as Special Representative of the UN Secretary-General allow you to do on the ground?

I cannot and should not say much at this point about what I can do on the ground. First, I have to listen to directives in New York, the Department of Political Affairs, which manages the dossier of Guinea-Bissau. With my colleagues in New York, listening to ECOWAS, the African Union, the CPLP, the European Union, we can forge a common thought and strategy. But most of all are our brother Guineans to say and decide on their future. The UN does not replace national leaders.

You have widespread international support, even in Guinea-Bissau. But given the past history of the country, what led you to accept a mission where so many others have failed?

Given the history of Timor-Leste with Guinea-Bissau, I could not say no to an invitation from the UN. Timor-Leste owes much to the UN and, in my experience, the organization can help the leaders and people of Guinea-Bissau to end the cycle of instability.

As you know, Portugal and the international community do not recognize the current government in Bissau. Do you think this situation will complicate your task?

No. We'll find a solution.

What means will you have to enforce the UN resolutions and fulfill your mandate on the ground?

The UN provides technical and human resources needed for each situation, not always great enough, but we need to know how to act and handle the situation with the resources that we have and not with the resources that we dream about. Sometimes people exaggerate on the resources, demand more, and in fact complicate things. And in the end, we end up spending too much time managing the internal aspects of the mission itself, instead of paying attention to the situation on the ground, for which we were mandated.

How will you approach your first test, the elections in Guinea-Bissau?

With serenity.

Let's talk about your country. Timor-Leste is much different today than it was a decade ago. Do you think that democracy and democratic institutions are already conveniently consolidated?

There is always room for improvement and need. Our institutions are young, so fragile. But the democratic culture is rooted.

What do you see as the role of Portugal since the independence of East Timor?

Timor-Leste will be forever grateful and indebted to Portugal for the central role that Portugal played for Timor-Leste's freedom with courage and dignity in the diplomatic arena. But we could never minimize the role of brother countries Angola, Cape Verde, Guinea-Bissau, Mozambique, and São Tome and Principe, Brazil, which were behind us on the diplomatic front as well.

Incidentally, before Portugal took the issue of Timor-Leste seriously, which only came to pass after 1991, these brothers from Africa, with the UN and the Non-Aligned Movement, ensured that the issue of Timor-Leste was not wiped off the international agenda.

At what point is the dispute over Timorese oil with Australia?

There is not exactly a dispute between Australia and Timor-Leste in this regard. The consortium of investors in Greater Sunrise is a multinational consortium of Australian, American, Japanese, etc.

The dispute, to use your expression, lies in knowing what is the best technology, the best way to explore the natural gas in the region, whether via a pipeline to an onshore plant in the south coast of East Timor, or a floating system [liquefied natural gas floating plant]. The dialogue is ongoing, and the various parties will find a solution with technical and commercial advantages for everyone.

Could oil also become a curse for Timor-Leste, as has happened elsewhere in the world?

Oil and gas are contributing to the modernization of our economy, reducing poverty, improving health, education, and food security.

The contribution of Portugal to Timor's State Budget was significant, with a focus on teaching and spreading the language and the consolidation of the military. But Portugal is undergoing a deep economic and financial crisis. Where are we with the promise of help in buying Portuguese debt with funds from sovereign wealth funds?

There was consensus in Timor-Leste to invest in Portugal's sovereign debt. But the government changed in Portugal, the arrival of the troika to Portugal, and there were elections in Timor-Leste, etc.

What I proposed at the time was a joint initiative of Timor-Leste, Angola, and Brazil to invest in the purchase of Portuguese sovereign debt to the advantage of all.

In Timor-Leste, you and Prime Minister Xanana Gusmão seemed to test the model followed in Russia, switching positions. Was this not a sign of weakness of the institutions?

Well… I'm no longer in power in Timor-Leste.

You recently told a newspaper that Portuguese language is gradually recovering its strength in Timor-Leste, with support by Portugal and Brazil. What is your assessment of the extent of this program?

The Portuguese language is gaining space, increasingly. But the effort must continue for another decade or two, so that the Portuguese language may gain irreversible roots in Timor-Leste.

As a Timorese in the wilds of Asia, as a diplomat, what is your vision of effective CPLP and its role in Lusophone?

We should not see language only through its geopolitical influence. Language and identity, citizenship, and history are all important factors to consider. Timor-Leste was forged by Portuguese colonization. And let's not underestimate the CPLP – given the enormous wealth they possess, Brazil, Angola, and Mozambique will emerge as major political and economic factors.

Your long political career has surely gained you both friends and enemies. Which is the most numerous?

As for me, I have no enemies. To those who may say that I'm their enemy I answer: You are my brothers! If I made mistakes I beg your forgiveness, because I am a simple human being who has failings and sins. Christ taught us to love, and love means forgiving those who hurt us. Life is so short. Fragile. Why waste it in quarrels, hatred?

Do you still have memories of the attack you suffered in 2008?

God wanted me to live on, to survive, but He left me with scars and some discomfort, permanent pain, a small ordeal that I must endure for the rest of my life. I live with this pain every day, thanking God for giving me the beauty of life, for imposing on me this suffering, so that I can better learn to appreciate the gift of life.

An article in the *Huffington Post*

Rohingya: Testing Democracy in Myanmar

José Ramos-Horta with Muhamad Yunus[20]

20 February 2013

When the Myanmar government considers its progress on reform towards an open and democratic system, it must address one of the most barbaric remnants of the recent past – the ethnic cleansing taking place in their midst.

One of the fundamental challenges of a democracy is how to ensure the voice of the majority does not trample the essential rights of the minority. In the founding of the United States this was addressed by the Bill of Rights, some form of which is integrated into most democracies today.

Even as we applaud and rejoice in the new freedoms enjoyed by the Myanmar people, the country's newly elected government must face this challenge as they evolve from autocratic rule into a democratic state. The tragedy of the Rohingya people, continuing to unfold in Rakhine State in the country's western corner, on the border of Bangladesh, will be its proving ground.

The minority Muslim Rohingya continue to suffer unspeakable persecution, with more than 1000 killed and hundreds of thousands displaced from their homes just in recent months, apparently with the complicity and protection of security forces.

The charge that the Rohingya are illegal immigrants to Myanmar is false. There is evidence that the Rohingya have been in present day

---

20   2006 Nobel Peace laureate Muhammad Yunus is an eminent economist and founder and former managing director of the Grameen Bank.

Myanmar since the eighth century. It is incontrovertible that Muslim communities have existed in Rakhine State since the fifteenth century, added to by descendants of Bengalis migrating to Arakan [Rakhine] during colonial times.

The borders between present-day Bangladesh and Myanmar have shifted back and forth throughout these periods, resulting in ethnic Rakhine Buddhists living in Bangladesh today, and ethnic Bengali Muslims such as the Rohingya in Myanmar. As the Rakhine Buddhists are rooted in their Bangladeshi communities today, the Rakhine State in Myanmar is the only home the Rohingya know.

A glaring injustice was done to the Rohingya in 1982 when the ruling junta instituted a new law excluding the Rohingya from the list of the 135 national races recognized by the Myanmar government, effectively stripping them of their nationality. Since that time they have been banned from traveling even short distances or from getting married without a permit. When a marriage permit is granted, they must sign a commitment to have no more than two children.

Half of the Rohingya population is estimated to have fled the periodic pogroms that have reduced their villages to ashes and left thousands killed or raped in horrendous massacres. After having lived side by side with the Rakhine Buddhist communities, today they are an uprooted and stateless population, with some 200,000 refugees estimated to still be living in neighboring Bangladesh and hundreds of thousands more having fled to other parts of the world.

The twentieth century gave us a term for the ugly phenomena of stripping individuals of their nationality and persecuting them for no reason other than the color of their skin, their religion, or their ethnicity: ethnic cleansing.

When the Myanmar government considers its progress on reform towards an open and democratic system of government, they must address one of the most barbaric remnants of their recent past, ethnic cleansing taking place in their midst, and right the wrongs done to the Rohingya population.

We wish the Rohingya to know that they are not alone. We hope to help share their plight with the world, in the hope and faith and trust that when the world knows of their suffering it will no longer turn its back on their persecution.

We humbly add our voices to the simple demand of the Rohingya people: that their rights as our fellow human beings be respected, that they be granted the right to live peacefully and without fear in the land of their parents, and without persecution for their ethnicity or their form of worship.

We ask the world to not look away, but to raise its collective voice in support of the Rohingya. In these days of public diplomacy the citizens, civil societies, NGOs, private investors and the business community have a vital role to play in the context of democratic reforms, human rights and development around the globe. We must use this voice.

We close with an appeal to the Myanmar government. You must amend the infamous 1982 law, and welcome the Rohingya as full citizens of Myanmar with all attendant rights. In doing so you will end the possibility of the radicalization of the Rohingya and channel their energies for the development of Myanmar. You will remove the impetus for extremism and terrorism being generated by the current mistreatment of this vulnerable minority. A strong, stable and democratic Myanmar is not only in the interest to countries of the region but will serve the cause of global peace and stability as well.

A government must in the end be judged by how it protects the most vulnerable people in its midst, and its generosity towards the weakest and most powerless. Let not the good work of this government be clouded by the continuing persecution of the Rohingya people.

Political, Military Elites Must be Aware of Existential Threats Guinea-Bissau Faces

12 April 2012 is not a date for celebration; it is rather the anniversary of one more coup d'état.[21]

Independent of the reasons that led the military to stage yet another coup, the truth is that, as a result, it brought a deep socioeconomic crisis and diplomatic isolation to the country.

I hope that, on this anniversary of the coup d'état, the transitional regime, the political and military elites of this country, will conduct a self-examination and be aware that, really, Guinea-Bissau faces an existential threat as a State, as a nation.

Without a strong State, a strong government, and solid political institutions, it will be extremely difficult for the country to face the regional challenges, the threats by organized crime, namely drug cartels of various origins and the other type of threat that each Guinean family experiences on a day-to-day basis, the threat of extreme poverty.

I must say, as a friend and brother of the Guineans, that the international community has always wanted, and wants, to help. But it is also tired. There is a real danger that the United Nations itself, the European Union and Guinea-Bissau's other friends and traditional partners may say no.

---

21   Statement by Special Representative of the United Nations Secretary-General José Ramos-Horta on the first anniversary of the 12 April 2012 coup d'état in Guinea-Bissau. Highlights of the statement were retrieved from the *Reliefweb* website with the dateline 5 April 2013.

I call on the political elites to reach an agreement on the promised road map – voter registration and the electoral calendar. Elections can be done this year, if the political elites understand what I'm saying, because the country is facing many challenges – I can even say existential challenges – as a State and as a nation.

They should come to an agreement and form a fully inclusive government as soon as possible to allow elections in a totally peaceful climate and with the prior knowledge that, in the face of the challenges of this country, there will be no winners or losers in the upcoming elections. This means that the political party with the majority of votes should have a sense of the higher interest of the State, should be aware of the seriousness of the situation, and be conscious that it alone cannot solve the problems of the country.

Extend a hand to each other, invite a third party and choose the best people – men and women – to form a fully inclusive Government, a strong Government, for the second phase of the process.

The first phase runs from now until the elections. The second – I will call it "reorganization" – is to rebuild the State and to garner international support so that the country can finally regain the prestige it had in the years of 1973, 1974, 1975. This is possible. This country is potentially rich, it has a fabulous people who have never been involved in bloody tribal wars, notwithstanding its multi-ethnic nature.

One Day with my Friend Kumba Yalá

3 August 2013

This is not meant as a political essay. It is just a short story about the charismatic, passionate, unpredictable political leader, emanating from an enigmatic ethnic community, the Balantas. His is a very horizontal society that discards hierarchy, unlike many other very hierarchical-traditional societies.

I have been wanting to share this story for a while now. It was many moons ago, before the rains started, when one Saturday I spent almost the whole day with this famous Bissau-Guinean, former President Kumba Yalá.

Mr Yalá was President of this unhappy country from September 2000 till 2003, when he was deposed in a largely bloodless coup.

I was Timor-Leste's Minister for Foreign Affairs and was sent to Guinea-Bissau in August of 2003, the month before, as the Special Envoy of the CPLP, to defuse the very palpable prevailing political tensions and prevent a widely rumored military coup.

I was not very successful in that coup-preventing mission! During my trip I had the sense that the coup was close to inevitable, given the almost general political malaise in the country towards Mr Yalá. I was right. On 14 September 2003, just a few weeks after my first meeting with him, he was removed from office in a military coup.

President Kumba Yalá was born 15 March 1953, in a very humble, poor, farming Balanta family. As a teenager, like most Bissau-Guineans, he joined the national liberation movement, the African Party for the Independence of Guinea and Cape Verde [PAIGC]. Many years later, disenchanted with the PAIGC leadership policies and their alleged exclusion of people of his Balanta tribe, Mr Yalá left the party in 1992 and founded a new one, the Party for Social Renewal.

Yalá says he studied theology and philosophy at the prestigious Catholic University of Lisbon. He is knowledgeable on the writings of ancient Greek philosophers. In conversation, this politician-theologian-philosopher will quote you Aristotle a hundred times.

Yalá was raised and first educated in a Catholic school until age 17 when, as he told me, his father threw him out of the house to "go out, be a man, make a living." Balantas cultivate a macho, warrior image, and young men are expected to be fighters.

In 2008 Kumba Yalá converted to Islam and took the name Mohamed Ialá Embaló. This conversion might not have been inspired by religious motives; as he told me, it may have been motivated more by criticism from the Bishop of Bissau and what Yalá felt was the Bishop's excessive involvement in politics. (The Bishop of Bissau, José Câmnate na Bissign, since 1999 the first Ginea-bissauan native Catholic bishop, is also from the Balanta community, a lovely, charming, humble prelate, widely respected by everyone, including his Protestant and Muslim colleagues.)

This is not meant as political essay. It is just a short story about this charismatic, passionate, unpredictable political leader, emanating from an enigmatic ethnic community, the Balantas, a very horizontal society that discards hierarchy, unlike many other very hierarchical-traditional societies.

The Balanta fighting spirit and military cunning contributed decisively to the 1973 defeat of the Portuguese colonial army. Of course, the then Soviet Union and Cuba provided military training and equipment, including portable anti-aircraft missiles, assistance that played no small part in clearing the skies of Portuguese air dominance.

When not at war, the Balantas are pastoral, sedentary agriculturalists, enigmatic, deeply embedded in their own mystical beliefs system. They reject wealth and ostentation. They resent being looked down at and excluded by the country's elites.

Kumba Yalá was, and still is, the eloquent voice of the Balantas.[22] There has been no more effective spokesperson for his people.

Today, one is hard pressed to find a positive note in the international media about Bissau-Guineans. Among the small and conspicuous foreign community in Bissau, one hears comments like "The politicians are all corrupt"; "The military are all involved in organized crime." And of

---

22   Former President Kumba Yalá untimely passed away from natural causes on 4 April 2014.

course there is a rising chorus echoing the refrain that Guinea-Bissau is the only "Narco-State" in the world. This is nonsense.

Colombia, Bolivia, Peru, Mexico, Honduras, Afghanistan, Myanmar, and others have far bigger drug problems and have much greater resources to fight back organized crime.

I have read a few papers on the drug problem and most seem to be quoting from each other. From all that I have seen and read, perhaps I am utterly naïve, but I am not persuaded that this is a "Narco-State."

It is a very fragile State, with extremely weak institutions. Corruption is pervasive at every level, undermining justice and democracy, good governance, pushing the country towards the abyss of a Failed State.

But Guinea-Bissau does not produce illicit drugs such as cocaine or amphetamines and does not consume these drugs to any noticeable degree. Yes, at times it is used as a transhipment point from Latin America to Europe with the active complicity of many. This does not make a country deserving of the title "Narco-State."

Other rumors heard frequently on the wind among the tiny expatriate community include the gossip that leaders like Kumba Yalá and General António Injái have become super rich off the country – something I have not seen borne out in fact.

I have been here for six months now. I have been in many parts of this not very pretty city and in the rural areas. I engage many local people, students, academics, journalists, small or richer business people, politicians, military, police, etc., in many different settings.

I am sharing with you some photos I took from my most recent visit with President Kumba Yalá and his family. From left to right, President Kumba Yalá, me, and his older brother, in his mid-seventies, seen here wearing a worn-out shirt or jacket, maybe some 20 years old, never washed. The house belongs to Mr Yalá's parents.

The older Yala still lives in the house, now ramshackle, where Kumba Yalá was born and lived until he turned 17. Their sparse food intake is cooked in open air in a clay pot, seen here also. Equally sad and heartbreaking is to see where the former President's older brother sleeps, on an improvised bench, outside the house.

I handed over [to] the older brother some money to buy himself new clothing. In my next trip I hope to bring him a proper bed and better cooking utensils.

Mr Kumba Yalá no longer lives in his *tabanka*.[23] He now lives in a very modest house in Bissau which I also visited. I was taken to every room by the former President. At some point he searched in a box for his favorite books of Aristotle, pulled out a book, and subjected me to another round of rambling citation of the great thinker.

It was by then a hot mid-afternoon. Kumba Yalá was very gracious and wanted to give me a tour of the town. I excused myself. I was tired. I was saddened by the story of this good man, somewhat eccentric and unpredictable, but essentially good.

He laments the two years that were robbed from him in 2003 by the coup, when he had just completed three years in office. I think of his destitute family, and he himself is poor. I am saddened by Kumba Yalá's story and I am saddened by the story of this often-betrayed people.

---

23   Small rural hamlet.

On Preventing Conflict, Ending Wars, Building Peace

October 2013

Sharing with you some reflections on Timor-Leste, Guinea-Bissau, Syria, the Israeli-Palestinian conflict, and other issues.[24]

I have just ended a three-day lecture tour[25] **in the Brazilian cities of Porto Alegre and São Paulo. The topic has been my lifelong commitment – preventing conflicts, ending wars, building peace.**

An estimated 2000 students, academics, and members of civil society organizations attended the talks and we enjoyed animated discussions around the issues. In São Paulo I also addressed a meeting on the Israeli-Palestinian conflict hosted by the Israel-Brazil Association.

The speaking tour was sponsored by *Fronteiras do Pensamento*,[26] a joint initiative of the University of Rio Grande do Sul, supported by some major Brazilian conglomerates that are committed to international dialogue and understanding of major peace and security challenges facing the world.

On the last day of the trip, 3 October, I caught an early flight to Brazil's capital for meetings with the Ministers of Foreign Affairs and Defence, other senior Brazilian diplomats, and political and security specialists to discuss developments in Guinea-Bissau.

---

24 Blogpost, in ramoshorta.com.
25 From 30 September to 2 October 2013.
26 Frontier of Thought.

The morning ended with a working lunch where I briefed some 20 ambassadors and answered pointed questions on the situation in the West African country.

I thought I would share some reflections on Timor-Leste, Guinea-Bissau, Syria, the Israeli-Palestinian conflict, and other issues with you.

On conflict prevention:

- The UN should be provided with more support to expand and enhance its political and conflict prevention mandate; it requires more financial resources to hire and deploy experienced conflict prevention specialists. Expanding and beefing up UN early-warning and preventive diplomacy mechanisms, more experienced specialists can be deployed to focus on regions or countries, looking at potential intra-state or inter-state conflicts, advising the Secretary-General and the Security Council to take timely action.
- Member States undermine the UN by not paying up their dues or even cutting off core and program funding for its many Agencies. There has been an irrational hostility by many in the US Congress towards, and a systematic assault on, the UN, undermining the very body the US helped to found in 1945.
- For the major powers, UN reform has meant draconian cost cutting, reducing its expenditure and personnel. It has not meant adjusting the distribution of power in the Security Council to reflect twenty-first century power balance. Powers like Brazil, India, Indonesia, Egypt, Nigeria should have Permanent Member status in the Security Council like any of the five aging major powers.
- Preventing conflicts must be a holistic approach that includes reduction of poverty and creation of prosperity through sustainable development strategies.
- Rich countries, with the notable exception of the five Nordics, have failed to allocate more of their country's wealth to Overseas Development Aid [ODA]. The UN has called for the allocation of at least 0.7 percent of the GDP of rich countries towards sustainable development in poorer countries of the South.
- At the onset of the US and European financial crisis in 2008, every western leader pledged in their speeches to the UN General Assembly in New York that "overseas development assistance would not be penalized as a result of the crisis." Every one of

them has betrayed their pledges and has drastically reduced their contribution to ODA by as much as 50–70 percent.

The UK is a notable exception. Not only has it not reduced its contribution; it has in effect increased its overseas development assistance to African countries.

- Weapons-producing countries from East and West have fueled tensions and wars by their unscrupulous weapons exports to volatile regions of the world.

On Syria:

- As I said in an interview with the respected daily newspaper *Folha de São Paulo*, the US President is right in being very prudent and not opting for a direct military involvement or the bombing of sites in Syria at this time.
- Criticisms of China and Russia for blocking UNSC action are not entirely fair. Even a unanimous UNSC resolution authorizing the use of force would not necessarily end the war – it could prolong the conflict.
- We must sometimes accept the fact that there are conflicts, and the conflict in Syria is a case in point, where the end of the war comes about not because of smart foreign mediation but simply and tragically because the two sides have exhausted themselves. This was the case in the Iran-Iraq war in the eighties. That war ended only after more than one million people had died and the two countries destroyed. They then sued for peace. This might be the case of Syria.
- What the international community can and must do is to expand its humanitarian assistance to Syrian refugees, and increase assistance to the neighboring countries that are overwhelmed by the inflow of refugees.
- The world will have to live with the legacy of the Syrian war brutality. The scars inflicted on its children and youth will be with them for many years to come.

On Egypt:

- Leaders bear the responsibility for the consequences of their policies and actions. A leader who fails to measure every step he or she takes, who drags his or her people into incalculable suffering, is a failed leader.
- Some leaders, when in power, lacking humility and wisdom, do not seek to embrace those on the other side. Such is the case with the deposed President Morsi of Egypt. After almost 100 years out of power, the Muslim Brotherhood had a chance to govern, but they had less than half of the country voting for them. Instead of walking halfway, building bridges, and embracing the other half, Mr Morsi attempted to impose his own beliefs on the rest of the country. He brought on himself and the country the coup and its aftermath. He failed because he miscalculated, underestimated the other side, overplayed his hand, overestimated his own strength.

On leadership:

In ending my remarks in my first public talk in Porto Alegre, I shared with the audience a passage of my farewell speech on 19 May 2012, when I handed over power to the newly elected President of Timor-Leste. I think it continues to be relevant today and beyond:

"I have often said, and I repeat again tonight, there is no greater justice than freedom, and, in 1999, Indonesia and the international community sanctioned the freedom for which we fought and died. This greater justice, our freedom and dignity, should prevail over the justice of the victors over the vanquished.

"We have built a unique relationship with Indonesia and Portugal as well as with all others who, at one time in recent history, were on the other side.

"Among our many achievements, one that is of great value is the reconciliation among the divided Timorese family. Our Maun Bot Xanana who led us to freedom when all seemed lost, has led this unique reconciliation process with courage, determination and compassion. I am proud of being part of a society that has shown a great heart in resisting the temptation to exercise revenge in the name of justice.

"In victory, be magnanimous; never seek to humiliate the adversary; if he is on his knees, hold his hands and plead with him to rise up; embrace him; walk halfway and meet the vanquished ones, embrace them, invite them to join in a new enterprise of peace, a new future for all. This has been my belief, and in many ways, this has been our practice since independence."

Asia Rise or Fall: Challenges and Opportunities

New Delhi, 4 December 2013

The 21th century could be Asia's Century.[27] Asia represents half of humanity; the largest, oldest, richest civilizations appeared and met in Asia. Only 50 years ago, our Continent was extremely poor. Today, it emerges as a center of world power.

I first set foot on this vast, sacred land of India in April 1992 in a private journey to Dharamsala, where many have journeyed before me to catch a glimpse of the Dalai Lama with the hope that one's soul is instantly cleansed and somehow our neurotic persona is transformed. But more than drawn by the promise of inner peace supposedly emanating from the springs of Dharamsala, to this very day I am still in awe by the greatest human being modern humanity has produced – the Mahatma Gandhi.

His has been India's greatest legacy to humanity.

I bow to all in India, past and present leaders, who have built up modern, free, democratic India, preserving freedom and democracy even in times of turmoil, never giving up democracy in spite of its imperfections.

Indians were never terribly interested in what was happening in Timor-Leste from 1975 till 1999. The Indonesian annexation of Portuguese East Timor was simplistically compared with India's takeover of Goa. At the United Nations, Indian diplomats instinctively and loyally sided with Indonesia in every single debate on the issue.

---

27 This lecture draws on the author's opinions put forward on 29 November 2012, in his *Lesson on Global Governance and Peacebuilding*, at the United Nations University, in Tokyo. The editors decided to include both conferences, though, as the *13th Lakdawala Memorial Lecture* broadens the scope of the analysis and includes a wealth of data which was not mentioned earlier.

But in 2003, after our independence, I came back to India as my country's Foreign Minister to begin a new chapter in our relations. I always hoped that somehow India would be tempted to adopt Timor-Leste as its protégé and would help transform my country in a single generation. This has not materialized but at least a considerable number of Timorese have come here to study.

Being a founding father of my country, I beg your indulgence to allow me to share with you the challenges and developments that are taking place there. Timor-Leste remains a success story in Asia. We have come a long way in a fairly short time, since the restoration of independence in 2002. Ten years on, we are proud that the latest UNDP Human Development Report accords Timor-Leste an HDI for 2012 that jumped to the value of 0.576, placing our country in the medium human development category; at independence in 2002 it was 0.375.

According to the UNDP-commissioned report, Timor-Leste, Cambodia, Ghana, Lao People's Democratic Republic, and Mongolia were the HDI growth leaders in the Medium Human Development grouping.

East Asia and the Pacific as a region have an average HDI value of 0.683 and registered annual HDI[28] value growth between 2000 and 2012 of 1.31 percent, with Timor-Leste leading with 2.71 percent, followed by Myanmar at 2.23 percent. The East Asia-Pacific region has the highest employment-to-population ratio (74.5 percent) in the developing world.[29]

Timor-Leste's economy continues to perform well. Bank deposits grew by 10.5 percent, year on year, in the first half of 2013. Private sector credit was 10.3 percent higher in June 2013 than a year earlier, reaching a new high of US$165.6 million.

Bank lending grew strongly as well in the first half of 2013 as credit to individuals rose by 13.1 percent and credit to commercial and financial companies grew by 25.2 percent.

Lending to agricultural producers also registered double-digit growth, which suggests expanded investment in coffee farms.

The value of merchandise imports was almost three times higher in the first quarter of the year than in the first quarter of 2012. The value

28   HDI is the United Nations Development Program (UNDP)-monitored Human Development Index.
29   UN Human Development Report, 2012.

of nonpetroleum exports posted very high growth, albeit starting from a low base.

Vehicle registrations in the first half of 2013 were 25.8 percent higher than a year earlier. Sales of electricity were 7.8 percent higher over the same period, following the completion of the national electrification program.

Since 2005, life expectancy at birth in Timor-Leste has increased by more than two years and now averages 64 years.

GNP[30] per capita increased 228 percent during the same period to over US$5,000. Average annual growth has exceeded 10 percent for the last four years and real non-oil GDP growth remains strong.

According to forecasts by *The Economist*, Timor-Leste is among the nine fastest-growing economies of the world in 2013.

School enrollment jumped from 63 percent in 2006 to well over 90 percent now for basic education, according to the 2010 National Census.

More than 300,000 adults have also graduated from illiteracy to functioning literacy since 2006, when we launched the adult literacy program, a program conceived with support from Cuba. It is anticipated that adult illiteracy will be eliminated by 2015.

Infant mortality, and child mortality under five, as well as post-birth mother mortality, have been halved. Incidences of malaria and dengue and the prevalence of poverty have decreased significantly. With less than one case of leprosy per 10,000 people, Timor-Leste is now considered by the WHO[31] to be free from this centuries-old disease.

As we feel proud of our achievements thus far, we are also very much aware of the daunting challenges still to overcome.

Poverty has seen significant reduction as its prevalence declined from 49 percent in 2007 to 41 percent two years later, according to estimates by the World Bank. But this means poverty is still high and remains a major challenge. However, the Government is determined to bring poverty levels down to below 15 percent by 2015.

Access to clean water, sanitation, public health, and education are key priorities that need robust investment now and for years to come.

---

30 GNP, Gross National Product, is the total value of goods produced and services provided in one country during one year. It equals the GDP, gross domestic product, *plus* the net income from foreign investments. In Timor-Leste's case, the latter are basically the financial applications of Timor-Leste's sovereign wealth fund, the Parliament-monitored Petroleum Fund.

31 The World Health Organization.

Like many countries in the early years of independence, Timor-Leste has had to confront social and political challenges. In some instances, like the 2006 crisis, violence flared up, rolling back the gains of previous years.

However, we have been able to quickly overcome these crises. As the UNDP Human Development Report and other indicators show, we have rebounded stronger from the brief periods of instability.

The political situation in Timor-Leste in recent years has been remarkably free of tension.

The governing coalition of three parties, led by Prime Minister Xanana Gusmão and the large opposition party FRETILIN, has committed itself to continue to further consolidate peace, national unity, reconciliation, and sustainable development.

We have a dynamic multi-party democracy with four parties in the National Parliament, and 37 percent of the elected MPs are women. Several women hold key ministerial portfolios.

While our democracy is young and therefore imperfect, nevertheless, Government and opposition have found common ground on key strategic priorities for the country and have been able to work together to consolidate peace and national reconciliation, creating an enabling environment for sustainable development.

Transparency in our public life is a process that we impose on ourselves to promote and to deepen with the assistance of the international community.

The Extractive Industries Transparency Initiative rates Timor-Leste as the best performer in Asia, and third in the world, in terms of accountability and transparency in the management of our petroleum resources.

In the pursuit of good governance and transparency, the Anti-Corruption Commission, working in partnership with the Ombudsman and the office of Prosecutor-General have shown to all that no one is above the law, and justice is being upheld for all.

Our security institutions, the Army and Police forces, are now more professional, disciplined, and better imbued with the culture of respect for human rights and the strict adherence to the rule of law.

We have ratified all major International Human Rights Treaties and complied with reporting obligations.

Our country stands out with its liberal, humanist Constitution that prohibits the death penalty and life imprisonment.

According to Reporters Without Borders, Timor-Leste has one of the freest medias in the region.

Our country has also set a successful policy of reconciliation and peace. On the national level, we have healed the wounds among the previously deeply divided Timorese family and with our Indonesian brothers and sisters.

Allow me to quote my own words, extracted from my farewell speech to the nation when I left office in May 2012:

"Among our many achievements, one that is of great value is the reconciliation among the divided Timorese family. Our Maun Bot Xanana, who led us to freedom when all seemed lost, has led this unique reconciliation process with courage, determination, and compassion. I am proud of being part of a society that has shown a great heart in resisting the temptation to exercise revenge in the name of justice.

"In victory, be magnanimous; never seek to humiliate the adversary; if he is on his knees, hold his hands and plead with him to rise up; embrace him; walk halfway and meet the vanquished ones, embrace them, invite them to join in a new enterprise of peace, a new future for all. This has been my belief, and in many ways this has been our practice since independence."

Today we enjoy unique excellent relations with our closest neighbors, Indonesia and Australia. I can state with confidence that there are no two countries anywhere in Asia enjoying better relations than Timor-Leste and Indonesia.

But far and beyond, we have developed excellent active relationships with China, Korea, Japan, the United States, the European Union, the Portuguese-speaking countries; and we look forward to soon join ASEAN and fully integrate into our natural region.

For all the above, for the peace our people are enjoying today, peace among us, and [being] at peace with our former "enemies," I may have contributed my share.

Allow me now to turn to the theme of my presentation for this occasion.

We are living in times of great challenges in much of the world, but also of hope and optimism for our peoples and our continent.

I'm a frequent visitor to Japan and have visited several times the historic city of Hiroshima, toured the Museum that so vividly walks a visitor through the corridors and chambers of horror of the devastation caused by the one single atomic bomb dropped on that city one clear day in August 1945, at the end of the Second World War.

No less heartbreaking have been my visits to the Holocaust Museum in Berlin that reminds us of the systematic cleansing of millions of Jews in Europe by the Third Reich.

In both cities we are sadly reminded of human beings' capacity to inflict destruction and pain on fellow human beings.

And Japanese people should not only be reminded of the horrors of the effects of the atomic bomb dropped on Hiroshima and Nagasaki. They should be truthfully educated about what brought about the destruction and death in Hiroshima and Nagasaki; as much as we must all revisit Hiroshima time and again, we should remember time and again the suffering and destruction caused by the Japanese Imperial Army in many parts of Asia during its years of aggression and occupation.

Unfortunately, human beings do not seem to ever learn from history. Soon after the end of the Second World War we had the Korean War, unleashed by the communist regime in the north of the Korean Peninsula as it attempted in a lightning surprise attack to overrun the people and forces of the south.

We had mad policies of Stalin in Russia and Mao in China, the 1965–66 mass killings in Indonesia, the Khmer Rouge Killing Fields in Cambodia in the mid-seventies, the genocide in East Timor beginning in 1975, the Rwanda genocide of 1994, the Balkan wars and ethnic cleansing in the 1990s, the ongoing tragedies in Darfur, Sudan, Somalia, Congo, Afghanistan, Libya, Syria.

Let us not forget the past wars of partition of India, Pakistan, Bangladesh, Biafra, the Iran–Iraq war, the invasion of tiny Kuwait by the Saddam Hussein regime, etc.

The catalogue of human brutalities is a far too long one and still ongoing that makes me wonder whether we ever learn!

As the US and NATO forces begin their phased withdrawal from Afghanistan, there is growing anxiety and fear among many Afghans about the future – about their hard-won democratic gains; will these gains survive the American withdrawal in 2014, or once again will the country and the people be overrun by the Taliban? And what will happen in Pakistan, facing its own internal Taliban and other security challenges?

I beg to disagree with a number of scholars who paint too rosy a picture about the emerging twenty-first-century Asia. Time and again we hear the claim that world power is shifting to Asia. I believe this is overly exaggerated and misleading.

The challenges we face in Asia are immense and complex. I daresay that our region is the most dangerous in the world, the most militarized, most nuclearized, with nuclear weapons neighbors; with complex land and maritime border disputes, regional rivalries, ethnic and religious conflicts that have exploded frequently in and among states.

Africa and Latin America have long freed themselves from the legacies of the Cold War. The conflicts still prevailing in the two regions pale by comparison with the security challenges we face in Asia. Africans and Latin Americans have created regional political bodies, democratic systems, rule of law and human rights practices, and monitoring mechanisms that make us Asians look like we still live in the feudal nineteenth century.

Only in Asia is there a regime like the one in North Korea, as barbaric as the worst of the Stalinist era; in parts of Asia we have Stone Age beliefs and practices that deny girls the right to go to school; in some parts of Asia acid is thrown on girls for daring to sit in a classroom; girls are married off or simply sold off. In parts of Asia a woman can be sentenced to death by stoning for committing adultery.

As long as all these horror stories occur daily in our region, as long as we have religious fanatics who want half of humanity, the women, to remain enslaved to ignorance and poverty, as long as too many in Asia believe in a God that is MERCILESS, and in His behalf kill those who disagree with certain interpretations of the holy script, the twenty-first century will not be ours.

As long as leaders and peoples of Northeast Asia [China, Japan, and South Korea] are not able to free themselves from the past, as long as Japanese officials and educators continue to rewrite history and trivialize the facts of the suffering caused by the Imperial war unleashed on Asians, and as long as leaders and peoples in China do not have the courage and magnanimity to free themselves from this chapter in their history with Japan, this century will be still the American Century, or it might be the African Century – an Asian Century will be elusive to us!

Our challenges are overwhelming, daunting. But we can overcome these challenges by pooling resources, solutions, in partnerships, without exclusions.

Asia must further develop partnerships with the US and the EU, technological powerhouses and large economic areas that have much still to contribute to global solutions.

Against the many negatives facts and complex challenges cited above, there is much good news, dramatic positive transformations. Hundreds of millions of people have been freed from poverty, in particular in China, India, Pakistan, Bangladesh, Vietnam, Indonesia, Malaysia, Cambodia, Laos, the Philippines, Thailand; others – the Republic of Korea, Japan, and Singapore continue to outshine much of the world in science, technology, and innovation.

As we enter the second decade of the twenty-first century, Asian economies have become the powerhouse of global economy.

China, the Republic of Korea, India, and Indonesia have been growing at annual rates of between six and 10 percent for sustained long periods.

The economies of China, Korea, Japan, and India put together already account for over $14 trillion[32] of annual GDP.

ASEAN,[33] another fast-growing economic region, represents some $2 trillion of combined annual GDP.

Asia economic powerhouses put together are already a formidable force, side by side with the $16 trillion of combined output in EU countries and the $15 trillion US economy, according with IMF[34] estimates for 2010.

And every day, the sustained high economic performance of leading Asian countries is helping pull smaller neighbors into the path of growth and economic development.

Excellencies, ladies and gentlemen, on the human rights front, there is also positive news. Compared with the immediate post-World War II period, up to the nineties, we could say there has been dramatic progress

---

32 Fourteen million million US dollars.

33 The Association of South East Asian Nations is a regional grouping promoting economic, political, and security cooperation among its ten members: Brunei, Cambodia, Indonesia, Laos, Malaysia, Myanmar, the Philippines, Singapore, Thailand, and Vietnam. Timor-Leste, the eleventh nation in the region, formally applied to full membership of ASEAN.

34 The International Monetary Fund.

in civil and political rights, and economic, social, and cultural rights, the two fundamental pillars of all human rights.

Colonialism and apartheid were obviously two of the worst manifestations of individual and collective abuses – of gross, systematic, and systemic abuse of human rights.

But sadly, and tragically, freedom from colonial rule didn't mean necessarily freedom from oppression. In fact, in too many instances, there were greater human rights abuses in the years after independence than during the colonial era.

Too many peoples in Asia, Africa, and Latin America were liberated from colonial rule to become victims of the new tyrants with different skin color and masks.

In Asia, for example, from the early fifties till the late eighties we saw horrendous human rights situations in China, Cambodia, Indonesia, South Korea, Bangladesh, and Burma.

Nevertheless, I would say that, overall, the human rights situation in the world today, viewed from the perspective of the two main international human rights conventions, has improved significantly.

In few words, the world has changed much. Asia is changing fast, and in the face of the financial and economic predicaments of the US and Europe, Asia must seek to be center stage and lead. But to lead is to inspire, to be able to forge partnerships, build bridges, and seek common ground.

Asia can and should lead on tackling the challenges we face in the twenty-first century: we have resources to alleviate and finally eradicate poverty; we master sciences and technology; we possess know-how to lead the search for global answers to the challenges of climate change and the need for sustainable increase in food production.

Asia can and should lead on reversing environmental damage and ensuring sustainable development while keeping up with the welfare of our peoples.

In our globalized world, Asia can lead only in partnership with other stakeholders, especially emerging countries. However, the challenges facing Asia as a whole are enormous and should not be underestimated.

Asia needs a road map of priorities and resource allocation to answer our challenges and it needs also leadership to establish and implement this road map, strengthening peaceful relations.

I believe that time has come for Asia to lead and guide the world while navigating the challenges of the twenty-first century.

Asian leaders should consider a 30-year Asian road map for integrated, sustainable Human Development, including goals to eradicate poverty, illiteracy, TB, malaria, etc., and restore the wealth and health of our forests, rivers, and seas.

With half the world's population, Asians extract a lot more from our planet to satisfy our needs of survival and development than any other peoples of the world.

For our own survival, in solidarity with our brothers and sisters from other parts of the world, we must act with vision and determination, we must do a lot more to free our people from extreme poverty and save our common planet.

Together, China, India, Pakistan, Japan, Republic of Korea, Indonesia, Singapore, Malaysia, Thailand, Turkey, Saudi Arabia, the rich Gulf countries have an unparalleled pool of know-how and financial resources to transform Asia into a prosperous, peaceful, and happy region for the four billion[35] that live in our region that spreads from Istanbul to Jakarta, Timor-Leste, and the Pacific Islands.

Our American and European brothers are enduring great sacrifices to overcome the crisis that is lingering on, since 2008.

We should sympathize with them and not gloat over their difficulties and pain. And I'm convinced that the USA and Europe will rise again, stronger, from this crisis.

The USA and Europe still lead in science and technology and they should invest even more on education, research and new technologies.

But Asia should create its own fund, the Asian Fund for Sustainable Development, that can be managed by an existing institution such as the Asian Development Bank, in partnership with UN Specialized Agencies such as UNDP, UNICEF,[36] WHO, FAO,[37] or NGOs with good regional or international reputation such as Oxfam.

Each country should mandatorily contribute to such a fund, according to their GDP. Maybe the various claimant States in the South China Sea

---

35   Four thousand million.
36   The United Nations Children's Fund.
37   The Food and Agriculture Organization of the United Nations.

dispute should agree to turn the whole area into a Zone of Peace and Joint Development.

Revenues from the oil, gas, and other wealth extracted from the area would go to such a fund, to be allocated and invested in the whole of Asia with a view to attaining our common dream of eliminating extreme poverty, preventable illnesses, illiteracy, saving our forests, rivers, lakes, and seas.

In few words, rather than engaging in dangerous brinkmanship and saber rattling, the claimant States in the South China Seas should engage in dialogue, build bridges of understanding, and search for common ground beneficial to all in Asia.

Asian leaders should rise to the challenges of the twenty-first century, to the dreams and hopes of a peaceful and dignified life for our people, and lead with vision and courage.

Asia is the most populous region in the world: we represent half of humanity; the largest, oldest, richest civilizations appeared and met in Asia. Only 50 years ago our region was extremely poor. Today, Asia emerges as a center of world power, and the twenty-first century could be Asia's Century; we have the brainpower, advanced technology, and financial means to make this dream come true.

We cannot continue to demand that the aging and impoverished Europe, or today's less powerful USA, come to our rescue and lead; much less should we take part in pointing fingers at industrialized countries for the ills of our planet.

If Europeans and Americans contributed the most to environmental degradation in the last 100 years, truth be told they also contributed the most towards advances in medicine, science, and technology, to the benefit of all of humanity.

The twenty-first century will be Asia's Century, Asia's Age of Enlightenment, if a new Mahatma Gandhi emerges who inspires and leads all, the four billion[38] people of this vast region that extends from the doors of Constantinople to Díli, a region of great civilizations, religions, and cultures, of great challenges and great possibilities; we need a new Mahatma Gandhi to unite us, to inspire, to have the courage to overcome the shackles of the past, face the present, and adopt a road map to build a Future of Peace, Freedom, and Prosperity.

---

38   Four thousand million.

Postponing Elections Means Postponing the Solution to Serious Problems

Bissau, 19 December 2013

I call Guinea-Bissau political leaders to unite around the ideals of their fight in the past, sit around the table to dialogue, and propose an agenda for Peace, Democracy, and Development.

The people of Guinea-Bissau unfortunately are not going to celebrate a happy Christmas like they used to do. The year that is just ending was a year of further suffering, disappointments, broken promises, fear, and impunity.

As the UN Secretary-General's Special Representative, I honestly cannot say that there was progress towards return to peace, good governance, justice, wellbeing.

I'm worried with regard to 2014, because nothing assures us that the situation will improve.

The postponing of the elections means postponing the resolution of Guinea-Bissau's serious problems.

The international community remains very skeptical about the political will of Guinean political leaders to assume their responsibilities and decisively find lasting solutions to serious problems of their country.

The international community cannot replace the national leaders. The international community can support those who demonstrably deserve support, who want to be supported.

I call Guinea-Bissau political leaders to unite around the ideals of their fight in the past, sit around the table to dialogue, and propose an agenda for Peace, Democracy, and Development.

The first step will be general elections in mid-March 2014. Not holding elections as promised to the people of Guinea-Bissau and the international community will inevitably exacerbate the very serious problems the country is facing. I therefore call on everyone to work towards the holding of free, fair, and credible elections, the formation of an inclusive, broad-based government and, together, mobilize the resources to rescue Guinea-Bissau from electricity and water shortages, extreme poverty, and instability.

I wish you all happiness in this Christmas time and, in advance, Happy New Year.

On the Conclusion of Voter Registration in Guinea-Bissau

Bissau, 7 February 2014

Now, we must all work even harder in the second phase of the electoral process, and this means the election itself, which will be held next month. Challenges remain, namely a decision by the political parties in Parliament and outside.

I applaud the decision of the relevant Guinea-Bissau transition authorities at the conclusion of the voter registration process, with a record-breaking 91 percent of the potential voter registration.

Based on the most recent national census of Guinea-Bissau (2009), the Office for the Technical Support to the Electoral Process, GTAPE, had estimated the [number of] potential voters at 810,961.

I have personally witnessed both the efforts by the relevant authorities and officials in bringing the voter registration to the remotest villages and islands of Guinea-Bissau, even where there were no roads: the electronic kits, as well as heavy generators, had to be carried on improvised transportation, or by foot, into remote areas. I also personally witnessed tens of thousands of common people standing up for hours, and days, to register.

There were many challenges, namely geographic conditions, inaccessibility in many areas of the country, adulteration of the equipment because of dust and humidity, lack of fuel for the portable generators, slow payment of kit operators and other personnel, etc. There was no lacking of challenges and obstacles along the way. However, in my view this has been an extraordinary effort, a success, and I commend with deep gratitude the national authorities, and their friends and partners, namely Timor-Leste, Nigeria, and the ECOWAS[39] countries.

Now, we must all work even harder in the second phase of the electoral process, and this means the election itself, which will be held next month. Obstacles remain, namely a decision by the political parties in Parliament and outside, together with competent authorities.

I commend other donors, namely the African Union, CPLP, the European Union, Portugal, the United Kingdom, China, and the Peace-Building Fund, that have so far pledged, and in some instances already delivered in kind, support or cash for this important democratic exercise that will bring to an end the transition period and usher a new chapter in Guinea-Bissau history.

---

39   Economic Community of Western African States.

An article in the *Huffington Post*

North Korea is the World's Worst Human Rights Crisis

27 February 2014

There is a tendency among many to be cynical about the UN, to dismiss it as toothless and ineffective. Now is a moment for the UN to prove its critics wrong.

North Korea is arguably the world's worst human rights crisis, in the world's most closed nation – but it can no longer be its most forgotten.

Last week's publication of the United Nations Commission of Inquiry report on human rights in North Korea, with its damning conclusion that the regime is guilty of multiple widespread and systematic crimes against humanity and its call for a case to be referred by the Security Council to the International Criminal Court, shines a long overdue light on the darkest corner of the globe.

The inquiry, led by Australian judge Michael Kirby, concludes that "the gravity, scale and nature" of North Korea's human rights violations "reveal a State that does not have any parallel in the contemporary world."

The 400-page report draws on hours of firsthand testimony by more than 320 witnesses, mostly North Koreans who have escaped from the country. It is the most comprehensive, detailed, and authoritative study to date, and provides compelling evidence to support its findings.

It details crimes against humanity, including "extermination, murder, enslavement, torture, imprisonment, rape, forced abortions and other sexual violence," as well as religious persecution and starvation. It concludes that there is "an almost complete denial" of freedom of thought, conscience, religion, or expression and association. "The unspeakable atrocities that are being committed against inmates of the Kwalliso[40]

---

40   North Korea's political penal labour colonies, sometimes also spelt *kwan-li-so*.

political prison camps," the report continues, "resemble the horrors that totalitarian States established during the twentieth century." Until now, no one has been held accountable. "Impunity reigns," it concludes, and the fact that the North Korean regime "has for decades pursued policies involving crimes that shock the conscience of humanity raises questions about the inadequacy of the response of the international community."

That the investigation has reached these conclusions is no surprise. The question facing the UN and all its member states now is what to do about it. The Commission of Inquiry sets out a number of recommendations, notably bringing a case to the International Criminal Court, imposing targeted sanctions against key figures in the regime guilty of these crimes, extending the mandate of the UN Special Rapporteur on Human Rights in North Korea, and establishing a UN-mandated system for collecting evidence and documentation "to help ensure accountability for human rights violations." The report puts the ball firmly in the international community's court, arguing that it "must accept its responsibility to protect the people of the Democratic People's Republic of Korea from crimes against humanity" because their government "has manifestly failed to do so."

There is a tendency among many to be cynical about the UN, to dismiss it as toothless and ineffective. Now is a moment for the UN to prove its critics wrong. Of course, the UN is only as good as the sum of its parts, and there are member states who can be expected to take an unhelpful position in response to this historic report – but for all member states with anything resembling a conscience, there is now no excuse for inaction. Even North Korea's few friends must now examine their consciences carefully.

For this to be simply another shocking report, which is then left to gather dust on a shelf, referred to academically in years to come, would be nothing short of a tragedy. Instead, it must be taken as a plan of action, a manifesto for the world to come together around, to stop the continuing suffering of the North Korean people. That task will not be easy, but no one should rest easy in the delusion that the inquiry's completion means our work is done. Indeed, quite the opposite – it is only just beginning. Yet of one fact we can all be sure: from this day on, no one can claim they did not know what was happening in North Korea. As the great British parliamentarian William Wilberforce said when he introduced legislation to end the slave trade two hundred years ago: "We can no longer plead ignorance. We cannot turn aside." The spotlight has finally shone on North Korea, and now its beams are cast on the international community for a response.

An article in the *South China Morning Post*

Asia Can No Longer Follow the West's Polluting Ways

José Ramos-Horta with Mohamed Nasheed[41]

18 February 2014

The threats to our nations are changing, and we must change accordingly. Huge standing armies or hi-tech weaponry won't protect us from the next super typhoon. In the climate battle our infantry will be mangrove forests and solar panels.

For decades, Asian leaders largely ignored climate change. It's a Western problem, we said. They caused the problem by dumping greenhouse gases into the atmosphere; let them clean it up. Instead, we Asian leaders focused on reducing poverty by growing our economies.

We were not responsible for the pollution, we argued, so we should not have to pay for it. Yes, Asia's industrialization was quietly building up toxic stores of carbon, but we were only following the rich world's prescription for success. Carbon equals growth, it said, and like those who took up smoking on the doctor's orders, we were not to blame.

There was a time when the assumptions underpinning this line of thinking were true. Not anymore.

Climate change has become malignant. It threatens to blunt Asia's growth and upend our development. Climate scientists are increasingly certain that catastrophic weather events – such as the 2011 floods in Thailand, one of history's costliest disasters, or last year's Typhoon

---

41   President of the Maldives, at the time of writing.

Haiyan, which killed thousands of people in the Philippines – will become more frequent and intense.

From small island states to delta settlements, Asia is the climate front line. Seven of the ten countries most vulnerable to climate change are in Asia and the Pacific. Millions of Asians are at risk. It falls to Asian governments, whose primary responsibility is to protect their citizens, to respond.

For decades, we left it to the West to solve the problem. And, for decades, they failed to do so. If Asian countries don't help push things forward, the United Nations climate summit in Paris next year – where world governments are due to sign a crucial agreement to curb emissions – could fail.

Three things need to happen. Firstly, Asian heads of government should reposition their countries ahead of the Paris talks. We should instruct our negotiators to leave behind entrenched positions and work positively towards a global deal.

It is difficult to admit, but sometimes we Asians have been less than helpful in the UN climate negotiations: using arguments about "equality" as a pretext to pollute; playing on post-colonial guilt to stymie progress; or claiming poverty when our per capita incomes sometimes rival Europe's.

One of the few positive outcomes from the Copenhagen climate summit in 2009 was the creation of a new group, the Cartagena Dialogue for Progressive Action: like-minded countries that refused to allow their differences in size, wealth, or geography stand in the way of their mutual desire to curb climate change. We need more of such cooperative action if we are to seal a deal in Paris.

Secondly, Asian countries should focus on building clean economies to boost growth, increase wealth, and reduce pollution. This isn't rocket science, but it does involve planning and preparation: we need electricity grids that can accommodate vast quantities of renewable energy, infrastructure that promotes green vehicles, and regulations that encourage energy efficiency.

Many Asian nations are already leading the way. South Korea is investing two percent of its gross domestic product in a plan for green growth. China – the world's biggest greenhouse gas emitter – is also the biggest investor in clean energy. In 2012, it poured US$65 billion[42] into renewables; over the next 20 years, it will add more clean energy than the US, Europe, and Japan combined.

Switching from fossil fuels to clean energy already makes economic sense in many countries, in large part thanks to the collapsing price of renewable energy, a trend likely to accelerate in future. The carbon/growth connection is being turned on its head, and Asian nations – many of whom are still developing – are well placed to get ahead of the curve.

Thirdly, Asian nations need to better protect their natural environments. Many, preoccupied with short-term profits, are guilty of the rapacious destruction of the natural world. But, as we are finding out, nature often provides the best form of defense against the storm surges, droughts, and typhoons that will progressively worsen in this century. Mangroves and coral reefs protect coastlines from storms, while rainforests help regulate local weather patterns; protecting forests is one of the most effective ways to cut carbon pollution, and a healthy natural environment protects human health.

The threats to our nations are changing, and we must change accordingly. Huge standing armies, or hi-tech weaponry, won't protect us from the next super typhoon. In the climate battle, our infantry will be mangrove forests and solar panels.

By strengthening our natural defenses, embracing clean growth, and leading the push for a global climate deal, Asian leaders can secure a more stable climate – and safeguard our development.

Asian people need a climate deal, and the climate problem needs Asian leadership. It is time for Asia to show the way.

---

42   Sixty-five thousand million US dollars.

How to Ensure UN Peace Operations Respond to Demands in a Changing World

Dhaka, Bangladesh, 19 January 2015

We undertook extensive worldwide consultations to listen to the experiences and concerns of member states, civil society, and think tanks about United Nations Peace Operations and solicit suggestions for consideration.

On behalf of my distinguished colleagues of the High-Level Independent Panel on UN Peace Operations and our dedicated support staff from UNHQ, I wish to sincerely thank our host, the esteemed Minister for Foreign Affairs Abul Hassan Mahmud Ali, and all the other authorities who have made possible this gathering in Dhaka and made us feel very welcome.

A word of appreciation is due to all the distinguished diplomatic representatives, experts, and civil society delegates based in Dhaka, and those who have come a long way from other countries in the Asia-Pacific region.

The panel held its first meeting in New York, in November 2014, and then in Geneva, in December 2014, where we interacted with a wide range of permanent missions, key UN inter-governmental bodies such as the Security Council and key General Assembly bodies and departments and agencies.

Today marks the first regional consultation of the panel. Others will be held in Africa, Europe, the Middle East, and Latin America. As of 2013, countries from Asia and Pacific provide the second most uniformed personnel to UN peacekeeping, accounting for about 42 percent of the total. During the preceding decade, of course, this region led others in contributions of uniformed personnel. In 2006, for example, more than half of all military and police came from Asia alone. This region's historical commitment to UN peacekeeping over the past decades is striking, and your men and women – including some pioneering all-female formed police units – are serving the cause of peace in far flung and dangerous environments.

This is also a region that is experimenting with new forms of mediation to resolve, and in some cases prevent, conflicts before they break out. Surely, we need more such efforts, knowing as we do the devastating human and social costs of war and the long shadow such trauma casts on generations to come.

Today, the nature of conflicts and the types of actors involved are changing. The roles allocated to UN peace operations also continue to evolve. The number of UN missions on the ground – peacekeeping operations and special political missions – is higher than ever. They are operating in some of the most demanding environments imaginable. And in a climate of financially constrained member states, the UN is being asked to do more with less.

For these reasons, the Secretary-General has asked our panel to undertake this review. His goal is to ensure UN peace operations are ready to face the current and future demands of a changing world.

The aim of our consultations today is to listen to the experiences and concerns of member states, civil society, and think tanks about UN peace operations, and to solicit suggestions for the panel's considerations.

Thank you for taking the time to join us in this city and offer us panel members your informed advice on:

- How the UN, to which we all belong and we all need, should better serve the cause of peace;
- How we should redeem ourselves after past and current failings, for they are many;
- How we should better anticipate, prevent, and deter conflicts;
- How we should better protect innocent peoples, women and children, caught in wars.
- How, when, and where should we deploy UN peacekeepers in a more timely fashion.

Additional questions are:

- How should we better mobilize resources, material and financial, to support the troops and the police the UN sends in harm's way – and to better reward them?
- How should we better assist peoples in healing wounds, promoting reconciliation, and consolidating peace?
- How we should we mobilize resources for post-conflict recovery and state-building?
- How can we better support women and children not only during but also after the conflict?

This is only my second visit to Bangladesh, the first being in November 2012 as a guest of the University of Liberal Arts Bangladesh [ULAB] to deliver the commencement address to an audience of about a thousand people, including more than seven hundred graduating students, their families, faculty, and staff.

My ULAB commencement address was entitled "The Rising Asia: Challenges and Risks." In that speech, I acknowledged both the impressive progress made by most Asian economies over the past thirty years and also the challenges of prevailing extreme poverty and inequality, unsustainable growth and environmental depredation, border disputes, ethnic and religious tensions and violence, regional rivalries, huge standing armies, and nuclear weapons.

I met with the Prime Minister, The Hon Sheikh Hasina, during which time I thanked Her Excellency for Bangladesh's active contribution to peace and security stabilization in my country during the early years of United Nations tutelage of Timor-Leste. I also paid a courtesy call on the head of the armed forces to extend my and my country's deep appreciation for the contribution made by the Bangladeshi army to restore peace and security in my country in the period of 2000–02 and 2006–08. During those early difficult years, I engaged often with the Bangladeshi peacekeepers, and was flown in helicopters by very able Bangladeshi pilots.

I also engaged with senior officers, soldiers, and police originating from India, Pakistan, Nepal, Sri Lanka, Malaysia, Singapore, Thailand, the Philippines, Republic of Korea, China, Japan, Australia, New

Zealand, Fiji, and Vanuatu. On different occasions, I had Bangladeshis and Pakistanis providing security to me.

We were privileged to have had over the years prominent Asians heading the UN operations in my country – we had two Special and Personal Representatives and Envoys of the Secretary-General, SRSGs from India, Kamalesh Sharma and Atul Khare; from Japan, Sukehiro Hasegawa; from Bangladesh, Ameerah Haq. We had peacekeeping force commanders and police commissioners from India, Malaysia, Singapore, Thailand, and the Philippines.

My country's history is so similar to yours and to many other countries in the region. My personal journey is similar to yours –being ignored, forgotten, betrayed, but never giving up, never losing hope and faith. I lived through almost every experience anyone can think of. I was born and grew up in one of the remotest villages in my forgotten country; I lost brothers and sisters who are still to be found and to be buried with honor and dignity; I founded or worked with many grass-roots civil society organizations in my country and overseas; I served as Finance Minister, Defence Minister, Prime Minister, and President.

I watched the UN at work – or at inaction – throughout the Cold War era, how it failed in Indonesia in 1965–66 and in subsequent years; how it failed the Cambodians during the Khmer Rouge dark era; how it was impotent for all the 40 years of the Ne Win dictatorship in Burma/ Myanmar; how it was important and indifferent for 24 years in my own country. The Rwanda genocide is a painful reminder of yet another failure by the world community.

But the UN is a sum of its members, the member states, and when we blame the UN we are actually looking at ourselves in the mirror because we are all the UN; we all have one vote, large and small, poor and rich; but most of us have less power and therefore we have much-reduced responsibilities for the failings of the system.

My country is an example of how much the international community, through the UN or bilaterally, can do to restore peace and hopes to a whole people. I can attest to the failings, but also the successes when there is compassion and political will by the powers that be.

The political and security challenges we as a whole face in this dawn of the twenty-first century is daunting. Complex civil wars are increasingly regional or international in nature. Many local non-state armed groups are aligning with, and financed by, transnational organized crime or international extremist networks, complicating efforts to define parties to a conflict and advance peace processes. Civilians, particularly women and girls, continue to be the target of attacks, sexual violence, and forced recruitment into armed groups.

The 2008–09 financial crisis originating in the US and Europe does not seem to have an end. In fact, the world economic situation is deteriorating further; the dramatic collapse of the energy market, namely the brutal fall of the price of oil, as a result of an old, simple question of supply and demand.

Consequences are being felt, or will be felt, not only by the oil-exporting countries, particularly those that are extremely dependent on this single source of revenue (Timor-Leste is among the most unfortunate ones) but also by those that refine and re-export crude; and as oil prices drop to such levels, there will be less incentive to continue investment in environmentally friendly energy, like solar and others.

These facts will have impact on peace and security around the world, further exacerbating social and political instability in many countries, from Asia to Africa and Latin America. Ladies and gentlemen, our esteemed Secretary-General Ban Ki-moon has encouraged the panel to be "bold and creative." We are here to encourage you to be bold and creative. I have said enough. In the next few days we are going to listen and learn from you.

To be Bold and Creative to Better Protect People Caught up in Conflicts

Addis Ababa, 11 February 2015

Our esteemed Secretary-General, Ban Ki-moon, has encouraged the panel to be "bold and creative." Those are his words. We are here to ask you, too, to be bold and creative, and help us craft a vision for our shared United Nations that can more effectively serve and protect people caught up in conflicts.

On behalf of my distinguished colleagues whom you have met, I wish to sincerely thank the government of Ethiopia and our colleagues at the UN office to the African Union [AU], and all the other authorities who have made possible this gathering in Addis and made us feel very welcome.

I also thank African Union Commission Chairperson Zuma for her kind invitation for the panel to visit the AU and we have already had good discussions with her and her team. Yesterday, we also had good discussions with the Foreign Minister. I was also very pleased to see that, during the recent summit, the assembly welcomed the establishment of this panel, and looked forward to our interactions this week. I share their view that an innovative and forward-looking UN-AU partnership is critical to the future of peace and security on this continent.

Another word of appreciation is due to all the distinguished diplomatic representatives, experts, and civil society participants, many of whom have come a long way from other countries in the region. I thank the governments of Norway and the United Kingdom for making it possible to have so many civil society friends from the region with us today and tomorrow. I would also like to thank our friends from the training for peace project: Accord, ISS [Institute for Security Studies] and NUPI

[Norwegian Institute of International Affairs] who worked so closely with our support staff at HQ to bring this event together.

The panel held its first meeting in New York, in November 2014, where we interacted with a wide range of permanent missions, key UN inter-governmental bodies such as the Security Council and key General Assembly bodies, as well as UN departments and agencies in both New York and Geneva. In January, we met with representatives of the Asia-Pacific region in Dhaka. Some of us have also visited Tokyo, Islamabad, and Delhi for follow-up discussions.

Following our discussions here, other regional consultations will be held in Europe, the Middle East, and Latin America.

Excellencies, today the nature of conflicts and the types of actors involved are changing and the tasks undertaken by UN as well as AU peace operations also continue to evolve. The number of UN missions on the ground – peacekeeping operations and special political missions – is higher than ever. They are operating in some of the most demanding environments imaginable. And in a climate of financial constraints, the UN – and the broader international community – is being asked to do more with less. For these reasons, the Secretary-General has asked our panel to undertake this review. His goal is to ensure UN peace operations are ready to face the current and future demands of a changing world.

Strong and strategic partnership with the AU, regional mechanisms, and regional economic commissions, and its member states will be key to more effective peace operations. Already, we see many important and varied forms of partnership across several operations today in Mali, CAR (Central African Republic), Darfur, and Somalia and between UN mediators and AU missions, or vice versa. The political coherence of these collective efforts, in particular, is very important. This week, we would like to better understand your views on this important partnership and your vision for the future.

The aim of our consultation today is to listen to the experiences and concerns of member states, civil society, and think tanks about peace operations, and what many of you refer to here as peace support operations, and to solicit suggestions for the panel's consideration.

Within UN operations, Africans are an important and growing stakeholder. At the close of 2013, Africa became the leading provider of uniformed personnel to UN peacekeeping, accounting for about

44 percent of the total. Our host today is the largest contributor from the continent. In addition, some 80 percent of all personnel serving in UN peace operations are in Africa. If we count the additional operations currently undertaken by all – including operations by the African Union and its regional mechanisms and regional economic commissions – 70 percent of all peace operations are currently in Africa.

Your envoys are working to support peacemaking efforts across the continent, often working closely with envoys of the Secretary-General and UN mediation experts. Many of the countries represented here have also championed the importance of prevention efforts. All of these dimensions – prevention, peacemaking, as well as complex issues related to the use of force and sustainable peacebuilding – are issues that the panel is wrestling with. For this reason, we have been very keen indeed to come to Addis and engage with you as vital stakeholders.

It cannot be questioned that, in many respects, the future of peace operations is closely tied to the future of efforts to advance peace and security across Africa. You all have deep experience and I look forward with great interest to our exchanges.

So, thank you for taking the time to join us in this city and to offer us panel members your informed advice and rich experience on many questions that are before us:

- How should the UN, to which we all belong and which we all need, better serve the cause of peace?
- How should we, individually as member states and collectively as the United Nations, redeem ourselves after past and current failings? For there are many.
- How can the UN and regional organizations work together on behalf of countries and peoples striving for a more peaceful future?
- How should we better anticipate, prevent, and resolve conflicts?
- How should we better protect the people – girls, boys, women, and men – caught up in war?
- How can we ensure women fully participate in crafting the political settlement after conflict and in ensuring sustainable peace and security?
- How can we deploy UN peace operations in a more timely, relevant fashion?

Given the central importance of the UN-AU partnership:

- What lessons have been learned about this partnership and the experiences to date?
- How can the UN, AU, and African member states work together toward a shared understanding and an agreed strategic partnership?
- How can the coherence of these respective efforts be strengthened and adequately resourced?

I personally know Africa reasonably well. I have traveled to many countries on the continent over the years, in the 1970s, 1980s, and 1990s. Several of your countries contributed to peace and security stabilization in my own country during the early years of United Nations administration of Timor-Leste, far from your homes.

Others of you I may know from my time as the special representative of the Secretary-General in Guinea-Bissau. During this time, I came to understand better the challenges of working to address conflict but also the wealth of spirit and energy that can help to build a strong future; the strength of communities and people, particularly women who play critical roles not only in the home but in the economy and political life. And the youth who I had the pleasure to work with – they are the future.

In Guinea-Bissau, ECOWAS[43] played an essential role and, through their efforts, I came to see firsthand the vital role played by regional organizations who are often the first to respond to crises.

Recently, Africa, particularly West Africa, has suffered greatly as a result of the Ebola outbreak. Not only Africa but many health workers around the world have responded, understanding that we are all part of an increasingly interconnected world. Allow me to say again that, mindful of this interdependence, my country, although poor, was among the first to deliver US$2 million in aid – $1 million in 2014 and $1 million this semester despite the dramatic decrease in the oil price.

As seen in the recent AU summit, serious peace and security challenges remain as well. Complex civil wars have recurred in some cases. In addition, non-state armed groups are aligning with criminal groups or international extremist networks, creating regional threats. Civilians,

---

43   Economic Community of Western African States.

and in particular, women and girls, continue to be the target of attacks, sexual violence, and forcible recruitment into armed groups.

Our esteemed Secretary-General Ban Ki-moon has encouraged the panel to be "bold and creative." Those are his words. We are here to ask you to be bold and creative, and to help us craft a vision for our shared United Nations and its partnerships with Africa that can more effectively serve the many people caught up in conflict and its destabilizing effects. We come to Addis to ask for your help, your wisdom, your experience, and your support. We come to Addis to work with you in partnership.

I have said enough. In the next few days we will listen and learn from you.

May God the Almighty bless and inspire us all as we search for solutions to our shared problems.

The Nippon Foundation's Decades-Long Effort Bears Fruit in the Fight to Eradicate Leprosy

Tokyo, 27 February 2015

Timor-Leste was declared medically free of leprosy in 2010 as the joint effort of my own government supported by WHO and the Nippon Foundation bore fruit in a remarkably short period of time.

It is a privilege to be here in Tokyo as guest of someone, Yōhei Sasakawa, Chairman of the Nippon Foundation, a living hero of the most outcast people in the world, the hundreds of thousands of our fellow human beings, our brothers and sisters, Children of God, the victims of this centuries-old illness: Hansen's disease, or leprosy.

While in Tokyo for this very important symposium and the world appeal, in response to a long-standing invitation, as currently the Chair of the High-Level Independent Panel on Peace Operations established by the UN Secretary-General, I and some of my colleagues who serve also in the panel have been engaging with senior Japanese government officials, civil society, academia, think tanks, and listening to their informed opinion that certainly will enable us to produce a comprehensive report and wise recommendations for our esteemed Secretary-General.

As we all know, our world is facing increasingly complex and dangerous challenges, ranging from decades-old unresolved conflicts like Somalia, Congo, and Afghanistan to the implosion of Middle Eastern states like

Syria and Libya, and new cases of implosion of fragile states like Central African Republic and South Sudan.

In the midst of these tragic events, that are the daily feature of mainstream media, there are also bright spots in the world where the actions of individuals can make a difference for the better for many fellow human beings.

Yōhei Sasakawa is not a Hollywood star or a billionaire who flies in and out of disaster areas with journalists and filmmakers, poses for pictures with poor, hungry children, and then leaves for the next popular cause.

Yōhei Sasakawa is not George Clooney, or Angelina Jolie; he and his family have devoted the last 40 years to raise awareness, to mobilize financial and medical support for the hundreds of thousands of victims of this terribly disfiguring disease that, for centuries, has made millions of our fellow brothers and sisters the most unwanted people in the world.

The Sasakawa family has also made generous and sustained contributions towards fostering dialogue, reconciliation, peace, and poverty alleviation through the Sasakawa Foundation.

A reading of the 2012 annual report offers an insight into the breadth and depth of the Sasakawa family's immense contribution to world peace in Asia, the Middle East, Africa, and Latin America, through generous grants in support of research, symposiums, training programs, rural development, building schools and hospitals, health clinics, clean water, and sanitation.

I did not hesitate one minute in accepting the kind invitation extended to me to be here so that, with Prime Minister Shinze Abe; our esteemed UN Secretary-General Ban Ki-moon (via video message); my good friend Dr Surim Pitsuwan, former Prime Minister of Thailand and former ASEAN Secretary-General; and Mrs Abe, the esteemed wife of Prime Minister Abe, we jointly support the Nippon Foundation Global Appeal 2015 on Leprosy Elimination.

There is no more noble cause than embracing our unfortunate fellow human beings, our brothers and sisters, beloved Children of God, afflicted by this illness and who, for this reason, are cast aside by society.

As a result of the joint efforts of my own government, supported by the World Health Organization and the Nippon Foundation, my country, Timor-Leste, with less than one case per 10,000 people, was declared medically free of leprosy in 2010, after centuries of affliction.

However, countries like Brazil, India, and Indonesia (particularly in Aceh and Papua) still have tens of thousands of new cases. The good news is that the new cases in the mentioned countries are gradually diminishing, leading us to be hopeful that with greater compassion and effort, leprosy can be eliminated in all afflicted countries around the world.

While elimination of Hansen's disease is an attainable goal, those cured often will still feel stigmatized and suffer discrimination in their communities and countries. We must all do more to return to them their full rights and dignity, embracing and providing all the support needed for their full reintegration in society.

In closing, I wish to greet all of you from many parts of the world who have converged to Tokyo for this symposium and appeal. Those of you who work in the field with our brothers and sisters afflicted by Hansen's disease, caring for them medically but also giving them love and hope, you have my deepest admiration. You are my living heroes and you, too, are children for God.

May God the Almighty and Merciful bless you all and continue to guide you in this noblest cause.

An article in the *The Wall Street Journal*

Repression in the Maldives

José Ramos-Horta and Benedict Rogers[44]

9 March 2015

The world can't turn a blind eye to a Muslim-majority nation slipping into dictatorship justified by religious zeal, even one so small as the Maldives.

On 22 February, Maldives police arrested the country's former president, Mohamed Nasheed, and charged him with terrorism. Mr Nasheed was refused bail, and the following day officers violently dragged him along the ground at the courthouse. The look of terror in his eyes as police officers ripped his shirt and injured his arm said it all.

A farcical trial has now begun in which Mr Nasheed is not allowed to participate in his defense. So far, judges have appeared as witnesses for the prosecution, other judges have been accused of leading the witnesses, and some witnesses have revealed they spent time with the police preparing their evidence in advance.

The arrest and prosecution of Mr Nasheed is blatantly political. If convicted, he could face up to 15 years in prison, disqualifying him from contesting the presidency again. Police have responded brutally to peaceful protests in support of Mr Nasheed, sending in thugs armed with iron rods and truncheons, and arresting dozens.

The country is run by the family of Maumoon Abdul Gayoom, who was Asia's longest-ruling dictator until Mr Nasheed won the country's first elections in 2008. In 2012, Mr Gayoom's allies staged a coup d'état, forcing Mr Nasheed from office. A year later, fresh elections were held.

---

44   At the time of writing, Mr Benedict Rogers was deputy chairman of the Conservative Party Human Rights Commission in the UK.

Mr Nasheed won 45 percent of the vote in the first round, just short of an outright victory, but the regime annulled the ballot before it went to a second round. When a second election was held a few months later, Mr Nasheed again won a plurality in the first round. But in the second round, his rival, Mr Gayoom's brother, Abdulla Yameen, played the Islamist card. He won the election by portraying Mr Nasheed as a secularist.

The Gayoom clan, now firmly back in charge, is seeking to prevent Mr Nasheed from challenging for power again. The charges against him relate to efforts to reform the legal system and establish judicial independence. Most of the country's judges at the time were Gayoom appointees. Many were unqualified, with only a very basic level of education. Unsurprisingly, they resisted efforts to remove those who failed to meet the proposed standards of educational attainment and ethical conduct.

The crunch came in 2012 when chief judge of the criminal court, Abdulla Mohamed, faced accusations of political bias. He had repeatedly acquitted political figures associated with the old regime despite evidence of serious crimes. Mr Nasheed's government tried every mechanism available to hold Judge Mohamed accountable, but all were blocked. Finally, the judge's refusal to honor a police summons led to his arrest. This is the basis of the terrorism charge against the former president.

The prosecutor general in Mr Nasheed's trial is a former associate of Judge Mohamed, and the lead judge had refused to take disciplinary action against Judge Mohamed as deputy head of the Judicial Services Commission. Another judge faces allegations of bribery, and the third has a criminal record.

President Yameen's behavior is increasingly erratic and paranoid. His foreign ministry officials resort to foul-mouthed abuse of critics as well as conspiracy theories about Christian missionaries and gay-rights activists joining hands to conquer the country.

So, what can be done? The glimmers of hope for a pluralist government seven years ago have been all but snuffed out. Yet, Mr Nasheed will never give up, and neither will his democracy movement. They deserve international support.

Options include targeted sanctions, freezing the overseas assets of senior members of the regime, and suspending the Maldives from the Commonwealth. Tourists should consider boycotting the Maldives, especially resorts owned by regime cronies.

The persecution of Mr Nasheed is an attempt to stifle demands for democracy and create a climate of fear. The world can't turn a blind eye to a Muslim-majority nation slipping into dictatorship justified by religious zeal, even one so small as the Maldives. The decision of India's Prime Minister Narendra Modi not to visit as planned this week is an important precedent. The Gayoom regime's refusal to allow an opposition party is a problem its neighbors in particular must address.

Message to the Oslo Conference

End Myanmar's Systematic Persecution of Rohingyas

Oslo, 26 May 2015

We must all contribute to create a climate of dialogue, mutual acceptance to move towards a road map leading to a Myanmar that is politically open, pluralistic, and embracing of all its ethnic and religious communities.

Hello, this is José Ramos-Horta speaking from New York. I regret not being able to be in Oslo at this time of this very timely, extremely important gathering, as Myanmar moves towards elections and hopefully consolidation of democracy, freedoms, rule of law.

I'm very familiar with Myanmar, although I could not claim to be an expert. For those of you who might not know much about my past activities or background, I first went to Burma then when hardly anyone paid much attention to Myanmar, in July of 1994. I went there, crossing the border from Chiang Mai, and I went to Manipur. There, with some colleagues, I conducted an international human rights and diplomacy training program for students, activists, many of whom I know today are back in their home country in Yangon, very much engaged in this process in Myanmar.

If today we can talk about one of the most neglected people in the world, one of the most forgotten, I would say it would be the Rohingya of Myanmar. We are all human beings in this planet. Myanmar is a mosaic of ethnic groups. It is a mosaic of cultures, of values, of different experiences – a crossroads from Asia, with many influences.

The Rohingya seem to have the least of rights, the least of privileges as citizens of Myanmar, as human beings. There have been extraordinary abuses, humiliation, killings, the expulsion of Rohingyas from their ancestral land. Whether they have been there for thousands of years or a few hundred years, or if they were there only some generations ago, they still have rights as people of Myanmar because they were born there, in Myanmar. They have been living there for generations, regardless of how long; thousands of centuries they have been there.

I do not wish to lecture any group in Myanmar. I do not wish to lecture authorities in Myanmar. I know the process of transition from dictatorship to democracy is a complex, tortuous, unpredictable, long one. We must all contribute to create a climate of dialogue, mutual acceptance, and maybe move towards a road map leading to a Myanmar that is politically open, pluralistic, and that is embracing of all its ethnic and religious communities.

However, I know that this is easier said than done, because there are suspicions, there are prejudices. That's what leaders are all about. Leaders at the community level, leaders at the national level who must embrace each other; who must act with compassion, with wisdom; who embrace everyone including the Rohingyas so that Myanmar can be a shining example in Southeast Asia, and in Asia in general.

Again, I wish to pay tribute to all those in Myanmar who for generations have struggled for freedom, for democracy, until today when you are on the eve of free general elections. I'm hopeful that all will be able to participate – the Rohingyas, the Muslim communities, and everyone, in an atmosphere of freedom, of no question, of no threats. When the election results come, it will be a new, promising beginning for Myanmar, a further step in the consolidation of democracy in your beautiful country.

I wish you all success in this conference and, as always, I pray to God Almighty and the Merciful to continue to bless the great people of Myanmar with wisdom, happiness, and prosperity.

The Credibility of the UN is Most at Stake Whenever its Ability to Protect is Under Threat

Kigali, Rwanda, 28 May 2015

Protecting civilians is not just the responsibility of uniformed peacekeepers. The primary responsibility lies with host governments as UN missions are slowly helping to build national capacity.

I am here as the Chair of the High-Level Independent Panel on UN Peace Operations and also as a former resistance leader and President of my own country, distant Timor-Leste.

Being here for the first time since the 1994 genocide, I bow in tribute to the 800,000 fellow human beings who were murdered during that period.

The Rwanda genocide will always stand as an indictment of the leaders of the United Nations and the international community at that time for their utter failure of moral leadership, compassion, and courage in making the decisions that peoples of the world expected of them, that they expected of the United Nations.

I bow in tribute to the people of Rwanda for the path of reconciliation you have pursued and for the extraordinary transformation your country has experienced, from tragedy to peace and prosperity.

Making sure that the United Nations never again leaves at a time when it is most needed, or betrays the most vulnerable at a time when their protection is most urgent, has been at the heart of the work of the panel.

Those who endure immense suffering are entitled to be angry; but those who are angry and yet forgive and live on, and let live their worst enemies, teach us all enduring lessons in courage, humanity, and wisdom.

I also applaud this initiative which links to the summit last September chaired by [US] Vice President Biden and President Kagame, among others. This year-long effort is focusing on mobilizing more countries to support UN missions as part of their global commitment to peace and security. I had the opportunity to participate in the European roundtable hosted by the Dutch in Amsterdam. I hope that the summit that will take place in the margins of the General Assembly this September will bear fruit.

Africa, for one, is now delivering. Africa now contributes more to UN peace operations than any other region. And this is in addition to your contributions to African-led peace support operations.

On behalf of the high-level panel on UN peace operations, I would like to take this opportunity to summarize our efforts since the Secretary-General appointed us in October 2014. I would also like to share our deliberations so far and hear from you, while we, the panel, are in the process of drawing conclusions, so we can present the final report to the Secretary-General on 16 June.

The panel has undertaken an intensive consultation process listening to the major stakeholders of UN peace operations; we have received, in total, 80 submissions from member states, regional organizations, UN bodies, and civil society.

The most recent submission we received was a very important and thoughtful one from the African Union.

We have also traveled to as many regions and capitals as possible in Asia, Africa, Europe, the Middle East, and Latin America.

We have held countless meetings with member states, regional organizations, international and national non-governmental organizations, in addition to relevant UN Secretariat, offices and agencies, funds, and programs.

Panel members visited three peace operations, in the Democratic Republic of Congo, Mali, and Dakar, to listen to the concerns of communities and host governments, as well as to the staff of peace operations and other partners on the ground.

We have met and spoken with many Special Representatives of the Secretary-General, special envoys, force commanders, and other senior mission leaders.

Throughout our work, the panel has maintained close communication with the UN Security Council Resolution 1325[45] Expert Study and the advisory group on the review of peace-building architecture to ensure a synergized approach to our respective areas of focus.

The protection of civilians featured heavily in all these consultations and it has become clear to the panel that protection of civilians is of critical importance.

Protection of civilians is the measure by which most UN peace operations are judged today. Ninety-five percent of UN peacekeepers have this mandate. It is what local communities and the international community expect from the UN. And yet there are so many challenges, particularly the gaps that we continue to see between mandates and resources.

Our panel has heard that some missions are making serious efforts to address armed groups that are threatening civilians, and that UN missions have saved many thousands of lives either by acting quickly, such as in CAR, or opening their gates to civilians, as in South Sudan.

In many cases, AU missions are doing even more in this regard and often with fewer resources to back them up or safeguard their own safety and security.

But we also have heard a lot of discontent from communities that UN personnel need to get out of their vehicles, be more visible, show that they are determined to act against the groups that are threatening civilians, and, as a last resort, even put themselves at risk when the lives of civilians are threatened.

Many community-based local NGOs think that the UN may prioritize negotiating an agreement between parties in conflict and are less concerned about the civilians caught in the crossfire. This misperception affects us all.

And the challenges of protecting civilians appear to be, if anything, increasing. Two-thirds of UN peacekeepers today are trying to protect

---

45   Approved in 2000, UN Security Council Resolution 1325 was the first to address the disproportionate and unique impact of armed conflict on women. It became the root source of the blueprint on gender and peacekeeping work for the DPKO.

civilians in the midst of armed conflicts, some in the presence of violent extremist groups. How do missions deal with these difficult environments? Rwanda knows these challenges well, as it has deployments in some of the most difficult countries in this regard, including Sudan and South Sudan. The challenges to logistics, mobility, and rapid response in these environments are very significant.

In Mali, the most dangerous place by far for peacekeepers today, the violence is not really targeted against civilians but against the mission and other international forces there. Peace operations need to be able to protect themselves in order to protect others.

Protecting civilians is not just the responsibility of uniformed peacekeepers.

The primary responsibility to protect civilians lies with the host government, and missions are slowly helping to build national capacity.

Civilians in all UN peace operations, as well as NGOs and, of course, the communities themselves, are all playing very important roles as well. Some are also effectively engaged in non-violent protection actions.

This burden also exists for peace operations.

We find ourselves within a normative framework with the responsibility to protect – endorsed at the 2005 World Summit – the Secretary-General's Human Rights up-front initiative and the increasing prominence of Protection of Civilians [POC] in Security Council mandates.

The United Nations Secretariat has developed guidance and training materials, and continues to adapt these as UN peace operations face evolving situations on the ground.

UN peace operations are deployed with protection advisors, dedicated civilian capacity with expertise on POC, the protection of women and children, and addressing sexual violence as a weapon of war.

However, it is with the ability to protect civilians under imminent threat that the UN's credibility is most at stake. And as we have heard and seen, there is a lot of room for improvement in this area. The responsibility to improve, however, is a shared one – the Security Council, the General Assembly, SRSGs, troop- and police-contributing countries, the US. We, as those obligated to serve and protect, need to better align our understanding and implementation of a POC mandate.

There are several ways to make sure peace operations deliver more effectively in implementing this mandate. These relate to how the mandates are formulated: better planning, better capabilities, better mobility assets and support systems, ensuring missions have more timely and better information on threats as they evolve, and better training and other efforts to address what some have called the "mindset."

More efforts need to be made to generate forces and capabilities that are tailored to the situation and can enable better and more effective protection by the UN in the future. More also needs to be done to make sure that the forces we deploy are able and willing to do so proactively.

When we say there is a mindset problem, what we really mean is that member states simply do not agree on whose job this is and just how far missions are supposed to go with the resources that they have been provided.

Are troop- and police-contributing countries fully aware of the situation and dynamics on the ground and are they ready to carry out this mandate?

Do the Security Council, the Troop Contributing Countries, and the Secretariat have a shared view on implementation and objectives?

You cannot protect everyone in all places. That is "mission impossible." So, who is responsible for closing that gap?

Is it the Secretariat's job to tell the Security Council who will and who won't be protected?

Is it the Security Council's job to give more restricted mandates covering, for example, a smaller area?

All of these issues must be very clear to everyone and, in our opinion, we are not there yet. I look forward to your thoughts and wisdom on this issue of the gap between mandates on the one hand and capabilities on the other.

Turning to the likelihood of success, it is one thing when you are trying to protect civilians in a relatively small country like Timor-Leste. But what about today, when peacekeepers are deployed in countries the size and scale of the Democratic Republic of Congo, South Sudan, Mali, and parts of Sudan?

These are missions in vast territories with limited infrastructure, and particularly difficult conditions with regard to terrain and climate. From a military perspective, it seems that the capabilities don't add up in several of these large-scale operations, but how much is enough in these massive environments? And how much is enough for the protection of civilians?

Planning and coordination is also very important – they are vital. The analysis and planning of missions have to be strengthened and POC has to be fully incorporated into every step of that process as a central objective of the mission.

The Secretary-General has to be as clear as possible with the Security Council on how mission efforts will be deployed and how priorities will be set. This also must be communicated much more clearly to communities.

There has been a lot of discussion around better information, analysis, and risk assessments for POC. It is clear that missions should have access to the technology they need to pre-empt threats and respond quickly to ensure greater safety for all.

Practical training is crucial because this is not the "usual" job of militaries around the world. It is closer to the work of formed police units around the world. Whether military or police, training in protecting civilians is needed.

The panel is very aware of the difficult situations where peace operations are deployed today. It is also acutely aware of the threats that exist to civilians and the expectations – and obligation we have – to proactively protect these civilians from imminent threats.

UN peace operations are deployed to pre-empt threats to civilians through non-violent means but also, within limits, with the use of force. Together, we have to make sure we do what is necessary.

All of these discussions link up closely to the broader questions around the use of force in UN peacekeeping operations.

As some former force commanders have pointed out to us, here we see a double standard where there are regular investigations when force is used and repercussions when it is deemed to have been used excessively – and this is only appropriate.

But where are the repercussions when mission personnel failed to act, even when they have the information and the ability to act on that information?

We need to ask what kind of signal that sends to those who are out there on the front lines of UN peacekeeping.

The push and the leadership to truly protect civilians cannot only come from those who are not participating in UN peacekeeping but also from those, like our hosts who are here today, who are acting on their words and on the lessons of the past.

Letter to the UN Secretary-General Ban Ki-Moon

Uniting our Strengths for Peace: Politics, Partnerships and People

New York, 16 June 2015

This report of the High-Level Independent Panel on UN Peace Operations: Uniting Our Strengths for Peace: Politics, Partnerships and People is based on an extensive consultation process across continents during the past six months. We hope that the Secretariat will take its recommendations into account in considering the implementation of the report and in other internal reviews.

Dear Secretary-General,

In October 2014, you honored us with our appointment as members of your High-Level Independent Panel on Peace Operations. As charged, we have worked over the last six months to undertake a comprehensive assessment of the state of UN peace operations, in light of the emerging needs and evolving challenges they face. Since then, the Panel has considered a broad range of issues facing peacekeeping and special political missions, including the changing nature of conflict, evolving mandates, good offices and peacebuilding challenges, managerial and administrative arrangements, planning, partnerships, human rights and protection of civilians, uniformed capabilities for peace operations, and performance.

United by our commitment to the Organization, and motivated by your encouragement to be bold and creative, we have worked to provide analysis and recommendations on how these instruments can better support the Organization's work to prevent conflict, achieve durable political settlements, protect civilians, and sustain peace. We have wrestled with challenging issues, such as the use of force, which have divided the Membership. We have endeavored to balance the principles with the practical as change is propelled forward through both of these motors.

I was humbled by your appointment as Chair of the Panel as I remain continually grateful for the opportunity to have served as your Special Representative in Guinea-Bissau. It was my opportunity to repay, in some small measure, a debt to the United Nations for standing by the people of Timor-Leste in our years of need. The United Nations is a powerful presence, but its challenges are also its weaknesses.

Even as the UN Mission in South Sudan struggled to shelter those fleeing violence, there were too many beyond the reach of the mission who had to look within for the courage and strength to survive. Nyakhat Pal, a three-year-old South Sudanese girl, walked for four hours by foot to a UNICEF-WFP rapid response distribution center in April 2014, leading her blind father. She had heard the UN was providing vaccines, food, and water. Nyakhat received the help she hoped for and returned to her village to await the return of her missing mother. Nyakhat looked up to the United Nations with hope. Her tenacity and bravery was rewarded; her story should touch the most hardened of hearts, as it did mine. But her story should also shame us, for we have collectively failed the people of South Sudan. Despite the courageous efforts of some, we have, as an international community, fallen short – and continue to fall short – in Burundi, Iraq, Libya, Palestine, Syria, Yemen, and Ukraine, among other places.

My fellow Panel members and I accepted this challenging assignment so as to contribute to a more credible, relevant, and legitimate United Nations, effective in preventing and ending conflicts, making and sustaining peace so that Nyakhat, and her peers, can live in security and in freedom.

It is with great honor that I submit to you the Panel's report: 'Uniting Our Strengths for Peace: Politics, Partnerships and People'.

The report and its recommendations are based on an extensive consultation process carried out during the course of the past six months. The Panel received more than 80 written submissions from

Member States, regional and other international organizations, civil society organizations and think tanks, and UN entities. These were of very high quality and greatly informed the Panel's thinking, but it is impossible to do them justice, and to address all the issues they raise, within the scope of this report. The Panel has therefore asked that if the entities which submitted them so agree, the Secretariat should make them available through appropriate channels. We hope that the Secretariat will take them into account in considering the implementation of our report and in other internal reviews.

In addition, the Panel held regional consultations in Asia, Africa, the Middle East, Europe, and Latin America, all of which were well attended by Member States, regional and international organizations, civil society and think tanks. The Panel also participated in thematic workshops on Protection of Civilians, Use of Force, Women, Peace and Security, as well as Prevention and Mediation and Sustaining Peace. To gather firsthand information on the concerns of communities and governments hosting UN peace operations, as well as to listen to staff, local, and other partners on the ground, Panel members visited three peace operations: MONUSCO,[46] MINUSMA,[47] and UNOWA.[48] Throughout, the Panel met many of your Special Representatives, Special Envoys, Force Commanders, and other senior mission leaders, as well as staff at all levels, at Headquarters and in the field.

In New York, the Panel met with Permanent Representatives of Member States, UN Secretariat and agencies, funds and programs, the Security Council, the Special Political and Decolonization Committee (the Fourth Committee), the Administrative and Budgetary Committee (the Fifth Committee) and the Special Committee on Peacekeeping Operations (the C-34). The Panel also maintained close communication with the Security Council Resolution 1325 Expert Study and the Advisory Group on the Review of Peacebuilding Architecture to ensure a synergized approach in our respective areas of focus.

During these past six months, we have encountered numerous examples of the dedication and commitment of staff and leaders,

---

46 UN Organization Stabilization Mission in the Democratic Republic of the Congo.
47 UN Multidimensional Integrated Stabilization Mission in Mali.
48 UN Office for West Africa.

both in field missions and Headquarters. Our deep appreciation and admiration goes to the national and international, civilian, and uniformed personnel of peace operations, as well as to their national and international partners on the ground, many of whom risk their lives every day in some of the most dangerous places in the world in pursuit of peace, security, and freedom. We are grateful to the many civil society organizations and think tanks who met with us and enriched our deliberations through their frank, rich, and grounding perspectives. We are also very appreciative of the support, financial and in-kind, provided by Member States to the work of the Panel. Our particular gratitude goes to Canada, Denmark, Finland, France, New Zealand, Norway, Sweden, the Netherlands, and Timor-Leste, as well as the Center on International Cooperation, the International Peace Institute, the Norwegian Institute for International Affairs, and the United Nations University.

I would like to thank the governments of Bangladesh, Belgium, Brazil, Egypt, and Ethiopia for hosting our regional consultations. The Panel is grateful by the hospitality extended to us by the host governments during our visits to China, Ethiopia, Finland, France, India, Japan, the Netherlands, Pakistan, the Russian Federation, Rwanda, Switzerland, the United Kingdom, and the United States. Finally, we thank the governments of the Democratic Republic of Congo, Mali, and Senegal and the leadership and personnel of MINUSMA, MONUSCO, UNOWA, and the UNOAU[49] for so warmly receiving and supporting our visits.

When we commenced our work, you encouraged us to be bold and creative; we hope our report meets that expectation. On behalf of the Panel members, allow me to thank you for the privilege and the responsibility you have entrusted to us. It is our hope that this report will contribute to a new generation of UN peace operations strengthened to meet today's and tomorrow's challenges.

Meanwhile, we are aware of the limits of the power of the United Nations to anticipate and prevent all tensions and violence and end wars. Expectations are naturally high, particularly among those most in need of our collective will, in need of the United Nations to act. But

---

49   The UN Office to the African Union.

we also must acknowledge the UN cannot be everywhere, every time, to solve every conflict in the world.

To my esteemed colleagues – Ameerah Haq, Jean Arnault, Marie-Louise Baricako, Radhika Coomaraswamy, Lt. Gen. (Retd.) Abhijit Guha, Andrew Hughes, Hilde Johnson, Alexander Ilitchev, Youssef Mahmoud, Ian Martin, Henrietta Mensa-Bonsu, B. Lynn Pascoe, Lt. Gen. (Retd.) Floriano Peixoto Vieira Neto, Rima Salah, and Wang Xuexian – I am profoundly grateful for their wisdom and dedication throughout these long months of travel, meetings, reading, and drafting in all regions of the world.

We are very different people, from all regions of the world, with our own beliefs, experiences, and sensitivities, but we have worked harmoniously together, united by our firm belief in the United Nations, its goals, ideals, and principles. I am particularly grateful to Ameerah who, as Vice-Chair, provided me with great wisdom and invaluable advice.

To the tireless, dedicated, and highly professional staff of the Panel Secretariat: Bela Kapur, Tamara Al-Zayyat, Heather Belrose, Paul Keating, Moritz Meier-Ewert, Madalene O'Donnell, Suman Pradhan, Jessica Serraris, and Mike Yuanhu Yuin, who supported the work of the Panel, my eternal gratitude and admiration. These staff members are the very best among the best serving the UN, dedicated, working many long hours and weekends and through holidays. I am deeply impressed by the quality of their work; they are highly competent international civil servants; they serve no government or country; they loyally uphold only the principles and values enshrined in the Charter.

José Ramos-Horta
Chair of the High-Level Independent Panel on United Nations
Peace Operations

Preventing Conflicts, Building Durable Peace

Uppsala, Sweden, 3 November 2015

Four essential shifts must be embraced in the future design and delivery of United Nations peace operations, if they are to realize their full potential for better results in the field and real progress is to be made.

It is an honor to be on this rostrum, following in the footsteps of greater luminaries who preceded me.

That you invited someone originating from a small village of a remote little country situated on the edge of the world to speak here in this august forum is an illustration of your generous heart more than it says about my possible worthiness.

Dag Hammarskjöld – diplomat, economist, author, and Secretary-General of the United Nations, 1953–61 – perished on 18 September 1961, just past midnight, as his DC-6 plane crashed shortly before landing in Ndola, a dot on the map of Northern Rhodesia, now Zambia.

The cause of Hammarskjöld's death remains shrouded in mystery, just as the murder of US President John F. Kennedy two years later does. There were enough people and interests who would want Dag Hammarskjöld dead as he searched for peace in the newly independent Congo, a private possession of King Leopold of Belgium until 1908.

It is fitting that I also pay homage to another great Swedish nobleman who preceded Dag Hammarskjöld as a dedicated and courageous mediator: Folke Bernadotte, Count of Wisborg, diplomat and nobleman, who was the first UN envoy sent to the Middle East in 1948 to try to bring about an acceptable solution to all parties, Palestinians, Arabs, and Jews.

As head of the Swedish Red Cross, Folke Bernadotte negotiated the release of 31,000 prisoners from German concentration camps, including 450 Danish Jews from the Theresienstadt camp.

Tragically, Folke Bernadotte, like many other great men of peace, was murdered by extremist elements as he searched for a fair and just settlement of the Israeli-Palestinian conflict; Jewish extremist elements assassinated Folke Bernadotte in 1948.

And long after the ultimate sacrifice of the two great Swedish statesmen, Folke Bernadotte and Dag Hammarskjöld, peace in the Middle East remains elusive and the UN is mired in Congo, one of the oldest and one of the most expensive United Nations peacekeeping missions in Africa.

We react in horror to the ongoing barbarities perpetrated by extremist groups operating in Syria and Iraq, but we should remember that extremism and violence are not evils that are particular to a group of people or religion; they are not particular to Arabs, Muslims, or Africans.

We are reminded of this as this year, across much of the world, the 70th anniversary of the end of World War II is celebrated; six million Jews, defenseless people, unprotected, unarmed, were executed, starved, and gassed. The Roma were equally singled out for extermination. More than 30 million Russians perished; an equal number of Chinese lost their lives during the period of Japanese occupation and aggression. These were not violence and wars waged by Arabs and Muslims.

More recent horrendous tragedies have faded in our collective memory; the 1965–66 killings in Indonesia; the 1971 Bangladesh–Pakistan War that devoured millions of people; the Killing Fields of Cambodia, with an estimated two to three million perishing under the brutal and insane rule of the Khmer Rouge; and the even more recent Balkan wars of the 1990s that happened in the heart of Europe.

And many more Muslims died in the last ten years in Afghanistan, Pakistan, Iraq, Syria, and Libya, slaughtered by fellow Muslims, than fellow human beings of other religious confessions.

In Myanmar, Buddhist supremacists are waging an ethnic and religious cleansing war on Burmese Rohingyas and other Muslims who have inhabited Myanmar for generations.

Your generous people and wise leaders contributed much towards world peace, freedom, and dignity of many millions. In the sixties and seventies, you protested the insane Vietnam War; in the sixties, you were the only Western European country advocating and actively supporting the struggles for the emancipation and freedom of the enslaved millions on the African continent.

You sheltered countless political refugees and provided them with material support and a free public platform to publicize and advance their struggles.

You were the most generous of all in the provision of development assistance to the newly independent Asian and African nations, from Vietnam to Tanzania, Guinea-Bissau, Mozambique, to mention only a few.

I haven't been here in many years, but I recall that it was here in Uppsala that, sometime in 1997, Swedish mediation experts managed to bring some Timorese compatriots and me for discreet talks with senior Indonesian officials as we began to explore the path of dialogue towards a resolution of the Timor-Leste conflict.

Sweden has faded away as a development partner of Timor-Leste, but you were with us in the first critical years, along with Norway and Finland, providing significant financial and technical assistance to our country.

Today, my country is free, peaceful, and on a relatively strong economic and development growth. The latest UN Human Development Index for Timor-Leste illustrates the progress we have made in less than 15 years.

On several social and economic indicators we are doing much better than Cambodia, Laos, Myanmar, India, Bangladesh, Pakistan, and Nepal, and all of Sub-Saharan Africa, with only two exceptions, Cape Verde and South Africa.

We in Timor-Leste do question the quality of past aid allocated to us by our friends, but we are grateful for the genuine commitment shown by our many friends around the world.

Australia, Brazil, China, Cuba, the EU, Germany, Ireland, Japan, New Zealand, Portugal, Republic of Korea, Spain, the United Kingdom, and the United States of America are among our generous, steady partners.

Beginning with small steps in 2003–04, Timor-Leste and Cuba developed a successful partnership in the health sector with the deployment of more than 200 Cuban doctors to Timor-Leste; 700 Timorese medical students were sent to medical schools in Cuba; all have graduated.

At the same time, Cuba set up our first medical school ever in Díli, where 400 students are being trained. By 2017, Timor-Leste will have more doctors as percentage of population than any country in Asia.

Our other friends and neighbors, Indonesia, Malaysia, Philippines, Singapore, and Thailand, have provided technical assistance, training, and scholarships, assisting Timor-Leste in a critical area of state building.

The United Nations system – agencies, funds, and programs – the World Bank and Asian Development Bank, have been in Timor-Leste from day one and continue to assist in our peace consolidation and development efforts.

After 24 years of an often brutal conflict, Timor-Leste and Indonesia enjoy an exemplary relationship at all levels; from day one of our Independence the leaders of our two nations wisely and pragmatically made a conscious and determined decision and opted to look forward, and chose the path of reconciliation and friendship.

Our people, though still bearing in their bodies and souls fresh wounds of the conflict, endorsed the leaders' wise decision to pursue a process of healing and reconciliation rather than allowing ourselves to be hostages of the past; we resisted the temptation of revenge.

Indonesian people and leaders, deeply absorbed in their own complex democratic transition, following the dramatic events of 1998–99, responded very positively to our approach; they met us halfway, accepted our hand of friendship, and together we have built an exemplary relationship.

As Europe faces exceptionally difficult times, I wish to express sympathy to all – sympathy to the policy makers and elected leaders who have to make difficult decisions in the midst of an unprecedented and prolonged severe economic downturn, financial precariousness, social stress, and political polarization.

I express my sincere admiration to those in Europe, particularly the average individuals and families and leaders who, in spite of the difficulties, nevertheless have shown heart-warming compassion and welcomed hundreds of thousands of refugees fleeing the wars in the Middle East and extreme poverty in Africa.

The old Europe that colonized much of the world, that displaced the original peoples and created new countries, that invented the slave trade to serve the European settlers in these new countries, is changing. The Europe that in part built its prosperity on the backs, sweat, and blood of the peoples it subjugated is now a safe haven for many that your ancestors conquered and subjugated.

A new Europe is emerging; and whether this new Europe will be peaceful and embracing of all, living in peace and harmony, and in continuing prosperity or not, depends on how Europeans of today, Europeans of different ethnic extractions and beliefs, want it to be, and whether, with vision and wisdom, they prepare the new Europe.

It will be a test of the quality of leadership, of political wisdom, a measure of the values of solidarity and justice that should be ingrained in European societies; it is a test for all in Europe, Christians and non-Christians, how they will jointly manage this fast-changing demography, and on them all depends a future, new, rejuvenated, and vibrant Europe, or a Europe mired in racial, religious, social, and political sectarianism and hatred.

Dag Hammarskjöld was an aristocrat. I am not. I come from a very different background. I grew up in places like Laclubar, Barique, Atsabe, Laga – as poor and as remote, forgotten, as any village anywhere in the world can be.

As a child I was mostly barefoot; I got my first pair of shoes for Christmas of 1957, and as I didn't want them to be worn out too quickly, I wore them only once for the midnight Christmas mass; after the mass I carefully put them away, saving them for the next Christmas. Every once in a while I would pull out my cherished shoes, looked at them lovingly and daydream about next Christmas when I could proudly wear them again. And when the next Christmas did arrive, to my utter shock, my feet no longer fit in those shoes; I was puzzled by how those shoes had shrunk.

I had never seen a car until one day, by an act of God, a beaten truck arrived in our village bringing some supplies for the lonely Chinese shop owner; the arrival of the old truck was cause for celebration. Children and adults, we were all in awe.

Fast-forward 20 years and I found myself in New York. Between 1975 and the late 1980s, I lived in New York, and to survive I did occasional menial work, including as a helper in a small Chinese take-away food business.

My first engagements with the UN began in December 1975 when, at age 26, on the eve of the feared invasion of the country, I was sent to New York to advocate and plead with the Secretary-General, General Assembly, and Security Council to prevent the much anticipated and feared invasion.

On 7 December 1975, following a State Visit to Indonesia by [US] President Gerald Ford and Secretary of State Henry Kissinger, Indonesian forces began what was to become a 24-year war and occupation of my country.

This was 1975, the height of the Cold War, and the immediate post-Vietnam War, a senseless war that ended with the mighty US being ignominiously defeated by an Asian peasant army.

Timor-Leste was a footnote of the Cold War, our people expendable and sacrificed in the name of God and anti-communism.

I have had about 30 years of engagement with the UN, primarily as an outsider, a victim, looking for help; I observed up close the paralysis and dysfunctionality in the Secretariat caused by poor leadership in the executive office of the Secretary-General and at key departments where personal ambitions and agendas, provincial-mindedness, and turf rivalries, exacerbated by the almost daily interference by member states, hampered the entire system.

But I was also fortunate to have met exceptional UN staff who, in spite of relentless pressures by member states and a senior management lacking in integrity and courage, truly embraced the ideals and principles embodied in the charter.

While I witnessed and learned sad lessons of blatant double standards and hypocrisy on the part of many member states, large and small, rich and poor, I was also fortunate in meeting diplomats who had a conscience.

Maybe because of this very unique, lifelong experience, with 30 years of intimate, daily engagement with the UN, and having served for 10 years as Foreign Minister, Prime Minister, and President, the esteemed UN Secretary-General invited me to be his Special Representative in Guinea-Bissau (2013–14); and later he thought I would be the right person to chair the High-Level Independent Panel on UN Peace Operations.

I was privileged to have served with 15 outstanding colleagues with very rich, diverse backgrounds, and [been] supported by a team of the best people drawn from the UN Secretariat.[50]

---

50 Panel members: Ameerah Haq, Jean Arnault, Marie-Louise Baricako, Radhika Coomaraswamy, Abhijit Guha, Andrew Hughes, Alexander Ilitchev, Hilde F. Johnson, Youssef Mahmoud, Ian Martin, Henrietta Joy Abena Nyarko Mensa-Bonsu, B. Lynn Pascoe, Floriano Peixoto Vieira Neto, Rima Salah and Wang Xuexian; Secretariat staff: Bela Kapur, Tamara Al-Zayyat, Heather Belrose, Paul Keating, Moritz Meier-Ewert, Madalene O'Donnell, Suman Pradhan, Jessica Serraris, and Mike Yuanhu Yuin.

We were tasked by the Secretary-General to review the UN peace and security architecture, its strengths and weaknesses, building on the Brahimi Report, and advise the Secretary-General and MSS on how to transform our organization to better address the new security challenges facing us all.

The challenges of the twenty-first century are enormously complex and overwhelming in their intensity and spread.

We are facing implosions of fragile states, like South Sudan and CAR,[51] and attendant mass atrocities against civilian populations by all sides in the conflicts; we are facing a non-traditional insurgency in Mali where the UN has become the main target of attacks without the human and technical resources proportional to the mandate assigned to it by the Security Council.

The UN peace and security architecture is under severe stress, with more than 100,000 armed personnel deployed in 16 peacekeeping missions and with more than 30 non-armed special political missions across the globe.

From the very first mediations, dizzying shuttle diplomacy, cease-fires and observer missions undertaken by Folke Bernadotte and Dag Hammarskjöld till our times, peacekeeping has evolved into peace enforcement and robust protection of civilian in armed conflicts; from being mere unarmed or non-combatant forces, the UN and/or regional organizations authorized by the Security Council have been mandated to use robust force to challenge armed groups, as in Congo and Mali.

While the UN peacekeeping budget at over US$9 billion[52] for 2015 may seem very high, in reality, the costs of UN peacekeeping operations are a minute fraction of US and NATO[53] costs per soldier deployed in Afghanistan and Iraq.

The overall UN core budget is modest by any standards of measurement; however, while there have been significant improvements and efficiency in management in the last ten years, there is urgent need and room for further improvement to end duplication, waste, and inefficiency.

---

51   Central African Republic.
52   Nine thousand million US dollars.
53   The North Atlantic Treaty Organization, which regulates the US-Europe Defense Alliance since 4th April 1949.

I am often baffled at how some Western leaders protest over the core cost of the UN and its peace operations as excessive, but gingerly they find hundreds of billions of dollars to rescue mismanaged banks, insurance, and housing companies, failed auto-industry companies.

The Secretary-General and his senior management team expect the Security Council to give the financial means and tools commensurate with the mandate; but for the organization to meet the expectations of its members and deliver peace and security, it must also change the way it is managed and how it operates.

On 16 June, after months of intense listening to all stakeholders – MSS,[54] United Nations' departments and agencies, SRSGs[55] and envoys, force commanders serving in the field, regional organizations, academics, civil society advocates, community leaders – and after reading through the more than 80 written submissions our panel received, my esteemed colleagues and I delivered to the Secretary-General our report entitled: *Uniting Our Strengths for Peace: Politics, Partnerships and People.*

Allow me now to share with you the key thoughts and recommendations contained in our 100-page report.

Four essential shifts

Four essential shifts must be embraced in the future design and delivery of UN peace operations if real progress is to be made and if UN peace operations are to realize their potential for better results in the field.

First, politics must drive the design and implementation of peace operations. Lasting peace is achieved not through military and technical engagements but through political solutions.

Political solutions should always guide the design and deployment of UN peace operations. When the momentum behind peace falters, the United Nations, and particularly member states, must help to mobilize renewed political efforts to keep peace processes on track.

Second, the full spectrum of UN peace operations must be used more flexibly to respond to changing needs on the ground.

The United Nations has a uniquely broad spectrum of peace operations that it can draw upon to deliver situation-specific responses. And yet, it

---

54 Mission Support Systems.
55 Special Representatives of the Secretary General.

often struggles to generate and rapidly deploy missions that are well-tailored to the context.

The sharp distinctions between peacekeeping operations and special political missions should give way to a continuum of response and smoother transitions between different phases of missions.

The United Nations should embrace the term "peace operations" to denote the full spectrum of responses required, and invest in strengthening the underlying analysis, strategy, and planning that leads to more successful design of missions.

Peacekeeping and special political missions are artificially separated, managed by two departments, leading to bureaucratic rivalry and infighting. Hence, the panel proposed the fusion of the two core UN peace and security functions into a single peace operations concept under a new deputy Secretary-General charged with the department of peace operations.

Sequenced and prioritized mandates will allow missions to develop over time rather than trying to do everything at once and failing.

Third, a stronger, more inclusive peace and security partnership is needed for the future.

A stronger global/regional peace and security partnership is needed to respond to the more challenging crises of tomorrow.

Common purpose and resolve must be established from the outset of a new operation and must be maintained throughout, through enhanced collaboration and consultation.

The UN system, too, must pull together in a more integrated manner in the service of conflict prevention and peace.

All of these partnerships must be underpinned by mutual respect and mutual responsibilities.

Fourth, the UN Secretariat must become more field-focused, and UN peace operations must be more people-centered.

There must be an awakening of UN headquarters to the distinct and important needs of field missions, and a renewed resolve on the part of UN peace operations personnel to engage with, serve, and protect the people they have been mandated to assist.

New approaches are needed to ensure that UN peace operations are able to reliably play their critical roles in the international peace and security firmament in the years to come, and significant change is required across four of the most important areas of the work of UN peace operations and of the United Nations.

Conflict prevention and mediation must be brought back to the fore. The prevention of armed conflict is perhaps the greatest responsibility of the international community and yet it has not been sufficiently invested in.

A decade ago, the World Summit, held from 14–16 September at United Nations headquarters in New York, brought together more than 170 heads of state and government. It was a once-in-a-generation opportunity to take bold decisions in the areas of development, security, human rights, and reform of the United Nations.

The agenda was based on an achievable set of proposals outlined in March 2005 by Secretary-General Kofi Annan in his report *In Larger Freedom*.

It called for collective Security Council action when national authorities are incapable or are unwilling to protect their own people from genocide, war crimes, ethnic cleansing, and crimes against humanity. It then went on to set up two new bodies, a peacebuilding commission to help countries in transition from war to peace, and a strengthened Human Rights Council. Whether these two institutions have delivered on their promise is a whole different question.

Member states have not sufficiently invested in addressing root causes of conflict; nor has the United Nations generally been able to engage early enough in emerging crises.

The UN must invest in its own capacities to undertake prevention and mediation, and in its capacity to assist others, particularly at the national and regional levels.

The Security Council, supported by the Secretariat, should seek to play an earlier role in addressing emerging conflicts, and must do so with impartiality.

At the global level, the United Nations must mobilize a new international commitment to preventing conflict and mobilizing partnerships to support political solutions.

It must find ways to draw on the knowledge and resources of others beyond the UN system through civil society – community, religious, youth and women groups – and the global business community.

Protection of civilians is a core obligation of the United Nations, but expectations and capability must converge.

Significant progress has been made in promoting norms and frameworks for the protection of civilians. And yet, on the ground, the results are mixed and the gap between what is asked and what peace operations can deliver has widened in more difficult environments.

The protection of civilians is a national responsibility and UN peace operations can play an important role in supporting governments to execute that responsibility.

UN missions and non-governmental actors have important unarmed and civilian tools for protecting civilians, working with communities.

The United Nations must rise to the challenge of protecting civilians in the face of imminent threat, and must do so proactively and effectively, but also with recognition of its limits. Protection mandates must be realistic and linked to a wider political approach.

Closing the gap between what is asked of missions to protect civilians and what they can provide demands improvements across several dimensions: assessments and planning capabilities, timely information and communication, leadership and training, as well as more focused mandates.

The Secretariat must be frank in its assessments to the Security Council about what is required to respond to threats to civilians.

In turn, member states should provide the necessary resources and lend their influence and leverage to respond to threats against civilians. When a protection crisis occurs, UN personnel cannot stand by as civilians are threatened or killed. They must use every tool available to them to protect civilians under imminent threat. Each and every peacekeeper – military, police, and civilian – must pass this test when crisis presents itself.

Clarity is needed on the use of force and in the role of UN peace operations and others in managing armed conflict.

While some missions are working to implement ceasefires or implement peace agreements, others are operating in environments with no peace to keep. They are struggling to contain or manage conflict and to keep alive the prospects for a resumption of a peace process.

The panel believes that the United Nations may see more, not less, of these situations in the future. Its existing concepts, tools, and capabilities for peace implementation do not always serve these missions well. For such situations there must be a new approach to mandating and resourcing missions, while also setting out the limits of ambition of what the UN can achieve in such settings. Every effort must be made to establish minimum conditions to ensure a mission's viability and to define "success" more realistically in such settings.

Where armed conflict is ongoing, missions will struggle to establish themselves, particularly if they are not perceived to be impartial. Although efforts are underway to strengthen capabilities, UN peacekeeping operations are often poorly suited to these operating environments, and others must come forward to respond.

The panel believes that there are outer limits for UN peacekeeping operations defined by their composition, character, and inherent capability limitations. Peacekeeping operations are but one tool at the disposal of the Security Council, and they should perform a circumscribed set of roles.

In this regard, the panel believes that UN troops should not undertake military counter-terrorism operations. Extreme caution should guide the mandating of enforcement tasks to degrade, neutralize, or defeat a designated enemy. Such operations should be exceptional, time limited, and undertaken with full awareness of the risks and responsibilities for the UN mission as a whole.

Where a parallel force is engaged in offensive combat operations, it is important for UN peacekeeping operations to maintain a clear division of labor and distinction of roles.

The panel has heard many views on the core principles of UN peacekeeping. The panel is convinced of their importance in guiding successful UN peacekeeping operations. Yet, these principles must be interpreted progressively and with flexibility in the face of new challenges, and they should never be an excuse for failure to protect civilians or to defend the mission proactively.

To sustain peace, political vigilance is needed. Peace processes do not end when a peace agreement has been signed or an election held. The international community must sustain high-level political engagement in support of national efforts to deepen and broaden processes of inclusion and reconciliation, as well as address the underlying causes of conflict.

Peace operations, like other actors, must work to overcome deficits in supporting conflict-affected countries in sustaining peace, including supply-driven templates and an overly technocratic focus on capitals and elites, and the risk of unintentionally exacerbating divisions.

Strong support for reconciliation and healing is also critical to prevent relapse into conflict.

Peace operations have a key role to play in mobilizing political support for reforms and resources for critical gaps in state capacity, as well as supporting others to revitalize livelihoods in conflict-affected economies. Engagement with affected communities should help build confidence in political processes and responsible state structures.

Missions must focus first and foremost on creating political commitment and the space for others to address important elements in sustaining peace. The security sector must be a particular focus, owing to its potential to disrupt peace in many countries, with the UN in a convening and coordinating role, if requested.

A significant change in policing approaches is needed to better support national police development and reform. These efforts should be linked to the whole "justice chain," ensuring an integrated approach between human rights and rule of law capacities.

In sustaining peace, the UN system must overcome structural and other impediments to working together, including through more innovative resourcing options.

Missions must work closely with their national counterparts and UN and regional partners to ensure that the least disruption is caused when they transition and depart.

These are the four core shifts in mindset and policies my colleagues and I have recommended to all stakeholders of our common effort to render our organization more reliable and efficient in the fight for peace.

I also want to mention that, in carrying out our work, the panel was mindful that the review of UN peace operations was taking place in parallel to two other important reviews related to the peace and security pillar of the UN's work – the review of the UN peace-building architecture [peace-building commission, peace-building support office, and peace-building fund] and the global study on the implementation of Security Council Resolution 1325 on Women, Peace and Security. In that regard, we consulted with the panels working on the other reviews and have advocated that changes and reforms that result from these processes must be coherent and not further contribute to fragmentation in the system.

In particular, I want to mention a common finding in all three reviews: that the UN is not doing enough to implement what has become known as the Women, Peace and Security agenda. Gender equality and women's empowerment on issues of peace and security must be made central to the UN's work in promoting peace, as women's participation is key to sustainable peace.

We are pleased that our report has received widespread support from all our partners. We are nevertheless concerned that the Secretary-General, in his own report to the General Assembly on 12th October, failed to strongly advocate for the full implementation of our core recommendations. One seasoned UN diplomat eloquently described the Secretary-General's report to the GA as a "decaffeinated" version of the report of HIPPO.[56]

The systemic weaknesses in the UN Secretariat, characterized by turf tensions and rivalries, are already emerging and threaten to undermine some of our key recommendations, namely in regard to mindset change in the Secretariat, entrenched HQ's ossified bureaucracy, and the respect and support due by the United Nations Headquarters to those operating in the field.

The panel called for several foundational changes in how the UN works in countries shattered by conflict. One important set of recommendations that I fear has not received the attention from member states that it deserves is related to bureaucratic reform.

We called for a decisive move away from the mindset of a headquarters bureaucracy not attuned to the needs of field operations.

Is real, lasting peace possible in our lifetime? For idealists, the answer is yes. Though I am a believer in the fundamental good of human beings, I also fear the human capacity for extreme inhumanity. From the time of our ancestors many thousands of years ago till present times, human beings have, with each passing century, perfected the art and science of war and killing.

Can we prevent social and political tensions from escalating into violent conflicts? Can we do better in bringing parties in a conflict to the table and restore peace? And how can we build durable peace?

In some cases, neutral and credible national and/or external actors may be able to discreetly or openly influence behavioral change and policies among competing actors, when those involved are committed

---

56   High-Level Independent Panel on UN Peace Operations.

to prevent escalation of the political conflict and welcome advice. But too often individual pride and egos block friendly, neutral help, domestic or external.

Too often, those in power do not have the wisdom and humility of the truly great in embracing the other half who disagree with them. And the opposition overestimates its own power, so it underestimates the adversary and miscalculates, making excessive demands amounting to ultimatum for surrender.

My humble advice: When you are at the top of the mountain, embrace those on the fringes of power and privileges; in victory, be magnanimous; embrace the vanquished adversaries; if they are on their knees, help them to their feet; invite them to join in the new enterprise of peace.

To those in the opposition my advice is: never surrender to violence and hatred; seize every opportunity to enter the political process, and advance your interests with patience, through dialogue and persuasion.

There are many simple ways to prevent conflicts and some old, tested methods are genuine, patient dialogue, consultation and empowerment of all, making all feel part of the nation. All it actually requires is serious investment in the mechanisms of dialogue – and "dialogue" means listening attentively and respectfully to the other side, accommodating their views as much as you can.

Leaders, supported by the international development partners, must carefully study and address the many obvious causes of tensions, namely: abject poverty of the majority, in contrast with opulence and ostentation of few; real or perceived discrimination and exclusion; they must engage community and religious leaders in developing strategies and inclusive policies that leave no one behind.

Corruption and ostentation are causes of inequality and tension; the more a country is free from corruption, the more leaders show humility and integrity, the more they are respected and are followed, the better the chances for peace to gain roots.

In too many countries, rather than embracing ethnic, cultural, and religious diversity as a blessing, leaders try to suppress particular ethnic groups, their language and religion, in the name of an artificial national unity – unity of the majority ethnic group. See the cases of Sri Lanka, Turkey, Spain under Franco, Myanmar.

When a particular ethnic/religious minority manages to achieve power (such as the case of the Alawites, in Syria), it builds a powerful minority army and intelligence apparatus to protect its community from the majority.

There are no shortcuts to peace or sustainable and equitable development; peace has to be built block by block; extreme poverty eradication is a moral imperative for all, and is a *sine qua non* condition for the attainment of durable peace.

ODA[57] has been, for decades, the prime tool employed to assist poorer countries in freeing themselves from chronic poverty and instability. Tragically and unwisely, in a simplistic and knee-jerk reaction to the economic and financial downturn that began in 2008, almost all OECD[58] countries, exceptions being the UK and the Nordic countries, opted to impose draconian cuts in ODA budgets.

The UK under Prime Minister David Cameron made the courageous and wise decision in increasing the UK's ODA budget to 0.7 percent of its GDP, thus becoming the only G7 country to do so; and Prime Minister Cameron's decision is the more commendable as this was done in the midst of the ongoing financial crisis.

As we have learned over several decades, there are no shortcuts to peace; there are no magic bullets that cure long-festering wounds and poverty. Both require long-term commitment and investment, and accepting that there have been, and there will be, relapses in the peace-building process, and with it, setbacks in the road to economic recovery.

Human beings (usually men) are the authors of conflicts and wars; and human beings are the only ones who can prevent the outbreak of violent conflicts, negotiate the end of wars, and build peace.

Peoples are the makers of history but peoples need leaders; when they are inspired by their leaders – leaders they trust, leaders who preach compassion and reconciliation – people follow, and peace grows.

To prevent conflicts, end wars, heal wounds, reconcile communities and nations, and build durable peace, we require leaders with vision, courage, determination, humility, and compassion.

---

57 Official Development Assistance.

58 Organisation for Economic Co-operation and Development.

Our community, called the United Nations, is made up of many parts, and the parts are we, the peoples of the world.

The UN of Dag Hammarskjöld, a UN fit for purpose, to serve the cause of peace, a UN of the people, is under severe stress and is challenged in many fronts.

I dedicated the panel report to my hero, a three-year-old girl from South Sudan, Nyakhat Pal. In April 2014, Nyakhat Pal walked for four long hours through treacherous treks, guiding her blind father, in search of a UN civilian protection center. They did reach the UN facility, were duly registered, interviewed, and assisted.

Her story, a story of resilience and survival, is also an indictment of the collective failure of the UN and its regional partners and neighbors of South Sudan for their inability to prevent the implosion of the country and the ensuing war; however, Nyakhat's story also underlines the indispensability of the UN; for all its weaknesses and limitations, the UN is in these conflict regions, its dedicated personnel facing extreme hardships and risks to their own well-being and life, and, working long hours, they feed, shelter, and save lives. We can do more; we can do better – we can prevail over hatred and extremism. Peace will prevail.

Your Royal Highness, I pray to God the Almighty and the Merciful to continue to bestow on the Majesties the King and Queen of Sweden, and their much-esteemed royal family, and the people of Sweden, bountiful health and endless happiness.

Totalitarian Ideology, Nuclear Arsenal, and the Human Rights Situation in North Korea

Seoul, 11 November 2015

We are not dealing with a regime that is about to collapse from within; nor is there a people that is ready to march in the streets.

It is a pleasure to be again in Seoul since my participation in the various events marking the 70th anniversary of the founding of the Republic of Korea and of the end of World War II, hosted by KBS TV on 24 August.

The people of the Republic of Korea can be proud of the extraordinary progress they have made since independence and the devastation caused by the Korean War.

There cannot be greater contrast between two countries and two realities: one, the people living south of the DMZ, the demilitarized zone, enjoying complete freedom and prosperity, and the other, north of the DMZ, living in fear, oppression, and extreme poverty.

While most of Asia has prospered and democratized, North Korea has been frozen in time.

The communist regime of the north, with its bellicose totalitarian ideology and nuclear arsenal, continues to be a source of tension and unpredictability.

Long after the collapse of the Soviet Union and of the totalitarian philosophies and ideologies, and with the few remaining communist regimes undergoing incremental political reforms and economic liberalization, the North Korean regime stands out as the last outpost of a gulag where millions of human beings are deprived of basic human rights, hostages of a communist dynasty.

The recent heartbreaking scenes of some long-separated Korean siblings meeting for the first time since their separation some 60 to 70 years ago only brought to mind the tragic reality of this Cold War legacy.

It is not my purpose to elaborate on the ongoing widespread, gross, and systematic human rights abuses in North Korea. Numerous eyewitnesses and defectors from the north have amply documented this over decades.

Our friend the eminent Justice Michael Kirby, and the international commission of inquiry he presided over, investigated and produced a far-reaching, damning, authoritative, and conclusive report on the human rights situation in North Korea.

The world is generally aware of the prevailing situation in North Korea; however, the regime has been extremely effective in impeding and suppressing a regular flow of information in and out of the gulag. Hence, the sad and tragic reality in North Korea is not a daily concern for the rest of the world.

And even if there were more regular flow of information about the shocking reality of life in North Korea, in the prisons and labor camps, there is still very little anyone can do to influence the behavior of the totalitarian regime in the north.

The supremely well-choreographed scenes of mass hysteria by Korean masses displaying their love to the "dear leader" illustrate, in my view, both a people intoxicated by propaganda reminiscent of the phenomenon of Nazism and Hitler in Germany and Austria, and a certain degree of genuine adulation.

We are not dealing with a regime that is about to collapse from within; nor is there a people ready to march in the streets.

There is no possible comparison between the situations in North Korea and any other in history. From an ideological perspective, the North Korean regime reminds me of the situations in Albania and Romania during the years of the dictators Enver Hoxha and Nicolai Ceaușescu, the two worst and most retrograde communist regimes of that time.

But neither had military capabilities of much significance.

Leaders and academics of the Republic of Korea know only too well the limits of outside influence, of how much and what can the international community do to influence the behavior of the regime in North Korea, a regime that shamelessly thrives in state gangsterism, blackmail, and brinkmanship.

Following Justice Kirby's report there was some media coverage; expressions of condemnation came primarily from Western countries and media.

From Asia to Africa to Latin America there was a deafening silence. For the people of North Korea we must raise our voices, even if this is all we can do; being silent and resigning to this seemingly mighty regime is not an option, at least for our conscience. Taking this matter to the international criminal court is an obvious option.

Three generations of communist leaders, from grandfather to son and now to grandson, have established a de facto communist monarchy in North Korea, of the mold of the Middle Ages, absolutist monarchies who ruled over their subjects in complete disregard for basic human rights and dignity. And this communist monarchy has assembled a mighty army and intelligence network that spy on and intimidate every North Korean family.

There is no light at the end of the tunnel, because this is a tunnel without an obvious end.

While there is every reason for us not to be hopeful for a peaceful transformation of North Korea and a happy reunification of the two separated peoples, let us remember that colonial empires generally lasted centuries; the briefest colonial occupation of any country must have been the Japanese occupation of Korea.

European colonization of Africa and Asia lasted much longer, from 100 to 500 years.

There is no valid comparison between the situation prevailing in North Korea and the situations experienced by the hundreds of millions of peoples in Africa and Asia conquered and colonized by the European powers from the Middle Ages till the twentieth century.

But at times it might be helpful to remind ourselves that empires and regimes built on falsehoods and oppression do come to an end; this has been humanity's history, from the ancient times to the twentieth century.

In the face of overwhelming force, fear or prudence prevails, and people appear to resign [themselves] to their fate; the wait can be long, too long. But the people always rise up when times has arrived. And time will arrive in North Korea when the people will rise up for freedom and dignity.

Armed Conflict Cannot be Answered Exclusively Through Security Approaches

Greentree, Manhasset, New York, 22 March 2016

How to make the multilateral system anchored in the UN "fit for purpose" on the face of new challenges of the twenty-first century.

I am honored to be the keynote speaker for the Independent Commission on Multilateralism's final, 16th retreat.

I do know this privilege stems from the kindness of our Chair, the Hon Kevin Rudd and Secretary-General Ambassador Hardeep Singh Puri; this is the only possible explanation for me being asked to share with this gathering of diplomatic and academic luminaries my thoughts on armed conflict, mediation, conciliation, and peacekeeping.

Supported by the governments of Canada, Norway, and the United Arab Emirates, the Independent Commission on Multilateralism is chaired by the Hon Kevin Rudd, former Prime Minister of Australia; and co-chaired by Børge Brende, Foreign Minister of Norway; [and includes] Hanna S. Tetteh, Foreign Minister of Ghana; Patricia Espinosa, former Minister for Foreign Affairs and current ambassador of Mexico to Germany; and myself.

The question that guides the Independent Commission on Multilateralism and permeates through the ICM's overall work is: Given the new challenges of the twenty-first century, how can the multilateral system anchored in the UN be made more "fit for purpose"?

In many parts of the world the UN is considered to be unique in its universality, and unmatched in its convening power. Seventy years since its creation, its successes in the normative and humanitarian and development fields are many, and undeniable. The recent adoption of the agenda for sustainable development and the Paris Agreement on Climate Change are singular achievements.

And yet, in other parts of the world, the UN's relevance as the pre-eminent epicenter of global governance is not taken for granted, and is disputed.

The failure of the Security Council to prevent the unspeakable human suffering caused by some of the contemporary conflicts give some of us a disquieting pause.

I have experienced violent conflict from the inside and witnessed it as an outsider. And I could not help [but] come to the conclusion that the real world does not confront decision makers with alternates of good and bad, but varying shades of lousy grey.

First, primarily as an outsider, a victim of injustice but also a beneficiary of UN peacekeeping, through the various Security Council-mandated missions, I related to the UN as an active partner, working with HQ[59] and the field missions during that long period of UN engagement with us.

Second, some 15 years later, I became a UN insider when our esteemed Secretary-General appointed me his Special Representative in Guinea-Bissau; and more recently, the Secretary-General invited me to chair the High-Level Independent Panel on UN Peace Operations.

This experience gave me an open window into the multilateral system. I witnessed and learned sad lessons of double standards on the part of member states, large and small.

For me, a naïve villager arriving in December 1975 in New York for the first time, and addressing the UNSC, was a memorable experience.

But gradually my naïveté was displaced by the realization that Realpolitik and pragmatism, national interests, real or perceived, as defined by national political elites, were, after all, the main driving force of the actions of states.

I experienced the dysfunctionality of a Secretariat that struck me as over-managed and under-led. I witnessed personal ambitions and

---

59   The United Nations Headquarters in New York.

agendas, provincial mindedness and turf rivalries, exacerbated by the almost daily interference by member states, at times paralyzing the entire system.

But I also met exceptionally dedicated international civil servants and seasoned diplomats with convictions and a conscience, who embraced the ideals and principles of the Charter [of the United Nations] in good times and bad.

I do not belong to the group that sees only failings in the UN; though a practicing Catholic, I do not see only virtues in a Vatican State led by the holiest of all Catholics.

I pay tribute to the many good men and women who have served, and are serving, in the UN across the world, almost always surviving with very basic material conditions, and often in dangerous conflict regions.

I also pay tribute to the HQ-based leadership and staff. Often unknown to the rest of the world, they work very long hours, round the clock, seven days a week, reading information from the field, dissecting conflicting intelligence, and producing irreproachable reports for the SG [Secretary-General] and member states.

Timor-Leste is a success story of post-conflict reconstruction, reconciliation, and recovery. This "success story" is the product of a number of enablers: a united and credible national leadership, motivated and determined to pursue dialogue and peace, working with, and supported by, an effective partnership with the international community coalesced around the UN.

However, as always, the road has been a bumpy one, and along the way sometimes, we careened off the track.

The challenges of the twenty-first century are enormously complex and overwhelming in their intensity and spread. We are facing implosions of fragile states like South Sudan and the Central African Republic and attendant mass atrocities against civilian populations by all sides in the conflicts.

We are also facing non-traditional insurgencies in Mali, and transnational organized violence is becoming increasingly the norm. In the asymmetric threat environments in which the UN is deployed, its peacekeepers have become targets. The UN flag no longer offers the protection its bearers used to enjoy.

Are we surprised by these turns of events?

Perhaps the UN presence in conflict areas is lacking the human and technical resources proportional to the mandate assigned to it by the Security Council. Perhaps peacekeeping missions cannot work properly where there is no peace to keep and where national and regional actors do not have a shared vision and commitment to prevent tensions, negotiate, and agree on a shared platform of peace.

From the very first mediations, dizzying shuttle-diplomacy, ceasefires, and observer missions in the 1950s, peacekeeping has evolved into multi-dimensional, integrated missions, often with a robust mandate under Chapter VII to engage armed groups or to protect civilians under imminent danger.

Today, the UN peace operation is under severe stress. We count more than 100,000 armed personnel deployed in 16 peacekeeping missions, and nearly 30 special political missions and good offices across the globe.

This is the context in which the SG invited me to chair the High-Level Independent Panel on UN Peace Operations. The panel's mandate was to take a comprehensive look at how United Nations peace operations could continue to contribute to the prevention and resolution of conflicts and be best designed to meet the challenges of tomorrow.

On 16 June 2015, after months of intense listening to all stakeholders – member states, UN Departments and Agencies, SRSGs and envoys, force commanders serving in the field, regional organizations, academics, civil society advocates, and community leaders – and after reading through more than 80 written submissions, the panel delivered to the Secretary-General its report entitled:

Uniting Our Strengths for Peace: Politics, Partnership and People – also known as the HIPPO report.

We are pleased that our report received wide support from many and varied stakeholders, both within and outside the UN, and equally pleased that the SG endorsed many of our recommendations.

We are nevertheless disappointed that quite a number of important ones were either ignored or received scant attention. The recommendations relating to the unarmed protection of civilian and the reform of DPA [Department of Political Affairs] and DPKO [Department of Peacekeeping Operations] come to mind.

Allow me now to share with you the key messages contained in the report. The members of HIPPO were of the firm belief that if real progress were to be made in the design and delivery of peace operations, four essential shifts must be embraced.

First, politics must drive the design and implementation of peace operations. Lasting peace is achieved not through military and technical engagements but through political solutions.

Over the last 20 years, we have seen an increasing militarization of UN operations, largely as a result of the Council's resorting to Chapter VII as a default response to situations where there is no peace to keep. It is not surprising therefore that we called for a re-commitment to the spirit and letter of Chapter VI, and to treating politics as the best force multiplier.

Second, the full spectrum of UN peace operations must be used more flexibly to respond to changing needs on the ground.

The UN has a uniquely broad spectrum of peace operations that it can draw upon to deliver situationspecific responses. And yet, it often struggles to generate and rapidly deploy missions that are well tailored to the context.

The sharp distinctions between peacekeeping operations and special political missions [SPMs] should give way to a continuum of response and smoother transitions between different phases of missions. Peacekeeping and SPMs are artificially separated, managed by two departments, leading to bureaucratic rivalry and duplication.

Hence the panel's recommendation for the merger of the two core UN peace and security structures into a single Secretariat entity under the overall direction of a new deputy Secretary-General.

Third, a stronger, more inclusive peace and security partnership is needed to respond to the challenging crises of today and tomorrow.

Crisis management needs to include responses at the national, regional, and global levels that address political, governance, development, and leadership failures that drive and sustain conflict.

Which brings me to the fourth shift the report advocates, namely: The UN must bring back to the fore conflict prevention and mediation and pursue a more field-focused and people-centered approach if it is to achieve the ultimate goal of sustaining peace where women and youth play a crucial role.

In fact, "sustaining peace" is the overarching concept also advocated by the two other peace and security reviews, namely the global study on the implementation of Security Council Resolution 1325 and the one dealing with the 2015 Review of the UN peacebuilding architecture.

The "sustaining peace" concept frees the peace-building enterprise from the short-term horizons that constrain it, particularly when it is conducted as part of a peace operation, which tends to treat the building of peace as a conflict management tool with few predictable resources to ensure its sustainability beyond the lifetime of the mission.

Also, the sustaining peace framework allows peace builders time and space to identify, engage, and support local actors and national structures that would strengthen and solidify peace.

More importantly, the "sustaining peace" framework breaks down institutional silos and allows for the integration of the Development, Peace and Security, and Human Rights pillars of the UN that are crucial for laying the foundations for a consolidated and inclusive peace.

As you know, member states have been discussing how best to take these common themes and related recommendations forward. The Security Council has already organized several open debates late in 2015 and earlier this year, and the General Assembly, after an initial discussion by its Special Committee on Peacekeeping, is planning a high-level thematic debate on May 10 and 11 to provide member states and others with a platform to discuss the way forward.

From what I can observe, some policy consensus seems to be emerging on where peace operations should be heading. Despite differences on certain critical issues, such as the financing of AU missions, or of Special Political Missions, my sense is that most member states are looking for ways to work together, differently, across structural divides.

As we have learned over several decades, there are no shortcuts to peace. Peace cannot be enforced when the human instinct to fight is stronger than the hope for stability and security. Violence and armed conflict cannot be answered exclusively through a single-minded security approach.

There are no magic bullets that cure long-festering wounds and poverty. Both require long-term commitment and investment. Accepting that there have been and there will be relapses in the peace-building process is also the key to sustainability.

Can we prevent social and political tensions from escalating into violent conflicts? Can we do better in bringing parties in a conflict to the table and restore peace? And how can we build durable, sustainable peace instead of building peace that has inherent time constraints?

Mediation as a peaceful means for moving warring parties from violence to politics is facing many challenges. Some of the reasons mentioned in the Independent Commission on Multilateralism discussion paper include the changing nature of the conflict, the plethora of national and regional actors with differing and competing agendas where the political, economic, and criminal motivations behind the violence are complex and intertwined, but also because of the multiplicity of mediators and envoys deployed by various countries or regional organizations to follow and influence the process and outcome of the mediation.

This analysis resonates with my experience in my own country, Timor-Leste, and in Guinea-Bissau.

In some cases, neutral and credible national and external actors may be able to influence behavioral change and mindset among competing actors. This can work when those involved are committed to prevent escalation of the political conflict and welcome advice. But too often individual pride and egos block help, domestic or external.

There are many simple ways to prevent conflicts. Some are old, tested methods that imply consultations and empowerment of all.

When we negotiate the end of wars and build peace, in the inclusion of all segments of societies lies the key to sustainable peace.

Above all, local and national actors should bear in mind their own communities' and countries' past experiences of conflict, and commit themselves to new approaches that genuinely accommodate the feelings and interest of every segment of the society.

In some specific situations there are too many outside mediators, and each with his or her own prescription. While it is politically correct to say "national solutions to national problems; regional solutions to regional problems," what happens when the country has run out of credible and impartial mediators?

What happens when neighboring countries have overlapping interests and are actually involved in the conflict?

And what to do in situations when a conflict spills over porous, unmarked artificial boundaries, and ethnicity and loyalties merge and clash across national boundaries?

When I was appointed as the Secretary-General's Special Representative to Guinea-Bissau, I quickly learned a few facts: listen to *everybody*, including the much-disliked military leadership – bring the UN to the people. So, I traveled exhaustively into every corner of the country to make the people feel the UN cares and listens to them. I had my critics in the UN. Some said I should not have visited the general army barracks, and [that] my many trips into the communities might raise false expectations.

I worked closely with all regional actors even though I knew of the strong differences and interests among Guinea-Bissau's neighbors. I worked also closely with the African Union even though I knew that some in the Economic Community of Western African States [ECOWAS] did not see eye to eye with their parent regional organization. I worked closely with the Community of Portuguese Speaking Countries [CPLP], even though some in CPLP had a strong view, different from mine, on how much and how far to engage national actors. I also worked closely with the EU, even when I was skeptical about the EU's dogmatic stance not to engage the very inclusive transitional government we helped put together with the task of preparing the country for national elections.

My message is that SRSGs must be uniquely qualified for their missions and, above all, try to earn the respect of all national and international partners; he or she must communicate with the people, and this means getting out of the UN compound, meeting all parties, community and confessional [church/religious] leaders. He or she must set their goals very clearly and stay focused.

On my desk I had two Security Council Resolutions on Guinea-Bissau with a multitude of operative provisions, the sort of "Christmas tree" favored by the Security Council drafters. I ignored most of these unattainable operative articles and instead focused on two key goals, and the first one was not even in the Security Council mandate and didn't have to be there:

1. restore faith and hope in the people, as this lessens tensions and contributes to a more constructive dialogue and agreement; and
2. Return Guinea-Bissau to constitutional order. This would not be possible without the first.

The work of the Independent Commission on Multilateralism and the seminal reports "Global Study on the Implementation of SCR 1325", the "2015 Review of the UN Peacebuilding Architecture," and HIPPO hopefully will inform the next Secretary-General.

Civil society and the United Nations General Assembly have laid out the criteria of qualifications for the next Secretary-General who, for the first time in the United Nations' 70-year history, will be chosen from a wider field of candidates, in a more transparent and democratic manner.

The next Secretary-General will not have more powers and resources than his or her predecessors. There will not be a powerful armada, a feared army, and an awesome air force at her or his disposal, to be activated at a second's notice.

She or he will not meet everyone's every expectations and solve all the world's problems; however, she or he will be someone uniquely qualified, with exceptional communication skills, able to inspire and engage the peoples of the world behind the UN in our shared duty to prevent conflicts, end wars, promote gender equality and fundamental human rights, eradicate extreme poverty, reverse the colossal damage done to planet Earth, and build sustainable, durable peace.

Last, but not least, 2016 is already proving to be an interesting year, a promising one. President Obama is visiting Cuba, the first American president to do so in almost a century.

Now the real news: I recently nominated the Cuban Medical Brigade for the Nobel Peace Prize. It occurred to me that, at the least, the Cuban Medical Brigade is as deserving of the Nobel Peace Prize as the many UN Agencies that were awarded the prize, namely UNICEF, UNHCR, Peacekeeping, etc.

Created in 1964, the brigade has deployed tens of thousands of doctors and nurses to over a hundred countries; they set up medical schools and trained thousands of doctors in the developing world.

In the last ten years, Cuba has trained close to a thousand Timorese medical doctors, now deployed in every village in Timor-Leste. On our independence in 2002, we had 19 medical doctors.

They are always first and fast on the front line in every major humanitarian catastrophe in the globe. And long after others leave, curtains drawn, lights dimmed, the Cuban doctors stay on, often in extremely precarious conditions.

I thank Your Excellencies for your kind patience and attention. You are all in my daily prayers to the Almighty, our Creator, as I plead with Him to bestow on each of you abundant health and bountiful wisdom as you undertake God's work – and that is the search for better ways to promote peace and harmony in the world.

At the St Antony's College 5th Southeast Asian Studies Symposium

On the State of Democracy and Human Rights in Timor-Leste and Southeast Asia

University of Oxford, 14 April 2016

ASEAN countries have performed well economically, with decreased poverty levels, and the rise of Human Development indicators. But there still are clear democracy deficits in good governance, transparency, and accountability.

My sincere appreciation to the University of Oxford Southeast Asia studies project for inviting me to this year's symposium, and I thank very specially Phyllis Ferguson for her hard work and flawless arrangements.

I will begin this presentation by sharing with you my views on Asia as a whole, followed by remarks on our immediate sub-region, Southeast Asia and Timor-Leste.

Asia is rising.

Led by 30 years of steady growth of the Chinese economy, Asia made impressive social and economic progress. However, the challenges confronting the countries of the wider region are numerous and complex.

Asia is the common home of half of humanity; in any given hour of the day, millions of people are in constant movement; millions are abandoning rural Asia and flocking into increasingly crowded cities. For their own daily survival, hundreds of millions continue to exert enormous pressure on exhausted lands, forests, seas, lakes, and rivers.

Asia is also home to the largest standing armies in the world, with nuclear weapons targeting rival neighbors, and intractable land and maritime border disputes, ethnic and religious tensions, and strategic rivalries.

In January 2015, as Chair of the High-Level Independent Panel on UN Peace Operations, I, with some colleagues, visited Bangladesh, India, and Pakistan, the three largest troop-contributing countries and police-contributing countries to UN peace operations.

Following fruitful discussions in Dhaka and Islamabad, my colleagues and I traveled to India. It would have been easier to fly out from Islamabad to Doha, and from there to Delhi. However, I decided to experiment [with] the most convoluted route – fly to Lahore and then drive about 40 minutes to the India-Pakistan border at Waga, where, a week earlier, extremist Taliban elements had committed an audacious attack, killing over 50 people during the daily change of guard.

There in Waga, as my panel colleagues and I, carrying our suitcases, went through the immigration controls on the Pakistan and India sides of the borders, I thought to myself this has to be the most dangerous region of the Earth.

Six decades after independence and partition, the two South Asian neighbors, both nuclear armed, are still facing off over Kashmir, host of the oldest UN mission in the world.

Moving east from South Asia, leaving behind the never-ending wars of Afghanistan and northern frontiers of Pakistan, there is another of Asia's dangerous flashpoints, the Korean peninsula, where an entrenched "hereditary communist monarchy," nuclear-armed and unpredictable, poses daily threats to its democratic and prosperous neighbor.

For the most part, Africans, Latin Americans, and Europeans have freed themselves from the Cold War legacy. Not so Asia. The communist monarchy inaugurated by Kim Il-sung has successfully resisted twentieth- and twenty-first-century transformations.

In some parts of Asia, as I have mentioned many times over, Stone Age practices remain pervasive, denying girls the right to go to school – acid is thrown on them for daring to sit in a classroom – marrying off or simply selling off girls to pay for family's debt, and in parts of Asia, sentencing women to death by stoning for alleged adultery.

Leaders of China, Japan, and Korea have not freed themselves from the legacies of colonial occupation and World War II. In part, this is because there haven't been Japanese leaders of equal stature of Germany's statesmen like Konrad Adenauer, Willy Brandt, Richard von Weizsäcker, as well as scholars and opinion makers who influenced post-war Germans to accept the collective burden of their national past.

Past Prime Ministers Tomiichi Murayama and Jumichiro Koizumi made unequivocal statements expressing "deep remorse" and "heartfelt apology" for Japan's war of aggression across Asia. However, some Diet [government] members continue to glorify the chief architects of the war with yearly visits to the Yasukuni Cemetery where a thousand war criminals are enshrined as heroes.

Another dangerous flashpoint is the South China Sea, and although a military clash may seem unlikely, the build-up by some claimant states increases the risks of escalation.

To complicate matters, in the face of a rising Asian economic and military superpower that dwarfs all others, some in the region feel the need to call on us to enhance their security protection; and whether on the South China Sea or Taiwan Strait, the world's only global power feels it is its "manifest destiny" to uphold "freedom of navigation" and "protect" its friends and allies in Asia, thus further raising the stakes.

Against the many negative facts and complex challenges cited above, there have been also impressive transformations.

In the last 30 years, millions of people have been freed from poverty in China, India, Pakistan, Bangladesh, Vietnam, Indonesia, Malaysia, Cambodia, Laos, the Philippines, Thailand; and the most developed Asian economies – the Republic of Korea, Japan, and Singapore – continue to perform very well, and excel in technology and innovation.

China, the Republic of Korea, India, and Indonesia have been growing at annual rates of between five and 10 percent for sustained long periods. The combined economies of China, Korea, Japan, and India account for over $15 trillion[60] of annual GDP.

Asia's economic powerhouses are a formidable force and stand side by side in output with the $16 trillion of combined output in EU countries and the $15 trillion US economy [IMF estimates for 2010].

Asia's rise has had profound impact on the environment and Asians should feel obligated to pull resources and lead on tackling the challenges we face in the twenty-first century, but leadership predicates the ability to build partnerships with other stakeholders, the emerging economies

---

60   Fifteen million million US dollars.

of the global South, and new partnerships, as equals, with Europe and the US.

Ladies and gentlemen, dear friends, Timor-Leste is the youngest independent country in Asia, barely 15 years since the restoration of independence in 2002. While challenges and failures are also evident, nevertheless, we have made progress that makes us reasonably content.

Our social and economic indicators speak for themselves: the UNDP Human Development Report accords Timor-Leste an HDI for 2012 that jumped to the value of 0.576, placing our country in the medium human development category; at independence, in 2002, it was 0.375.

According to the UNDP-commissioned report, East Asia and the Pacific – the region – has an average HDI value of 0.683 and registered annual HDI growth values between 2000 and 2012 of 1.31 percent, with Timor-Leste leading with 2.71 percent, followed by Myanmar at 2.23 percent.

At the time of independence in 2002, life expectancy at birth in Timor-Leste was 57 years, and now averages 67 years. In 2002, there were 19 Timorese doctors in the country. Now, we have more than a thousand medical doctors, thanks to Cuban solidarity.

Incidences of malaria and dengue and the prevalence of poverty have decreased significantly.

Infant mortality and child mortality under five, as well as post-birth mother mortality, have been halved.

With less than one case of leprosy per 10,000 people, Timor-Leste is now considered by the WHO to be free from this centuries-old disease.

School enrollment jumped from a modest 63 percent in 2006 to well over 90 percent for basic education, according to the 2010 national census.

In addition to the thousand medical doctors trained in Cuba and in Timor-Leste, hundreds of Timor-Leste youth and civil servants were sent abroad under full government scholarships for advanced diplomas, Masters, and PhD studies.

As we have some reasons to feel pleased with the achievements thus far, we are acutely aware of the daunting challenges still to overcome.

Like many countries in the early years of independence, Timor-Leste has had to confront social and political challenges. In some instances, like in the 2006 crisis, violence flared up, rolling back the gains of previous years.

It is on the civil and political rights core elements that we have made the most progress, and where we feel we have not failed to live up to the ideals of independence.

Timor-Leste has ratified every Human Rights treaty and is in compliance in all categories of Human Rights; our constitution prohibits the death penalty, and the maximum prison sentence is set at 25 years.

We have a very free media and active civil society; tensions do occur from time to time between governing leaders and the media, however, not a single media entity has been closed down or a journalist jailed in the 15 years of our independence.

While the situation of women still lags in some areas, Timor-Leste has a high representation of women in the legislative and executive branches.

The building of an independent and competent judiciary has been slow, and remains in its infancy. I have the deepest respect for our prosecutors, judges, and public defenders and lawyers, and for this very reason it is a cause for concern that in some instances the prosecution and trial of some high-profile cases reveal serious irregularities.

A judiciary whose professional competence and integrity is irreproachable is the crucial pillar of democracy and rule of law.

While political leaders must show utmost respect for the independence of the judiciary, the judiciary must earn this respect by way of its irreproachable competence and integrity as it handles alleged corruption and other cases brought before it.

Ours is an imperfect democracy with the many flaws common to democracies in Asia, Africa, Latin America, and parts of the West.

The only time when money did not play a role in our election outcome was in 2001–02. Was this because we were all honest in 2001–02, or because no one really had much money then to influence voters?

However, our innocence did not last long. We soon learned the Asian style of democracy, a money democracy very much in vogue throughout Asia, and in fact in most of the world in varying degrees. By 2007 money began to influence voters, and in the 2012 elections millions of dollars changed hands.

How did we learn all this so quickly? Did we learn it from Indonesia? The Philippines? Thailand? Brazil? The US? There's no lack of examples to emulate.

However, for all the imperfections of our developing democracy, and isolated, rare incidents of violence notwithstanding, our regular elections have been largely peaceful and passable in terms of fairness and transparency.

Timor-Leste enjoys friendly and proactive relationships with its two giant neighbors, the Republic of Indonesia and the Commonwealth of Australia, and both countries have played central roles in assisting our efforts in state building, peace building, and national development.

With Indonesia, we have almost completely resolved our common land border demarcation and are to begin maritime border negotiations.

However, our relationship with Australia is clouded by its refusal to entertain negotiations to define our joint maritime boundary.

In 1972, Australia and Indonesia agreed on their joint maritime boundary based on an antiquated "continental shelf" principle. The "median line" principle is the accepted norm.

At the time of the conclusion of the 1972 Australia-Indonesia maritime boundary, Australian and Indonesian scholars said Australia took Indonesia "to the cleaners."

Ever since our independence, Australia has tried to push down our throats the same arrangement that it unfairly managed to sell to Indonesia.

The Timor-Leste chief negotiator at that time, Mr Mari Alkatiri, resisted Australia's demand for a maritime boundary based on the antiquated "continental shelf" principle. Hence, we opted for a resource-sharing agreement and the deferment of a permanent maritime boundary to a later stage.

However, some facts have emerged that compelled our government to seek redress through reopening of negotiations on maritime boundary – Australia's unfair acts of espionage through blatant bugging of Timor-Leste government offices during the negotiations.

I hope and believe that common sense and justice will once again prevail. The Labor opposition has pledged that if elected into office in the coming federal elections, it will reopen negotiations with Timor-Leste on a permanent maritime boundary. I do hope Australian voters will do justice.

In the meantime, as the Australian government continues to refuse to negotiate a permanent maritime boundary with Timor-Leste, our government launched a request for compulsory mediation by the United Nations under the United Nations Convention on the Law of the Sea.

Other than this disagreement – which is no small matter – our two countries continue to cooperate in almost every field, with Australia being still our largest development aid partner; our bilateral defense and police cooperation has been exemplary. Hundreds of Timorese students are studying in Australian colleges and universities under full Australian government scholarships or fully sponsored by our own government.

The Australian people, as we have known for decades, are instinctively sympathetic to the underdog, and Australians of all walks of life have shown genuine solidarity towards the people of Timor-Leste; they reject the elitist conservative political leaders' hard-line approach on the maritime boundary issue.

And all this has only to do with the vast reserves of oil and gas that lie in the Timor Sea which, under a median-line maritime-boundary agreement, would be 100 percent Timor-Leste's.

Timor-Leste and ASEAN membership

From day one of independence, Timor-Leste stated its desire to join ASEAN, the sub-regional organisation of the Southeast Asian nations.

The ASEAN charter of 2008 clearly stipulates a number of fundamental requirements for membership, a *sine qua non* requirement being that the applicant country must be in Southeast Asia's footprint.

Article 6 outlines a number of other conditions, including recognition by all ASEAN states and the ability to carry out obligations, etc.

Timor-Leste is geographically on Southeast Asia's footprint and has demonstrated its ability to develop normal, proactive, and constructive relations with all ASEAN states and beyond.

Timor-Leste is an active member of the United Nations and all major multilateral bodies, including the Bretton Woods institutions.

Timorese police officers, army engineers and UN volunteers served, or are serving, in many United Nations missions, from Afghanistan to Africa and the Middle East.

In the 2014–16 biennium, Timor-Leste presides over CPLP, the Community of the Portuguese Speaking Countries, which brings together countries from four continents.

In the last 10 years Timor-Leste has contributed over US$30 million in emergency relief assistance to countries affected by major natural disasters, including Myanmar, the Philippines, Indonesia, China, Cuba, Haiti, and others.

In the eighties, ASEAN leaders did debate the pros and cons of early admission of fellow Southeast Asian countries Cambodia, Laos, Myanmar, and Vietnam; each presented a different set of challenges, ranging from outright military dictatorship to one-party communist regimes; there were, and there remain, considerable social and economic disparities among them.

But these challenges notwithstanding, the rational for early admission of the four mentioned Southeast Asian countries is entirely applicable to Timor-Leste today; regardless of the disparities among the four newcomers and other fellow ASEAN countries, the debate was welcome and gradually steered them towards full integration.

We have been respectful of those in ASEAN who were, or are still, skeptical about Timor-Leste's capacity to meet the demands of ASEAN membership; we understand that as some ASEAN member countries still face internal security and economic challenges, the addition of a potentially unstable new member may be cause for hesitation.

With all these aspects in mind, we have worked harder to convince fellow ASEAN member states that Timor-Leste will be a responsible member.

We thank all of them for their support, particularly the ASEAN Secretariat and the ASEAN-Timor-Leste Taskforce led by Singapore for their diligent advice and steady assistance.

The State of Democracy and Human Rights

Across Southeast Asia, from the vantage point of the momentous developments of the last 40 years, in reviewing the state of Democracy and Human Rights, I submit that there have been significant gains and some setbacks.

While, overall, ASEAN countries have performed well economically, with decreased poverty levels and the rise of Human Development indicators, there still are clear democracy deficits – deficits in good governance, transparency, and accountability; there still are serious challenges in the judiciary, in which some countries face overwhelming political interference.

ASEAN countries have a long way to walk in fostering genuine democracy and rule of law, and in empowering women and youth. Leaders have to address challenges of sustainable development, equitable distribution of wealth, environmental degradation, over-fishing, and destruction of corals, food security, etc.

Governments have to be more forthcoming in listening to their own people's voices, and open in accommodating critical views.

Long-lasting peace and stability in Southeast Asia requires a comprehensive, integrated strategy encompassing all of the above, as peace cannot be achieved through a security-based approach.

Member states must firmly address security threats emanating from extremist ideologies, but intelligent security approaches are the ones that encompass dialogue, accommodate critical views, and embrace ethnic and religious diversity and political plurality. Heavy-handed security approaches do not suffice to ensure stability and lasting security.

In twenty-first century politics, in the era of social media, of cyber- and instant journalism, power is more diffused and inevitably shared with the common person, the restless youth, students and intellectuals, workers and farmers.

Decision making is no longer an exclusive privilege of political dynasties or hereditary monarchies and the rich.

ASEAN policy-makers must innovate to catch up with the fast-changing dynamics in the cities, communities, and streets, and to lead rather than be dragged along by events.

City street demonstrations in countries from Brazil to Turkey, the Occupy Wall Street movement, the protests of city dwellers in the UK, France, and elsewhere alert us to the fact that there is more to individuals and societies than economic growth and glossy trade figures.

I submit that Indonesia, the Philippines, and Timor-Leste are the three Southeast Asian countries with the freest media and most political pluralism and inclusion, and there have been setbacks and dangerous trends in some other countries of our region.

There has been undeniable progress in Myanmar. As in Indonesia, in the weeks and months following the fall of the Suharto regime in 1998–99, Myanmar is beginning what promises to be a difficult transition to an open political and public space.

In 1998–99, Indonesia was jolted by widespread ethnic- and religious-based violence, as in Kalimantan, where thousands of people were killed during the Dayak–Buginese confrontations, or in Ambon, where Christian–Muslim pogroms took place. And, as we know, for decades the Indonesian-Chinese communities were subject to official policies of exclusion, discrimination, and sometimes widespread violence.

Some 15 years later, Indonesia is a very different country. It resolved two separate conflicts, in Timor-Leste and Aceh, that invited international criticism and occupied much of Indonesia's attention. And it has since recovered its status as the regional economic, security, and diplomatic powerhouse.

Myanmar is going through similar challenges. Cease-fire agreements, demobilization, disarmament, integration of ethnic fighters into meaningful civilian life, national dialogue, healing, and reconciliation, addressing the sensitive issues of the Rohingya communities, and the relationship with the Muslim minority require strong leadership, courage, and serenity by all involved.

Harsh judgments of Daw Aung San Suu Kyi over her apparent evasiveness in addressing these challenges are premature and unfair. As any wise leader would, Aung San Suu Kyi is exercising maximum prudence by managing sensibly the conflicting interests and forces in the country, carefully weighing every step in the long and arduous journey towards a truly free, democratic, and inclusive multi-ethnic Myanmar.

We must give her and her colleagues in the new government time and space to manage a very new situation as they begin transitioning from a past of violent conflict, sectarianism, and exclusion, absence of freedom and of the rule of law, and a weak existing judiciary into a functioning democracy.

We know from experience how hard is the building of a modern, functioning state. We, too – Timorese leaders – were criticized, and rightly so, by some in our own country and abroad, for refusing to support the creation of a special international tribunal to judge past crimes in Timor-Leste.

Then and now, we believe that the cause of Justice, Human Rights, and Democracy in Timor-Leste and Indonesia, and in fact anywhere in the world with similar challenges, are best served through a process of Truth and Reconciliation, recognition and respect of victims, establishing an institute of memory so that future generations will not forget past injustices and crimes as well the sacrifices and bravery of many.

Remembering and learning from the past, the bad and the good, must be an exercise to honor our martyrs and heroes, and as a pedagogy on nonviolence, forgiveness, and reconciliation.

It would be a tragedy if the process of remembering the past provoked anger and hatred instead of healing the soul and being an education on nonviolence and forgiveness.

I congratulate the University of Oxford and the Southeast Asia Project for bringing about this series of Southeast Asian symposia.

A region with nearly 700 million people spread over an area of 4.5 million square kilometers[61] with a combined GDP of almost US$2 trillion[62] cannot be a footnote of studies in European universities.

The twenty-first century will be Asia's century, Asia's Age of Enlightenment – if a new Mahatma Gandhi emerges, who inspires and leads all, the four billion[63] people of this vast region that extends from the doors of Constantinople to Díli, a region of great civilizations, religions, and cultures and of great challenges and greater possibilities. We do need a new Mahatma Gandhi to inspire and unite all peoples.

---

61 1. 7 million square miles.

62 Two million million US dollars.

63 Four thousand million.

On Freedom and Peace

Jakarta, 5 May 2016

Peace and freedom coexist, evolve, mature, and consolidate together. Conflicts arise and peace is broken when freedom is denied to people, whether to a nation as a whole or a particular ethnic or religious group.

Thank you – *terima kasih* – for inviting me to come here. I thank the organizers of the ASEAN Literary Festival for inviting me to this conversation on freedom and peace.

The world has changed forever, mostly for good, and Indonesia has also changed, hopefully forever, and for the better.

The main architects of Indonesia's 1975 Timor policy have passed away – in God's judgment – but too many Indonesians are uninformed or misinformed, or are in denial about the tragic chapter of their history of connection with Timor-Leste. Everywhere, anywhere, societies should always learn about the past with courage to face the honest, unfiltered, unadulterated truth, even when the truth is too painful.

Seventy years ago, Europe was engulfed in the most devastating war that the world had ever witnessed. And that war, their war – and I underline "their war" – was brought to the shores of far-flung countries, causing destruction and death. After the war, great statesmen, accepting the heavy burden of their collective responsibility, led Germany to confront their history with courage.

Their nation atoned for the crimes committed by the Third Reich, and from the ashes of the war, Europe emerged more united and stronger.

Peace and freedom coexist, evolve, mature, and consolidate together. Conflicts arise and peace is broken when freedom is denied to people, whether to a nation as a whole, or a particular ethnic or religious group.

And what is freedom?

- Freedom of belief, and of practicing one's beliefs.
- Freedom of thought, and of public expression of our thoughts.
- Academic and intellectual freedom to explore and question policies and laws; to criticize and challenge beliefs, whether these beliefs are religious or secular, old or modern.

Indonesia and people in Asia who were once colonized do understand what freedom and peace mean. Much of Asia was once conquered and colonized. They fought and prevailed from South Asia to Southeast Asia – freed themselves from European colonial domination, and later, in the twentieth century, Asians fought and died for freedom from Japanese aggression. Asians fought and died in the so-called French Indo-China; and soon after they died in the American war in Vietnam, Cambodia, Laos.

But not long after the colonial era, new forms of tyranny were imposed on Asians through either communist totalitarian regimes or through right-wing military regimes, both suppressing freedom and inviting reaction and war.

Timor-Leste is the youngest independent country in Asia – only 15 years old since the restoration of independence. Challenges and failures are evident, but we have made progress that make us reasonably content.

At independence, at 2002, life expectancy at birth in Timor-Leste was 57 years, and now it is 67.

In 2002, there were 19 Timorese doctors; now we have more than one thousand medical doctors – and this with thanks to the exceptional generosity of and cooperation with the Cuban government. We sent 700 students to Cuba, and they all returned; and 400 [more] are studying in Timor-Leste in a new medical school set up by the Cubans.

Incidents of malaria and dengue and the prevalence of poverty have decreased significantly, and by 2020, malaria will be eliminated.

Infant mortality, and child mortality under five, as well as post-birth mother mortality, has been reduced by half.

With less than one case of leprosy per 10,000 people, WHO declared Timor-Leste now free this centuries-old disease.

School enrollment jumped from a modest 60–63 percent in 2006, to well over 90 percent now.

In addition to the thousand medical doctors trained in Cuba, and in Timor-Leste, hundreds of Timor-Leste youth and civil servants were sent abroad, under full government scholarship, for advanced diplomas, Masters, and PhDs, in regional universities like the Philippines, Indonesia, Thailand, Australia, and as far away as Brazil and Portugal.

We are pleased with achievements, but we are conscious of the challenges still to overcome; and we admit that we could have done much more to improve the lives of the urban and rural poor.

However, it is on civil and political rights where we have made more progress, for elements of civil and politic rights, economic-social rights, is where we have excelled. We have not failed to live up to the ideal of independence.

We have ratified every Human Rights Treaty, and we are in compliance in all categories of Human Rights.

Our Constitution prohibits the death penalty. And the maximum sentence is 25 years. We do not have life in prison. Death penalty is a notion that shocked our collective mind and belief. For us, it is unthinkable that Timor-Leste would join the rest of Asia in instating the death penalty. We advocate a worldwide moratorium on the death penalty and its abolition, but we do not feel we are in a position to lecture those in favor of it.

While the situation of women still lags in many areas, Timor-Leste has a high percentage of women in the legislative and executive branches.

The building of an independent and competent judiciary has been slow, and it remains in its infancy.

Ours is an imperfect democracy with many flaws common to democracies in Asia, Africa, Latin America, and parts of the West.

We enjoy friendly relations – friendly and proactive relations with our two giant neighbors, the Republic of Indonesia and Australia. Both countries have played, and continue to play, an important role in assisting us in the long and difficult process of statebuilding, peacebuilding, and national development.

We have developed excellent relationship with our Southeast Asian neighbors, establishing embassies in all 10 ASEAN capitals.

Malaysia, Singapore, Thailand, and Philippines have provided substantial assistance to Timor-Leste, particularly in the field of Human Resources development and capacity building.

Hundreds of Timorese have graduated, or are in the process of graduating, from universities and technical institutions in several ASEAN countries. In Indonesia alone the reported figure is four thousand students enrolled, and some say even more than four thousand.

Overall, ASEAN countries have performed well economically with poverty level decreased and human development indicators up – but there is a democracy deficit, a deficit in good governors, transparency, and accountability.

There are serious challenges in the judiciary, in which some countries face overwhelming political interference. Long-lasting peace and stability in Southeast Asia requires comprehensive, integrated strategy encompassing all of the above – strengthening of judiciary, the rule of law, and empowering women and youth.

Peace cannot be achieved through an all-out security-based approach.

And high-digit growth does not always translate into sustainable and equitable distribution of wealth, benefiting all proportionally.

And we know from our own experience in Timor-Leste, we have had double-digit growth for several years – now, less – but this impressive double-digit growth is natural in a country starting from zero, and with strong capital investment from the government. However, it does not necessarily translate into significant improvement in the lives of the people in the rural areas.

It is always a challenge for leaders and policymakers to adopt and implement policies that accommodate every segment in a multi-ethnic, multi-cultural, multi-religious society. In too many such countries, myopic sectarian leaders from a particular ethnic and/or religious belief, rather than pursue inclusive policies, seeking to include and embrace all, tend to favor the people belonging to their particular religious belief. Hence, they sow the seeds of discontent, and as discontent increases, they use increasing force to suppress, and this in turn provokes further anger, and sometimes insurgency. This is what we witness around the world.

If each of us look at the root causes of conflicts around the world, including in the Middle East, we will find some commonalities on how conflict started.

It is to be expected that the State firmly address security threats emanating from extremist ideologies, but the use of measured and proportional force might, at times, be required – at *times* it might be required – but a wiser and more effective strategy is one that encompasses dialogue, accommodates critical view, embraces ethnic and religious diversity and political plurality. A heavy-handed security approach alone will never suffice to ensure permanent security. It produces the opposite effect.

In twenty-first-century politics, in the era of social media, or cyber- and instant journalism, power is more diffused, and inevitably is shared with the common person – the restless youth, students, and intellectuals, workers and farmers. Decision making is no longer an exclusive privilege of political dynasties or hereditary monarchies and the rich.

We can see from the street demonstrations from cities in Brazil, Turkey, the Occupy Wall Street movement, protests in the past in cities in the UK and France – these alert us to the fact [that] there are more to individuals and society than economic growth and trade figures.

Will the ASEAN community be a community of actual communities, with shared values and a people for people's solidarity, or it will be a copy of the overly bureaucratized and overpaid European Union, Brussels-based bureaucrats disconnected from the real people of Europe?

Ambassador, I am sorry for criticizing the European Union, but I gave a speech once in Brussels, at the European Parliament – I was there on a State Visit as President – and the part where I got the biggest applause from all the Parliamentarians was when I referred to EU bureaucracy. So, it seemed like I was not alone in criticizing the European bureaucracy.

One way to bring the 700 million people on the ASEAN region closer to each other is through literature, art, and music.

Maybe there should be more effort in having the great works of Southeast Asian, Indonesian writers translated into the many languages of the region, and made available by way of subsidized prizes.

If the economies of ASEAN, the government leaders of ASEAN, really want to connect the people, one way is to subsidize literature – to subsidize arts, in different languages of the ASEAN region, to bring people really close together.

It is one way. I am not saying it is *the* way.

I submit that Indonesia, the Philippines, and Timor-Leste are the three Southeast Asian countries with the freest media and the greatest political plurality and inclusion.

And there have been setbacks and dangerous trends in some other countries in our region – as [happened] in Indonesia, in the weeks and months following the fall of the Suharto regime in '98/'99, Myanmar is beginning what promises to be a difficult transition to an open political space.

In '98/'99, Indonesia was torn by widespread ethnic and religious-based violence, namely in Kalimantan where thousands of people were killed during the Dayak-Buginese confrontations; or in Ambon, where Christian-Muslim violence took place.

Myanmar is going through similar challenges, and it might wish to learn from Indonesia how to manage the complex process of transition from an authoritarian regime to a full-fledged, dynamic, multi-party democracy, with all its imperfections.

Indonesia remains very much an inclusive and tolerant society where many ethnic and religious groups live side by side. Intermittent or frequent anti-Christian violence does not obscure this factor. With the largest Muslim majority in the world, and hundreds of ethnic minorities in a multitude of faiths, Indonesia continues to stand out, most particularly when compared with other states around the world.

The new Myanmar leaders, led by Aung Suu Kyi, must address the sensitive issue of the Rohingya communities and their relationship with that Muslim minority. It requires strong leadership, courage, and serenity.

Suu Kyi is attempting to do what wise leaders do, and that is to exercise maximum prudence, to manage sensibly the conflicting interests and forces in the country, to carefully weigh every step in the long and arduous journey towards a truly free, democratic, and inclusive multi-ethnic Myanmar.

We, too – Timor leaders – were criticized, and rightly so, by some in our own country and abroad for refusing to support the creation of a special International Tribunal to judge past crimes in Timor-Leste.

I was often criticized by our NGOs, by Amnesty International, for actively opposing the setting up of an International Tribunal for the violence of 1999. Our critics are entitled to criticize us, and they stand on high moral ground when they do so. There is no question about that. Their position of criticizing us is irreproachable from an intellectual, moral point of view.

However, then and now, we believe that the cause of justice, human rights, and democracy in Timor-Leste, and in Indonesia, and in fact anywhere in the world with similar challenges, is best served through a process of truth and conciliation, recognition and respect of victims, establishing, in our case, an Institute of Memory so that future generations will not forget past injustices and crimes as well as the sacrifice and bravery of many.

However, remembering and learning from the past, the bad and the good, must be an exercise to honor our martyrs and heroes, but, as well, a pedagogy on non-violence, forgiveness, and reconciliation.

It would be tragedy if the process of remembering the past, instead of healing the soul and being a pedagogy on non-violence and forgiveness, provoked anger and hatred.

A true, honest, meaningful process of truth and reconciliation is one that is, or should be, accepted by the victims, and enables them, in their hearts and minds to feel that they finally have closure. Finally, they can turn the page of the past and live in peace and freedom the rest of their lives. And [that] their children and their grandchildren, stigmatized since childhood, also feel liberated and able to enjoy a new life, a better one than their parents and grandparents had.

Indonesia can inspire and lead by example – the example of wisdom and compassion – by the way leaders and policymakers promote policies of inclusion and national cohesion, where all are treated equally, where the most neglected and abused feel their dignity restored.

Peace and freedom are attainable within the same multi-ethnic, diverse nation state. So, you make humane, compassionate, inclusive policies that respect the unique culture and belief of each community that make up a rich, diverse country. If all are equal in the eyes of God, and in the provision of the Constitution, then all must be treated with equal respect for their identity, culture, beliefs, and in proportion to their specific needs.

And last, but not least, I hope that the organizer of the ASEAN Literary Festival considers holding the next festival in Timor-Leste. I am sure our national institutions, public and private, would wholeheartedly welcome and support you. If I'm President again, and if you don't criticize me (just joking...), I will support the organization of such an initiative.

Uniting our Strengths for Peace: Politics, Partnerships and People

New York, United Nations Headquarters, 10 May 2016[64]

The UN may be a convenient scapegoat for many conflicts that resulted from the utter failure of national leaders, but let's be frank: the UN is not responsible for the outbreak of wars and their ensuing ramifications.

My esteemed colleagues and I of the High-Level Independent Panel on UN Peace Operations – I recognize in the room Ian Martin, Alexander Illitchev, Youssef Mahmoud, Rima Salah – worked closely with member states, the SRSGs,[65] force commanders, troop-contributing countries and police-contributing countries, regional and sub-regional organizations, think tanks, and civil society from all regions of the world over several months. In addition, we received and digested 80 comprehensive submissions. The report, *Uniting Our Strengths for Peace: Politics, Partnerships and People*, is our collective work, yours and ours, all of us who are deeply committed to a world free of the scourges of wars, of violence against women and children, a world free of extreme poverty, a world at peace.

As you might all recall, I dedicated our report to a little heroine in South Sudan, the brave three-year-old Nyakhat. The real-life story of little Nyakhat is in fact an indictment of the leaders of South Sudan and of all

---

64 High-Level Thematic Debate: A World at Risk - Peace, Security and the United Nations, on the implementation of the Report of the High Level Independent Panel on UN Peace Operations.
65 Special Representatives of the UN Secretary-General.

of us, policymakers, diplomats, envoys – an indictment of the whole UN – for our utter failure in preventing the implosion of South Sudan. But this is also a story of the indispensability of the United Nations insofar as its presence on the ground has saved many thousands of lives, providing safe haven, shelter, food, and water to hundreds of thousands who otherwise would have perished and joined the unfortunate hundreds of thousands who died. Since we handed over the report to our esteemed Secretary-General in June 2015, my colleagues and I have remained actively engaged in numerous in-depth conversations in New York and across the world on the more than 100 recommendations contained in it. As you know, we made detailed, substantive, bold, and creative recommendations which, if implemented, would go a long way in helping the United Nations measure up to the changing global security threats of our time and help meet the expectations of the people it is called to serve. In view of the constraints of time and in respect to other speakers, I shall recall some salient elements, just three:

- Any UN peace operation must be grounded on a political strategy. This means that beyond operational security and stabilization activities, sustaining peace should be the single most important goal to which all mission efforts should be dedicated. Panel members noted, and were concerned, that in responding to crises, the UN was deploying peacekeeping operations to conflict zones where there was no peace to keep and where the emphasis on securitized responses in the face of asymmetric threats may not serve the cause of peace and may not make the peacekeepers safer. Mali is a case in point. In this regard, we made it very clear that peacekeeping, as currently configured, should not be involved in counterterrorism activities.

- The second set of recommendations aim to make the UN Secretariat more field-oriented rather than making the field comply with headquarters-centered administrative and budgetary processes and guidelines that treat peace operations as exceptions to the rule. Member states need to take the lead to overhaul this antiquated system and stop investing in procedures that tend to control rather than empower the field. We made suggestions on how this can be done, including the establishment of mechanisms for greater accountability by managers. As things stand now, it is regrettable that these suggestions did not receive the attention they deserve.

- Last, but not least, we have made a case for restructuring the compartmentalized Secretariat entities entrusted with implementing the peace and security agenda of the organization. The sharp distinctions between peacekeeping operations and special political missions should give way to a continuum of responses and smoother transitions between different phases of missions. Hence, we have called for the United Nations to embrace the term "peace operations" to denote the full spectrum of responses required on the ground on the basis of sound strategic analysis and planning.

Sequenced and prioritized mandates will allow missions to develop over time rather than trying to do everything at once and not succeeding. I am gratified to hear that sequencing and prioritizing is being considered for Mali ahead of its forthcoming mandate renewal. It is hoped that the new Secretary-General will take the lead, in inclusive partnership with member states, in taking these recommendations forward, building on synergies between our report and the other two seminal reports that examined other pillars of the UN peace and security architecture.

With more than 100,000 armed blue helmets deployed in 16 theatres of conflict in a vast area of the globe, the UN is like an overstretched empire, the Secretary-General an emperor without clothes, hopelessly presiding over a vast domain without adequate financial resources, men and women in uniform sent into battle without adequate modern hardware and software.

The UN may be a convenient scapegoat for many conflicts that resulted from the utter failure of national leaders, but let's be frank: the UN is not responsible for the outbreak of wars and their ensuing ramifications. It might be responsible for the deterioration of the conflicts because of inaction, but blame should be apportioned closer to home. These manmade catastrophes are caused primarily by national leaders of all sides in a given situation, because of their lack of wisdom, courage, and humility, and because of inflated ambitions and egos that dominate their thoughts and actions; and, hence, they are not able to engage each other in constructive dialogue and forge a national pact beneficial to all. It has been shown from the wars in the Congo in the early 1960s to today's wars in South Sudan, Somalia, Syria, Afghanistan, and Palestine that there are limits to what the international community anchored on the UN can do; there are limits to what even a well-intentioned mighty global power can do. If force alone could prevent or resolve the outcome of social-, religious-, and ethnic-based wars, then the mere appearance on the horizon of an awesome fleet and the intimidating display of fighter formations in the skies would suffice to freeze, in fear, all warring factions.

More often than not, the end to wars and durable peace comes about through patient dialogue where all concede some. With humility, we believe that if our recommendations are implemented, we, as the UN, may better prevent the outbreak of wars; we may more timely deploy credible means to prevent the deaths of innocent civilians, usually the first casualties in a conflict; we may better mediate the end of wars and help build lasting peace and reconciliation.

You all are in my daily prayers.

No Fortress Europe can Stem its Demographic Transformation

Vienna, Austria, 28 June 2016

The demographic transformation from a predominately aging Judeo-Christian continent to a vibrant, younger, multi-ethnic, multi-religious, and multi-cultural Europe is unstoppable. Let's make this a windfall of opportunities for its peoples.

You are convening here at a time when Europe and much of the world are confronted with a multitude of ever more complex and interconnected social, political, economic, and security challenges that threaten to unravel even a multinational institution as solid as the European Union and some of its constituting States.

Many are still trying to make sense of the result of the UK referendum on EU membership. Rather than uniting and strengthening European unity and cooperation in the face of the ever more complex challenges faced by all, there are centrifugal forces tearing Europe apart. Those in England, the so-called Eurosceptics who sowed the seeds of British exit from the EU, have paved the way for a much-diminished UK in size and influence in Europe and the world.

Will the Queen be able to prevent the splintering of the Kingdom? It seems inevitable that Scotland will now go its own way and Northern Ireland will reunite with the Republic.

The cauldron of the Middle East wars and the endemic poverty plaguing much of the African Continent have uprooted more than 60 million people, and of these, many have sought, and are seeking, shelter and a new life in the old [European] Continent.

Some European leaders and people have shown great heart in welcoming their fellow human beings fleeing wars and deprivation, but, understandably, other European leaders and communities have been less generous, reacting often out of ignorance and fear. And let me clarify that when I use the word "understandably", I am not condoning the xenophobic mindset of many in Europe; I am simply saying that in any given society different people act or react differently in similar circumstances.

The US, Canada, the Latin American States, Australia, and New Zealand are very much a product of the religious wars and extreme poverty in Europe that prompted the greatest movement of people ever in previous centuries. We are living witnesses to an ongoing and irreversible demographic transformation of Europe, a continuation or repetition of the massive movement of people in previous centuries caused by wars and poverty in Europe, prompting millions of Europeans to flee to the Americas.

No matter how high and thick your walls are, there will be no Fortress Europe that can stem the tide of people fleeing wars and poverty. The demographic transformation of Europe from a predominately aging Judeo-Christian continent to a vibrant and younger, multi-ethnic, multi-religious, and multicultural Europe is unstoppable. These phenomena are not always entirely peaceful, and, sadly, many will suffer immensely, but with wisdom, determination, and compassion, Europe would emerge rejuvenated and stronger in the long run.

Some decades ago the principle of inviolability of colonial boundaries inherited by the newly independent African States, carved out by nineteenth-century European powers, was strictly upheld by all.

The first to challenge this taboo was the Eritrean People's Liberation Front, waging a successful protracted war, resulting in the secession of Eritrea from Ethiopia. The second successful secession case was when Christian South Sudan seceded from the Northern Arab majority of Sudan. In both cases, secession didn't result in peace, greater freedom, and prosperity. The euphoria didn't last long as the newly independent South Sudan imploded with extraordinary ferocity and untold destruction. Eritrea is a tragic story of a dream turned nightmare.

These phenomena that were thought of as a malaise of the developing world seem to have contaminated the well-established European Nation-States.

But, in reality, the fragmentation of twentieth-century European Nation-States was unleashed more than 20 years ago when the shaky ground upon which the mighty Soviet Union was erected collapsed. Americans and Western Europeans celebrated the dismantling of the Berlin Wall, the demise of the USSR, the end of post-World War II Yugoslavia, and did not think twice in moving EU and NATO boundaries eastward, ever closer to the gates of the weakened and hungry Russian bear. But, again, the euphoria lasted only as long as it lasted.

The above snippets of past, recent, and ongoing phenomena should help us reach some conclusions. Empires, regimes, governments, elected, and non-elected come and go. From the glittering Roman Empire to the rise and fall of the Third Reich, the rise and fall of the Soviet Union, American triumphalism, and the rise of China and India, all are passing phenomena and only the people are a permanent feature – born and surviving in the midst of wars, starving and dying of poverty in the midst of the opulence of some. The people will always be there.

The lesson is that whenever we think of and design institutions and projects, we must always endeavor to serve the people. The institutions and projects must be peoples-based, connected with the people; and the institutions may adapt as peoples' needs, desires and priorities evolve, change.

The other lesson is that no power is eternal. Empires and emperors come and go, the strong and the rulers of today may be the weak and servants of tomorrow. So, we must always embrace the virtue of humility and compassion, sources of greater and longer-lasting power.

When we are at the peak of power and privileges, our power is enhanced when we embrace the virtues of humility and compassion, embracing those on the fringes of power and opportunities. If you have triumphed in battle, do not seek to humiliate the vanquished ones. Walk towards them, your sword pointing down. Invite them to rise up. Embrace and invite them to join in celebrating peace and freedom for all.

Timor-Leste is a country of only a little more than one million. We survived and prevailed through centuries of colonial rule, occupation by the Japanese Imperial Army, recolonization by Portugal, and occupation by Indonesia.

In victory, in 2002, we celebrated our freedom and honored our former adversaries; we forgave our captors and tormentors without demanding or waiting for an apology; we rejected an international tribunal to try those who committed war crimes and crimes against humanity.

Those who tortured and killed did not apologize for their crimes, and they continue in denial, unable to summon enough courage to accept their part of guilt.

But this is their problem. They live with their crimes on their conscience, the screams and faces of their victims still haunting them, every day, every night. We are now free and refuse to be hostage to anger and hatred.

Ladies and gentlemen, my European brothers and sisters: look eastward and seek to engage Russia. Instead of moving planes, tanks, and troops closer to the Russian border, you might seek to understand the reasons of Russian pride, fears, and actions. Sound bites about Putin being the new Russian Tsar, and Russian expansionism, are not going to help bring back Europe and Russia to normal levels of cooperation and the recovery of Crimea.

This now-impoverished region of the world – I mean Europe – of great nations that did great things for humanity, but also invented the Inquisition, colonialism, two World Wars and reinvented slavery, must reinvent itself now as a region of solidarity and compassion, to reconnect with its peoples and reach out to the great Russia.

I am not a romantic pacifist who believes that force must never be used. Sometimes, the use of force is necessary, when it is the only option available to prevent genocide. Bosnia, Rwanda, the Killing Fields of Cambodia are just some reminders that non-use of force to prevent genocide and mass atrocities is equivalent to surrender of our morality, a betrayal of the victims.

However, the preferred option should always be prevention of conflicts, dialogue and mediation to settle disputes, and when these are actively, creatively, and patiently exercised in a timely fashion, more often than not they produce better results.

National actors, rather than external, are best placed to engage in conflict prevention processes at every level, from community to national level. External actors are not the best substitute and should not be the first responders; however, in some situations, credible threat of sanctions, including use of force, may help domestic actors leading prevention and mediation actions in their efforts to prevent conflicts from erupting.

I had the unique privilege of chairing the High-Level Independent Panel on UN Peace Operations appointed by the Secretary-General Ban Ki-moon (2014–15) and I am Co-Chair of the Independent Commission on Multilateralism, a project of the International Peace Institute, both endeavoring to deliver a better, more effective, and credible multilateral system anchored on the UN.

My colleagues and I, a 16-panel membership, produced a comprehensive report with more than 100 recommendations on how to improve overall the UN's role in conflict prevention and mediation, on more agile and effective deployment of peace-enforcers, and on sustaining peace. We also made far-reaching recommendations on improving leadership and coordination at the UN Secretariat.

We expect that the next UN Secretary-General, to be elected this fall, will make it an absolute priority the full implementation of the High-Level Panel's Report and of the two other complementary reports, namely on Peace Building Architecture and on Women, Peace and Security. Procrastination and failure in undertaking speedy and full implementation of the three seminal and complementary reports and recommendations will inevitably result in the UN sliding further into irrelevance.

There is universal agreement that prevention should have primacy over intervention. However, while prevention might appear simple, nothing is ever simple when we are confronted with human frailties like the inflated ego of leaders, ignorance, prejudices, and fear.

Take the tragic example of Syria. I sum up in few words three main obstacles: overestimating one's own power; underestimating the adversary's; miscalculating.

In my view, all have erred. The Assad regime erred for not making real efforts in reaching out to those wanting more freedom. The opposition erred in overestimating their own power, refusing to negotiate with the regime, demanding instead its resignation, and underestimating the staying power of the Assad regime, and failing to understand the fears of the Alawite minority in power that inspired its actions. Europeans and Americans who underestimated the Assad regime misread the complexities of the so-called "Arab Spring" and, euphoric with their

Pyrrhic air campaign against Muammar Gaddafi, of Libya, believed they could arrange another regime change. All miscalculated, and we all know the consequences of this miscalculation. The consequences of this is what you see, right in your midst, in Europe: the hundreds of thousands of Syrians pleading with you to shelter them.

Europe and Russia cannot continue to drift apart. This vast region with endless resources and highly motivated and educated people working in honest and innovative partnership for peace and progress can transform the world; there is more in common between Europe and Russia than what divides you.

The US should also rethink its relationship with Russia and China, treating them as equals and not as second-class powers. Whether the US likes it or not, China is inexorably emerging as a modern twenty-first-century Asian power. This inevitably leads to fear among China's neighbors and this being the case, it is China, an aspiring world power, that must behave as a responsible and benevolent power and reassure its neighbors.

For many in China and Russia, and indeed in many other countries, US policies are always inspired by its strategic hegemonic goals and selfish economic interests. This is an exaggeration, although it is understandable, as they view the US through the prism of many past US policies.

I have a more innocent and benevolent view of the US. I am a great fan of the Kennedys, of the immense good they did in their time. Their legacy has lasted for generations, long after they have gone. American society has produced thousands of great achievers, scientists and millionaires whose roots can be traced back to impoverished towns, ghettos, and villages around the world. Another great American president[66] will soon leave active office.

In regards the above, it is easier said than done. How can Europe or the US normalize relations with Russia in the face of the annexation of Crimea?

My best advice is: set aside what are, for the time being, irreconcilable differences, re-engage each other, explore areas and ideas of common interest, namely on how best to address the global economic and financial crisis, bring an end to the Syria conflict, address the refugee crisis in a

---

66 President Barack Obama, whose term would end close to seven months later.

holistic manner, both in its humanitarian dimension and political and economic dimensions, address extremism and terrorism in a holistic manner, both through sharp intelligence and prudent action, and through understanding and action on the root causes.

Wars are not inevitable, and every war brings immense destruction and suffering, exacerbating tensions, rivalries, and generating more enemies. Almost every military victory is a Pyrrhic victory.

So, we must do more to enhance – multiply – preventive diplomacy mechanisms and initiatives, undertake research on innovative prevention processes and mediation. There are no shortcuts to peace; we build peace in our homes, families, villages, towns, block by block. Peace is the work of patient and dedicated people with missionary zeal, people who have empathy for those who suffer the most – women, children, the elderly. Peacemakers must have a heart and compassion.

Europe is at a crossroads. The challenges are daunting. But Europeans faced greater challenges in the past. You regrouped, reconciled, and rebuilt a greater Europe after World War II. You can do it again, and do better still.

The Missing Priority: Child Safety and Development

Huffington Post, 14 March 2017

We all have the moral responsibility to raise our voices against the exploitation of children, support efforts, and initiate more concrete robust measures to safeguard children.

There is a common misperception that we live in a civilized world. At the core of our community are the values of progress and peace. It is, therefore, unfortunate that even though we have transcended galactic boundaries, we have failed to universally uphold these values.

Today, one of the largest and most shameful crises faced by humanity is the issue of children's safety and development. Children in crisis are refused asylum. They are used to propagate violence. Around the world children are sold as inanimate objects for physical and sexual exploitation. And it is the children who suffer the worst outcomes of war.

All children deserve a life free of violence and fear, a life of hope and dreams. However, the previous century's hasty development agenda has neglected their needs. Today, we stand again on the brink of leaving behind an entire generation. To alter the circumstances, we need to build a strong foundation which prioritizes children and their protection.

For this reason, fellow Nobel Peace laureates and world leaders gathered in a Children Summit in New Delhi, in early December last year, hosted by Kailash Satyarthi, the 2014 Nobel Peace laureate, and the President of India to strategize towards the goal of ensuring that no child is left behind in our policies, programs and promises.

Satyarthi, his wife, daughter, son, and in-laws, and the rest of their extended family are all deeply involved in the noble pursuit of freeing children from slavery held by powerful economic groups. Braving threats and physical violence and over several decades they have saved over

100,000 children from slavery, sheltered, educated, and prepared them for a life in freedom and dignity.

The New Delhi outcome document called the *A Will for Children* underlined the moral responsibility of the laureates and leaders to raise their voices against the exploitation of children, support efforts, and initiate more concrete and robust measures to safeguard children across the world.

Some Nobel laureates who attended the summit in New Delhi were also present at the 16th World Summit of Nobel Peace laureates in Bogotá, Colombia, earlier this month, as was I.

The direct outcome of our discussions and collective will, as reflected in the final declaration, was the recognition of children's issues as the key to building pathways to a lasting and sustainable peace. The Nobel laureates emphasized inclusion and financial prioritization of children's issues, and the need for adequate laws and their effective implementation.

They reaffirmed the importance of youth voices in creating policies. In the post-World-War era, the impetus has been on international coalitions and technological investments for a resilient and more peaceful world. But the gaps in our economic policies have proliferated child marriage, the number of children out of school, children in exploitative sexual and labor conditions, and, most of all, the disparity of opportunities between children of different ethnicities, regions, and backgrounds.

Besides being an acute moral dilemma, protection of children's rights is an urgent economic and development priority. International and regional governing bodies must ensure that the mistakes of the past are not repeated.

Albeit a little late, the protection of the totality of children's rights is finally gaining momentum on the world stage. And, even more promising is the fact that it is slowly uniting the world.

Ending Myanmar's Blame Game

José Ramos-Horta with Janelle Saffin[67]

13 April 2017

There is an urgent need for stronger commitments to help provide services, defend the rule of law – in Rakhine and in Myanmar generally – and search for lasting solutions to the current crisis.

YANGON – Human-rights abuses in Myanmar's Rakhine State have led to mounting international condemnation and calls for a United Nations Commission of Inquiry. The atrocities there must be investigated and their perpetrators held to account. But the situation in Rakhine is now fueling criticism of Myanmar's de facto head of government, State Counsellor Aung San Suu Kyi, in a way that is obscuring the military's responsibility in the crisis.

Condemning Suu Kyi, a former dissident and Nobel Peace Prize winner, for not using her position as a megaphone to address the problem may be emotionally satisfying, but it does not help those most in need. It is simply wrong to say that Suu Kyi has done nothing in the face of the horrors being perpetrated in Rakhine. One must remember that Myanmar is undergoing a fragile political transition, under a constitution that gives the military a leading role in national politics while constraining Suu Kyi.

Given that atrocities are still being committed, it would be premature to excuse or defend any of Myanmar's leaders. But we should identify the right targets for criticism. Suu Kyi has been hung out to dry while

---

67 Chair of the Australian Labor Party's International Party Development Committee and former chair of the Australia-Myanmar Parliamentary Group. This op-ed was first published by project-syndicate.org.

Myanmar's generals – who misruled the country for decades – have been allowed to step back as the conflict escalates.

And Suu Kyi's critics should recognize that the generals have reserved the capacity to step back in, should she suffer too much political damage. Myanmar's 2008 military-decreed constitution allows them to stage a coup d'état whenever they deem it necessary to restore order. The international community should not let itself be held hostage by this possibility; but it must be borne in mind.

Although Suu Kyi led the National League for Democracy to an overwhelming victory in the 2015 parliamentary election, she does not have complete authority over the government or the state. The fact that she was barred from occupying the presidency, and forced to accept the title of "State Counsellor," speaks to the inadequacies of Myanmar's constitution. The generals never intended to let a civilian government hold them to account.

As State Counsellor, Suu Kyi has the same responsibilities as other heads of state, but not nearly as much power. The military's commander-in-chief, General Min Aung Hlaing, meanwhile, has little responsibility, but far more power than Suu Kyi.

So, rather than focusing solely on Suu Kyi, the international community should be pressing the military and the Rakhine State parliament to work alongside the government and other parties toward peace. They can start by helping to implement the recommendations of the Advisory Commission on Rakhine State, led by former UN Secretary-General Kofi Annan. Suu Kyi has already committed her government to enacting the commission's recommendations, and it is now time for the military and Rakhine officials to do the same.

There is also an urgent need for stronger commitments at the international level: to help provide services, defend the rule of law – in Rakhine and in Myanmar generally – and search for lasting solutions to the crisis. Curtailing development aid, as some of Suu Kyi's critics have proposed, would only serve the military's interests. Simply put, creating a culture that respects human rights and the rule of law – long ignored and violated in Myanmar – won't happen overnight.

That is why the international community should back a long-term strategy of support for Myanmar, while condemning abuses when they occur. International inquiries and fact-finding missions will not put an end to the violence, and could even inflame an already volatile situation. According to the International Crisis Group, developments in Rakhine took a "dangerous turn" in October 2016, when Rohingya Muslim militants – who have been radicalized, armed, and funded from abroad – launched a series of attacks against border-guard outposts.

Among all of the stakeholders, Myanmar's military has the most power to end the conflict. An armed insurgency was allowed to radicalize and foment strife and division in Rakhine on the generals' watch. If the generals cannot move beyond their traditional *modus operandi* of command, control and, in this case, containment, they should bear the blame for the crisis.

Myanmar's government, despite having far less power than the military, has taken action to find long-term solutions that will secure a lasting peace. But achieving peace will be a long, painful process. Rakhine State has not experienced peace or prosperity for more than half a century. After decades of colonization, military rule, ethnic and religious conflict, and civil wars, Rakhine has been left in a state of abject poverty and division.

This grim history includes the Japanese occupation during World War II, which precipitated the 1942 Arakan massacres – a period of communal violence between British V-Force-armed Kamam Muslims (today's Rohingya) and Buddhist Rakhine villagers. Today, against the backdrop of the North Arakan Muslim League's demand for annexation to Pakistan and the Mujahid Party's effort to secure an autonomous state within Rakhine, a separatist Arakanese Independence Movement has been actively, and often violently, pursuing independence.

No UN Commission of Inquiry can unpack this history. Creating a peaceful, prosperous state and society in Rakhine will take slow, deliberate actions that are aimed specifically at building trust and a culture of respect for human rights and the rule of law.

Only Hlaing, the military's commander-in-chief, has the power to launch a genuine reconciliation effort. He would do well to ignore Suu Kyi's critics, and to listen to those who are calling on him to work collaboratively with her government. There is no other path to peace.

The Media's Role in Advancing Peaceful, Just and Inclusive Societies

Jakarta Convention Center, 1–4 May 2017

The relative peace, ethnic, cultural, and religious coexistence and tolerance that fortunately many enjoy in countries in Asia, Africa, and Latin America should be nurtured; the media should alert us to tragedies, but it should also report on the oasis of peace and tranquility, of those success stories that inspire and give hope, where hope of a better life has been taken away.

It is a privilege to join such distinguished thinkers on this occasion marking World Press Freedom Day. And, needless to say, it is always a pleasure to be in this dynamic Asian metropolis. I regret that constraints on my agenda do not allow me to stay longer in Jakarta.

I thank Your Excellency Prof. Irina Bokova, Director-General of UNESCO, for the kind invitation extended to me to share my thoughts on this critical theme, and I warmly congratulate you and UNESCO partners for this timely initiative at such challenging times for freedom of expression and civil and political rights in many parts of the world.

I am particularly grateful for the opportunity to be here not so much to speak words of wisdom but rather to listen and learn from you: media practitioners, authors, academics, human rights advocates and civil society activists, government leaders, and leading members of the business community.

On this day I bow to the memory of journalists killed at the front lines while reporting for us, the public, to connect us with fellow human beings, victims of conflicts; journalists murdered by criminal gangs and also by security elements co-opted by organized crime. I pay tribute to the journalists working in dangerous trenches, leaving behind the safety and comfort of their homes, in order to inform and connect us with near and far-away realities.

We are witnesses, actors, and some are just bystanders in these times of uncertainties, in a world of fast-moving events, a world that is changing fast, and not for the better.

The periphery of the unwanted and unwelcome poor, living at the edges and shadows of the minority of affluent and ostentatious part of humanity, are inching themselves into the midst of the wealthy few, changing the demographics of the countries of the rich North.

This twenty-first-century mass exodus of people could have been prevented if the richer North that recovered from the devastation of World War II thanks to the visionary men and women in the US who conceived and implemented the Marshal Plan for Europe had gathered the same vision, political will, and resources and had conceived a Marshal Plan on Education and Poverty Eradication for Africa and Asia.

I could elaborate more on what went wrong with much of the foreign aid that failed to lift people out of poverty and chronic instability, but this is reserved for another time and another forum. For now, I must add only that failures are to be shared by many at both ends, the providers of the so-called aid and the receivers. It would be unfair and hypocritical to assign blame to just one party in the donor-recipient equation.

Weapons-producing countries are also harvesting the violence they inflame with the technology of death they produce and profit from; rival neighbors in the Middle East, the Gulf region, parts of Asia and Africa, out of fear or of desire for aggrandizement, acquire ever more sophisticated weaponry, including fighter jets where they don't even have an airspace to practice flying; weapons-producing countries provide armaments to those they consider "moderates" to fight a supposed common enemy of today only to find out that these weapons often end up being used against them by the allies of yesterday. This has been going on at least as far back as the first of the many Afghan wars.

We all know the consequences of a nuclear war, the certain decimation of human civilization as we know it. Yet enlightened leaders of the major powers continue to perfect their nuclear arsenals. And some in

Asia believe that possession of nuclear weapons is a shortcut to super-power status.

In Europe there are two nuclear powers, France and the U.K., and I can assure you they are not targeting each other; in Asia we have fraternal neighbors, blood brothers and sisters, who spend an exaggerated percentage of their national GDP on Defense and mutually targeted nuclear weapons.

And we have the DPRK that targets everybody else, its near neighbors and its imagined distant enemies. I think we in Timor-Leste are among the lucky few safe from Kim Jong-un's long range missiles only because being too small, the North Korean unreliable missiles would miss us anyway.

Africans and Latin Americans have the wisdom not to acquire nuclear weapons. In Asia many believe that there are shortcuts to super-power status and prestige; one does not have to resolve the tragic realities of extreme poverty, of millions of people without access to clean water, sanitation, and basic education. All that is required is to assemble some scientists, take money away from education, health, agriculture, and food security and put it in the development of nuclear weapons.

Fortunately, ASEAN leaders have shown greater wisdom in rejecting nuclear weapons and have maintained Southeast Asia as a nuclear-free zone. This position has been emphatically stated at every ASEAN Summit.

Back in the late sixties, as a young dreamer reading about Watergate and *The Washington Post*'s courageous pursuit of the story which resulted in the resignation of a powerful President, my early admiration of, and infatuation about, the US and everything American was confirmed. As a high school teenager I remember telling my high school fellows when President Nixon was forced to resign: "See, this happens only in America. A newspaper brings down a President."

For a while my nickname was "the American," as I talked up the Kennedys, Martin Luther King, the Apollo programs, etc. As the merciless carpet bombing of Vietnam was being waged, back home across the US Americans were on the streets protesting the war. And in 1975 the US suffered its first military, political, and moral defeat, not in confrontation with another nuclear super-power, but in an unequal war waged by the mighty super-power on an Asian peasant country.

President Trump has declared war on select American TV network and print media; the venerable *New York Times* seems to have been elevated to enemy No. 1. If you read the news and opinion pages of this old paper, you will find exceptionally well crafted, challenging stories and essays, mostly unkind and unflattering of the new US President.

In recent weeks I came across a *New York Times* columnist I had never read before. His name is Charles M. Blow; I am now an avid reader of Charles Blow's column; he writes elegantly, devastatingly, and is unforgiving in his attacks on the US President.

Yet, the point I want to make here is that Mr. Charles Blow has not given any indication that he is being followed, hassled, and harassed by people wearing raincoats, hats, and dark glasses. Newspapers have not been forced to close down, TV networks declared enemies by the President have not been pulled off the air, no journalist haunted by the Secret Service.

And maybe alone in his vast sumptuous rooms, sometime between 2 and 4 am, the restless President cannot resist and reads the much maligned *New York Times*; he gets infuriated by what he reads and share his anger with his legions of Twitter fans.

How many politicians anywhere in the world are that fast with their fingers in churning out tweets and have such a legion of loyal followers? I am jealous. I do have a Twitter account that was never used, not once. But I am reasonably active on Facebook.

A friend of mine, a former UN Under-Secretary-General, Head of the Department of Public Information, author of 16 books, boasts two million Twitter followers in his or her country. I am not saying his or her name. You can start guessing; you are allowed to Google, and during the Q&A period you may say his or her name.

This is the difference, ladies and gentlemen, between them – the US democracy and its exceptionally strong democratic institutions – and some of us, and by "us" I mean many of our countries in Asia, Africa, and Latin America where freedom of thought and expression, oral or written, has not been lost simply because it was never there to lose. In some countries, where there was a sort of Democracy Spring and Free Media Spring, journalists and bloggers are now being jailed.

Of course there are notable exceptions everywhere, where media is largely free, inquisitive, and courageous, and there are all types, high quality with irreproachable professionalism, and there are those who serve political and economic interests, sycophants of the powers of the moment.

I am proud that in my infant country, Timor-Leste, we have complete freedom of thought and Press; not a single newspaper or radio has been stopped by decree, even when some in Government are deeply offended and injured in their rights and dignity by unsubstantiated allegations splashed in the media. Not a single journalist has been jailed for real or perceived offence to those in public office.

Our young journalists' badge of honor is to attack Government ministers and senior officials, accusing them of KKN[68] (Corruption, Collusion, Nepotism); but too often their stories jump past the basic What + Who + When + Where + How. Investigation is not one of their strengths.

In my country it is always up to the injured person to deny the accusations of corruption and nepotism leveled at them, and when the Prime Minister or a Minister goes through our tedious legal process to clear their name, the unelected missionaries of Media Watchdog cry "witch hunt of journalists." But I still say it is better to have journalists as loose cannons than not having a free media at all.

But I submit that freedom creates obligations; individual rights must be balanced by obligations and duties; community rights must not be sacrificed by the narrow interests of individuals or of financial and economic interests; as much as an individual cannot freely burn a private or public property, as much as an individual cannot freely set on fire a forest, our individual freedom, freedom to write, demands from us prudence and absolute professionalism and integrity in our investigations and writings; and we must never forget that whatever we write as journalists, however irreproachable the facts are, at the other end there is a man, a woman, a family, whose lives may be forever affected. So, we must think twice, we think again and again, before we release the story. At least, this is my belief.

The actions of those in public life must be scrutinized by everyone and anyone, as citizens with rights and obligations, or by legally established bodies, such the Public Prosecutor, Anti-Corruption Commissions, and Ombudsmen, whose competence and integrity must be irreproachable.

---

68 From the acronym in Indonesian for 'Korupsi, Kolusi, Nepotisme'.

The background notes prepared by UNESCO encapsulates the truths of what constitutes ethical journalism with highest values and professional standards. I completely agree with them and I am pleased to read out passages of this excellent text.

On quality journalism:

[A] public good for just, peaceful and inclusive societies...

Sustainable Development Goal 16 aims towards just, peaceful and inclusive societies, where fundamental freedoms are guaranteed through effective institutions.

This is only viable through a free, independent and pluralistic media sector that reflects these characteristics.

Quality journalism, on- or offline, based on professional and ethical standards, is quintessential in this regard, as it supplies the much-needed information for good governance and decision-making.

As a public good, quality journalism greatly contributes to the free flow of information and maximises development efforts as well as their impacts. The more people participate in this flow of information, the more valuable it becomes and the greater the common benefit.

It is vital to empower each member of society in taking part, especially those who are marginalised politically, economically or socially. The fundamental freedoms of expression and information need to be guaranteed for any significant steps forward.

One of the key components of sustainable development is "ownership" of this ambition, whether it is personal, national, regional, or international. For positive change to take root, people need to become their own agents of change.

Communication and information can foster this ownership by enabling public participation in decision-making processes and encouraging dialogue. Seeking, receiving, and imparting information by every member of the general public helps to build the foundation for the overall achievement of the 2030 Agenda for Sustainable Development.

High-quality public-interest journalism is costly, and the societal benefits are not always visible to those who own media for primarily political or business reasons.

The financial challenges, in part due to the crisis of traditional business models, can often dissuade media outlets from striving towards high professional standards.

When there is significant demand from critical audiences for in-depth and well-researched stories, such as by audiences empowered with Media and Information Literacy competencies, quality journalism is able to thrive and to contribute to just, peaceful and inclusive societies.

I could not agree more!

But this UNESCO paper refers to an ideal world, to "Alice in Wonderland." The reality is that long before the emergence of social media, of Facebook and blogs, of instant "journalism," of the legions of "columnists" with millions of loyal followers, gutter journalism was well in existence, entrenched, shamelessly unethical and unprofessional, engaged in orchestrated falsehoods and in instilling racial and political prejudices and violence.

Some of the best newspapers in the world are *The Guardian, The Independent, The Observer,* and *The Economist* magazine in the UK, *Le Monde* and *Libération* in France, *The New York Times, The Washington Post, The Los Angeles Times,* and *Newsweek* and *Time* magazine in the US. But these countries also hosted many politically biased, shamelessly unethical media, radio, print, and TV long before the proliferation and onslaught of instant digital journalism.

The latter group of media and politicians of the extreme right deliberately fuel prejudice, racism, and are responsible for the rising violence in many cities and towns across Europe and the US, targeting refugees and immigrants, most of whom were either born there or living there for many years, and helped built the economies of their elected countries.

Some of the worst crimes committed in our times, in the Balkans and Rwanda, were in part possible when local media allowed themselves to be used, or in the absence of an independent and critical media, people were intoxicated by official propaganda fueling prejudice and hatred, using radio and TV, that resulted in the genocides in Bosnia, Kosovo, and Rwanda.

I first visited Jakarta in 1974 and traveled around on a scooter and on becaks [cycle rickshaws]. How much the world and the region has changed since, how much has Indonesia changed, from an autocracy to a vibrant if imperfect democracy.

This rich multiethnic and multi-culture country of 250 million spread over the largest archipelago in the world experienced waves of violence in its history that threatened its national unity. The process of nation-building and national unity gained roots thanks to the vision and determination of generations of Leaders who forged national cohesion in diversity through policies of tolerance and inclusion. I am sure Indonesians are the first to admit that more must be done to embrace all and make all feel they are truly citizens of this great country.

In this regard, a critical independent media that questions and challenges policies deemed to be discriminatory towards particular social, ethnic, and religious groups may contribute to greater unity, as they alert policy makers to perceived discriminatory, exclusionary policies that may fuel resentment and undermine national cohesion.

Again, I agree with the following UNESCO's assertion:

Sustainable Development Goal 16 aims towards just, peaceful and inclusive societies, where fundamental freedoms are guaranteed through effective institutions.

This is only viable through a free, independent and pluralistic media sector that reflects these characteristics.

Quality journalism, on- or offline, based on professional and ethical standards, is quintessential in this regard, as it supplies the much-needed information for good governance and decision-making.

The rising intolerance and violence in Europe and the US can be reversed; there, millions of good men and women of all ages who share our humanity are doing their part in opposing discrimination, exclusion, prejudices, and violence. We must do our part in reversing the rising intolerance and violence in and among communities in Southeast Asia and elsewhere in Asia.

Traditional media, TV, radio, and responsible social media have a moral duty to take part in national, regional, and international efforts in fighting prejudices, intolerance, racism, and extremism.

While measured and well thought out security approaches are often required and may be effective in anticipating and preempting plans by extremist elements to execute their terrorist plans, policy makers must also make every effort to understand the root causes of this nefarious phenomenon that tears apart entire countries, by looking at religious, social, and political strategies that may more effectively neutralize them.

The example of Indonesia where the two largest and most respected Islamic organizations have launched educational strategies against violence, and for tolerance and inclusion, is one such example to be studied and replicated elsewhere. And in this strategy, the role of media, both mainstream and modern social media, is crucial to its success.

The relative peace, ethnic, cultural, and religious coexistence and tolerance that fortunately many enjoy in countries in Asia, Africa, and Latin America should be nurtured; the media should alert us to tragedies, but it should also report on the oasis of peace and tranquility, of those success stories that inspire and give hope, where hope of a better life has been taken away.

As our peoples watch the tragedies unfolding in Syria, Yemen, South Sudan, and with the unwanted Rohingya, to mention but a few of a long list of man-made catastrophes, we must ask ourselves: Do we want these tragedies to befall our own people, our families, our children who now live in peace and harmony?

Obviously, we don't want our families, friends, and neighbors to meet the same fate; and this being so, we must be attentive and vigilant to detect groups instigating prejudice and hatred. In this regard, on the critical area of prevention of conflicts, a free, independent, and critical media and an informed, free, and critical society do play indispensable central roles.

Terima kasih … and I wish much success for this seminar, and bountiful happiness to all in your professional and personal lives.

I pray to the Almighty and the Merciful to continue to bestow on us endless wisdom as we try to realize His teachings of love and compassion, of tolerance and forgiveness.

The Grand Challenge: Protecting the Rights of Refugees and Migrants

Sydney, 8 May 2017

Labor migration has the real potential to drive national development in Timor-Leste if properly supported and harnessed by the State to ensure protection of Timorese abroad and helping to ensure funds sent home are put to good use.

> *An individual has not begun to live until he can rise above the narrow horizons of his particular individualistic concerns to the broader concerns of all humanity.*
>
> **– Rev. Martin Luther King**

I thank the esteemed Vice-Chancellor and President Professor Ian Jacobs for the kind invitation extended to me to share with you what I intend to be some provocative words for reflection and debate on this topic at these challenging times for us all, and I warmly commend you and all at UNSW for launching this thought-provoking and soul-searching moral and intellectual discussion series. I thank UNSW staff and students, alumni, generous and wise donors.

I have been associated with UNSW for almost three decades, and during this time I witnessed the growth of UNSW into a premier university with modern infrastructure, cutting-edge equipment, and the highest academic standards in every field of sciences and humanities, including, seminally, law. Congratulations to all who made this possible.

I thank my ever loyal mentor, Mother Superior Janelle Saffin, without whom I always feel intellectually and emotionally barefoot, so to speak.

And thank the ever hardworking Alexander Weilsmann, who ensures that my visits to Australia always run with Swiss clock precision.

Janelle Saffin was a Labor Member for Page, in Northern New South Wales, and she narrowly lost her seat in Parliament; Janelle has devoted over 30 years of her life to Timor-Leste and Myanmar, advising, strategizing, fixing problems, helping overcome challenges, and even mothering many of us children. Petite, as you can appreciate up close, but respected and feared by all in our often sleepy and obstructive bureaucracy.

I acknowledge the presence of Mme Estela Ferreira, Goodwill Ambassador for Timor-Leste, and her husband, Fernando Ferreira. They are from Portugal and have been residents for decades. Fernando came in 1970, and Estela in 1999. They are among the great builders of this country. Fernando arrived having only small change in his pocket. Their firms have now employed over 600 people and all pay substantial taxes. Estela and Fernando are also generous philanthropists, having donated several hundred thousand dollars of their own money to two major humanitarian and educational projects in Timor-Leste, an orphanage, in Baguia, where she and friends have built a new building, and helping a great Franciscan friar, Friar Filipe, of Laleia.

Two other persons in the room tonight are Sakib Awan and Neelo Awan, husband and wife, who come from Pakistan and settled in Australia more than 30 years ago, under Australia's [business] skills transfer migration program.

In 2000, Sakib and his family moved to Timor-Leste, having sold their assets and successful export award-winning business in Darwin to develop business in Timor-Leste. They employ over 200 Timorese.

Here with us is also: Wilson da Silva, Portuguese Brazilian, over 30 years now an Australian national [and] a great science writer with UNSW Science for Society Centre. And, more important, he is the father of my best friend in Sydney, four-year-old April – yes, she is my best friend.

The name dropping could go on and on, as I know people, great people, from many different countries, ethnicities, and cultures who make up Australia.

I begin with the words of Rev Martin Luther King, an exceptional human being who, in times of great challenges, of racism, anger, and violence, responded with powerful messages of non-violence and reconciliation.

Rev King's memorable speech, "I Have a Dream," delivered on the 28th August, 1963, at the foot of the steps of the Lincoln Memorial, in Washington, [D.C.] entered towns and homes across the US, visiting and touching the most hardened of hearts, inspiring tens of millions of blacks and whites, Asians and Chicanos, Republicans and Democrats, propelling them into action. And together they realized a part of the dreams of emancipation of the then called Negro men and women, the descendants of the slaves, and other excluded peoples.

Through the power of non-violence, reconciliation, and compassion, Rev King contributed to breaking centuries of the chains of slavery and racism, and secured rights that had never before been recognized, rights as human beings, living as free men and women, with equal rights and opportunities.

Rev King's message reverberated beyond the US, echoing around the world, inspiring and mobilizing tens of millions struggling toward positive change. Rev King belongs to that unique class of individuals who shaped their time, made history, and are forever remembered.

Are Rev King's messages relevant to our discussion today? Are they relevant to the security and humanitarian challenges we face? Are they relevant to the 60 million refugees and displaced persons caused by ongoing wars, man-made (and, yes, they are predominantly man-made), and natural disasters, with the resulting extreme poverty and famine?

Surely, they are. In these dangerous times, the world is lacking in moral leadership, wisdom, and compassion, in a leadership that would guide us to the Promised Land, in a world littered with mines and swamps of human depravity.

I had been literally stateless and homeless in New York, from the snowy days of December 1975, when I first landed there with a simple message from our revered national hero Nicolau Lobato: "You go to the UN to present, advocate, and argue our cause."

I did manage to not only reach New York but then address the United Nations Security Council at a very young, romantic, inexperienced age. After what seemed to have been a truly successful diplomatic achievement, and as I was looking forward to returning home soon, I realized that that wouldn't be so. The supposedly binding UNSC unanimous resolution calling on Indonesia to withdraw its military forces from East Timor "without delay" was not intended to be taken seriously. Weeks turned into months, months turned into years, and into two and a half decades.

I did not have a US resident visa, had not applied for refugee status. I didn't think about or know the first thing about obtaining a "green card."

In fact, the first time I heard about a green card was from a waiter in a small Chinese eating place. He would smile when I showed up. One day, when the place was empty, he asked me where I was from. I say, "I am from East Timor." He looks at me, curious, and exclaims: "You are Eskimo! I not met Eskimo!" Well, me either! I never met one before, I explain. I repeat more slowly that I am from East Timor. Ah, now I hear you. You from Istanbul! Did you see *Midnight Express*?"

Midnight Express was in cinemas in New York at that time and I ended up going to see the film as my friend sort of recommended it.

Between my heavy accent and his unintelligible English, we managed to communicate over many takeaway orders of "fly lice." One day, after he better understood my country's history, he told me sympathetically in an uncle's tone of voice, "Don't go back there. No safe, no good. Get green card."

After 15 years of surviving in New York, sometimes enjoying it, sometimes hating it, by 1989 I was literally burned out and decided to migrate to Australia under the family reunion scheme. It was from here that I would continue advocating for self-determination for Timor-Leste.

Being based in Australia meant that my international travels increased exponentially, having to fly back as many times as necessary for lobbying in the UN, the US Congress, and throughout Europe and Japan.

The application process to migrate to Australia was a straightforward one – tedious, yes, but not unreasonable at all. From the moment I lodged my application papers, it took roughly one year before I was granted permanent residence status.

And thus began my association with UNSW, now almost three decades old. It was soon after I arrived in Sydney, at the end of 1989, that Professor Garth Nettheim, John Scott-Murphy of the Evatt Foundation, and I established the Diplomacy Training Program, or DTP as it is called. The UNSW Law Faculty agreed to lend their name and space to this innovative concept of imparting knowledge in international human rights values and norms and their practical application in the field.

Since then, many thousands of indigenous representatives and human rights advocates from across Asia and the Pacific have enrolled in DTP courses that have been delivered throughout the year in cities and towns in the region.

In this regard, I acknowledge and thank Patrick Earl, who tirelessly and diligently has steered the Diplomacy Training Program for the last 10 years. Emeritus Professor Paul Redmond, thank you for being always so gracious and supportive, and for being here tonight.

We are living in extremely challenging and dangerous times, in a world that is changing fast, and not for the better. We are witnesses to these man-made tragedies; we can be actors or agents of change for the better, if not globally; or regionally, if not nationally. Let's try to be agents of positive change locally, in our own communities, or in communities of the forgotten, the poor, the unwanted. But there are many who choose to be mere bystanders.

Partly because of the economic and financial crisis that originated in Washington during President George W. Bush's eight-year spending spree and deficit ballooning, partly because of donor fatigue or selfishness, private, personal, social, and humanitarian contributions have decreased dramatically; in some instances they have completely stopped. OECD countries have drastically reduced their ODA[69] contributions.

Sweden and Norway are the only two countries that have kept up their level of development aid corresponding to one percent of their GDP. The UK, under David Cameron, was the only G7 country that increased its ODA to 0.7 percent of GDP. Every single traditional donor country has introduced drastic cuts in ODA, Australia leading the pack by far in aid cuts.

We are living witnesses of a massive dislocation of peoples without precedent in modern history. The millions of unwanted and unwelcome, *les damnés de la terre*[70], barely surviving on the periphery, at the edges and shadows of the affluent and ostentatious minority of humanity, are inching themselves into the midst of the wealthy few, changing the demographics of the countries of the rich North.

---

69   Official Development Assistance.
70   After a book by Franz Fanon

The old Europe that colonized much of the world emerged from the Second World War destroyed and quickly rebuilt, prospered, and reconciled, has done much for the rest of the world, being the single-largest provider of development assistance to countries of the poorer South.

It is undergoing tectonic changes, with extremist right-wing ideologies reminiscent of the thirties, inciting divisions on ethnic, skin color, and religious bases, causing a spiral of racially motivated violence in many European cities, and the possible breakup of the world's most successful regional integration, the European Union.

British demagogues of the likes of a Mr Farage, who has the manners and speech of a discredited second-hand car dealer, lied enough and convincingly so as to cause the Brexit, and with it a weakened Europe and a much weakened England.

Some good news out of Europe, more precisely out of Paris: Marine Le Pen, the right-wing presidential candidate, was sent away by the electorate to manage a *boulangerie.*

Ladies and gentlemen, my forecast on French elections posted on my Facebook page on 25 April proved right! Let me share with you what I wrote then:

The French electorate is more educated and more open-minded than the American.

The French will NOT elect Marine Le Pen President of the French Republic. If in the extremely unlikely scenario of a Le Pen victory, violence would inevitably spiral in France—I am referring to rightist inspired violence against Jewish, Muslims, Africans and Asians—ISIS would rejoice and escalate attacks in France and against French interests and symbols elsewhere. Mrs Le Pen has stated she would pull France out of the EU. France would be under siege, isolated and severely weakened.

A weakened and discredited France, and Europe, is a nightmare scenario.

I am sure the French electorate, which is very informed and more sophisticated than the average American electorate, will vote the moderate, centrist and decent Emmanuel Macron over the demagogue, xenophobic, racist and dangerous Marine Le Pen and her National Front.

The moral of my retelling this story here is that if you wish to be better informed and thus be able to make better decisions in your life, including how to vote here in Australia, follow me on my Facebook page!

The Europe that built its prosperity on the backs, sweat, and blood of the peoples of its colonies has been, for decades, the destination of choice, a safe haven for millions fleeing wars and extreme deprivation.

A new Europe, multi-ethnic, multi-culture, and multi-faith, is emerging, pushed by the approximation of the tectonic plates of Africa/ Middle East and Europe. This tectonic clash is not a geological one; it is, rather, several human plates coming together, the poor South pushing toward the rich North.

Whether this new Europe will be peaceful and embracing of all, living in peace, harmony, and prosperity, depends only on Europeans of today, of different ethnic extractions and beliefs, and whether they have the wisdom and courage to prepare the new future Europe, sharing their common fate.

It will be a test of the quality of leadership, political wisdom, and a measure of the strength of the values of solidarity and justice that are the foundation of modern Europe. It is a test for all in Europe, Christians and other faiths, how they will jointly manage this fast-changing demography, and on them all depend a Europe rejuvenated and vibrant, or a Europe mired in racial, religious, social, and political sectarianism and hatred.

This twenty-first-century mass exodus of people could have been prevented if the richer North that recovered from the devastation of World War II – thanks to the visionary men and women in the US who conceived and implemented the Marshal Plan for Europe – had gathered the same vision, political will, and resources, and conceived 50 years ago a Marshal Plan for Education and Health, Sustainable Rural Development, and Water and Food Security for Africa and Asia.

I could elaborate more on what went wrong with much of the foreign aid that failed to lift people out of poverty and chronic instability, but this is reserved for another time and another forum. For now, I must only add that failures, and there were many, are to be shared by both ends, providers of the aid and receivers. It would be unfair and hypocritical to assign blame to just one party in the donor-recipient equation.

Weapons-producing countries are also to blame for the spiraling of the violence across much of the world; because of them, with their greed and their irresponsibility, we are harvesting the violence they inflame with the technology of death they produce and profit from. Rival neighbors in the Middle East, the Gulf region, parts of Asia and Africa, out of fear or of desire for aggrandizement, acquire ever more sophisticated weaponry, including fighter jets where they don't even have an airspace to practice flying.

In the Syria quagmire of quicksand and shifting alliances, we see how supposedly wise leaders in the USA and Europe provide armaments to those they consider "moderates" to fight a supposed common enemy of today, only to find out that these weapons often end up being used against them by the allies of yesterday. This has been going on at least as far back as the first of the many Afghan wars.

We all know the consequences of a nuclear war, the certain decimation of human civilization as we know it. Yet, enlightened leaders of the major powers continue to perfect their nuclear arsenal. And some in Asia believe that possession of nuclear weapons is a shortcut to superpower status.

In Europe, there are two nuclear powers, France and the UK, and I can assure you they are not targeting each other. Africans and Latin Americans have the wisdom not to acquire nuclear weapons. In Asia, many believe that there are shortcuts to superpower status and prestige. One does not have to resolve the tragic realities of extreme poverty, of millions of people without access to clean water, sanitation, and basic education. All that is required is to assemble some scientists, take money away from education, health, and agriculture and food security and put it into the development of nuclear weapons.

And we have the Democratic People's Republic of Korea [North Korea] that targets everybody else, its near neighbors and its imagined distant enemies. I think we in Timor-Leste are among the lucky few safe from Kim Jong-un's long-range missiles only because being too small, the North Korean unreliable missiles would miss us anyway.

Fortunately, ASEAN leaders have shown greater wisdom in rejecting nuclear weapons and have maintained Southeast Asia as a nuclear-free zone. This position has been emphatically stated at every ASEAN Summit.

This country, sometimes called "the Lucky Country," or "Down Under," in modern times populated by the poor of Europe, by the tens of thousands who were rightly or wrongfully convicted by the Courts of

England and deported here, is not immune from the social and political tectonic movements taking place elsewhere.

This is a country of the original inhabitants, the Aboriginal people who had been here for over 50,000 years before the arrival of the "white ghosts." But it is also now the home of Irish, Scottish, Welsh, Italians, Maltese, Lebanese, Portuguese, Spaniards, Vietnamese, Cambodians, Chinese, Timorese, Somalians, Tamils, Kurdish, Croats, etc., all being Australians with equal rights and equal opportunities. What a beautiful tapestry of an ethnic, cultural, social, religious mix from all corners of the world, all coming here together, seeking peace and comfort, together transforming Australia into a bastion of peace and democracy and a prosperous nation.

From the first batch of alien arrivals on Australian shores in the eighteenth century till the Second World War, almost all came fleeing deprivations in their home countries; they fled justice or were simply victims of England's ambitions to expand the size and importance of the little island that sometimes desires to be European, and sometimes feels the urge to affirm its separateness.

I ventured into Australia for the first time in the early 1970s with a younger brother, Arsenio, crisscrossing this vast continent, from Darwin to Sydney, hitch-hiking, by bus, and by an occasional lift.

My observation then was that Australia was far less accommodating of non-Anglos; even the proud Greeks emanating from the cradle of civilization were not seen as good enough to be here; maybe it has to do with their suntanned complexion and thick moustaches. Chinese and Indians were even less welcome. Cuisine in the mainly Anglo cities and towns was as bad as it was in England – my brother and I didn't speak much English and didn't have much money, so we ate mostly fish and chips, in brown bags.

Later, in the 1970s, as hundreds of thousands of Vietnamese fled their country, many came to Australia. I recall what a charming, talkative, Sydney Greek taxi driver told me: "They used not to like the Greeks. Now they don't like the Vietnamese, so they forgot about Greeks. We are OK now." And he laughed, as Greeks and Mediterranean peoples know how to.

Some 20 years ago, in one of my many visits to Melbourne, I met the then newly elected Mayor, a relatively young gentleman of obvious

Chinese origin who spoke English with a heavy Chinese accent. John So was Melbourne's first directly elected mayor, originating from the Tiananmen generation, having managed to flee, and reaching the safety of Australian shores.

Some 20 years earlier John So would not be recruited even to a modest office job anywhere in Australia, let alone being elected Mayor. When we left his office, I thought to myself how much this country has changed for the better; how it has become more open and enlightened.

Some 10 to 15 years ago I was at a gala dinner table in Dublin, hosted by the American Academy of Achievements. To my right was a charming gentleman, and naturally I asked him, "Where are you from?" He answered, "I am from Australia." and I asked, "what you do?" He answered, "I am a businessman." "What kind of business?" I asked. He answered, always quietly, politely, "I own the Westfield."

I was familiar with the Westfield mall in Liverpool, where I lived for a while, and it was a favorite hangout of my mother, Dona Natalina, and many Timorese. Like an Australian immigration officer asking many questions of a visitor, I asked: "You mean you own the Liverpool Westfield shopping mall?" The gentleman answered, smiling: "Yes, I own that one and many others around Australia, in the UK, and the US."

I said, "Hmmm, you must be rich! What's your name?" He said, "Frank Lowy."

Frank Lowy, Holocaust survivor, arrived here without a penny. A chance of a new life was granted him and he built an El Dorado that employs tens of thousands of people, many being refugees and migrants like himself. Imagine if Australia had not given sanctuary to Frank Lowy and many others?

Following the outbreak of civil war, in August 1975, several hundred Timorese and Portuguese citizens were evacuated by ship to Darwin. We could say they were some of the first "boat people" to reach Australia. I want to share with you that one of those Timorese "boat people" happens to be the MP for Katherine, in the Northern Territory Parliament. She is also my niece, and my family are, of course, quite proud of her.

The experience of Timorese in Australia was largely a very positive one. They were welcomed and helped to settle. Most found jobs and worked tirelessly and honestly until retirement age. Their children and grandchildren growing up in this welcoming country were able to study, and acquired university degrees and/or vocational skills contributing to the well-being of their new country, Australia, and some have had the good fortune of going back to serve in their country, Timor-Leste, after 1999.

Let me share with you excerpts of a profiles series made by a good friend in California, Mary Wald, commissioned by NASA. The Women at NASA's Jet Propulsion Lab [JPL] site profiles 15 women at the forefront of space exploration. The site was built to inspire young girls to go into science, technology, engineering, and math. It tells the stories of how these women came to JPL, what they are working on, and what their advice would be to young girls who want to work in science, or, to use JPL's motto, young girls anywhere in the world who "Dare Mighty Things."

It was only after the site was completed that the producers noticed that nine of the 14 modern-day Galileos were either immigrants, children of immigrants, or war refugees.

MiMi Aung was born and lived as a child in extreme poverty in Burma. She was fortunate to have been taken to the US, where she grew up and studied. This is a Burmese refugee, an Asian migrant in the US.

Today, one of the top scientists at NASA's Jet Propulsion Lab, MiMi is the head of a project to design and develop a helicopter that will fly on Mars in 2020. It's very small, because there is so little atmosphere on Mars that there is little draft. But it is a type of flight that has never been attempted by man or woman and that is flight on another planet.

These profiles include Ana Maria Guerrero, the daughter of Mexican immigrants who came to the US and worked at menial labor to put their children in college. Ana studied computer science and now runs the telemetry area of JPL, developing the software for all the digital communications in and out of JPL's missions in deep space.

Melanie Chau-Budiman, at 15 years old, was on a boat out of Saigon with her two younger brothers and 2,600 other refugees. They were picked up at sea by the Red Cross. Today, Melanie is an IT manager at JPL.

Khanara Ellers dreamt as a child in Cambodia of working in the space program, before the Khmer Rouge killed her father and all of her male relatives. Today, she is a systems engineer at JPL.

Another migrant, one of the richest men in the world, Carlos Slim, originates from a small village in Lebanon, anda whose wealth is estimated to be grander than that of Bill Gates. And it was this Lebanese-

Mexican billionaire who rescued *The New York Times* from closure with the acquisition of that mighty American institution with several hundred million dollars some 10 years ago.

In my life's journey I was blessed to have met in Australia, Asia, Europe, the US, and Latin America countless individuals from all over the world with similar stories, stories as fellow human beings searching for a better life and succeeding. Not all will turn out to own shopping malls or to be NASA scientists, Hollywood stars, or sports heroes; many are doctors, academics, journalists, engineers, architects, many own modest takeaways, food outlets, churning out kebabs during busy lunchtimes. Sikhs in Manhattan dominate the Yellow Cab fleets; Indians dominate the IT space with their genius.

Bangladeshis, Filipinos, Mexicans, Hondurans, Algerians, Tunisians, Moroccans, Malians, Togolais – tens of millions of peoples are working on any given day, anywhere in the richer countries, keeping commerce, high tech, automobile industries running, and making sure that, at fruit-picking season, millions of cartons of fruits destined for overseas markets are all ready for shipment; they also look after the children of the busy middle classes and the rich.

If you travel across the US as I have done (and I would bet I have been to more states, cities, and towns in the US than any American, or any living person) you would be surprised to see peoples from so many regions of the world in management, banking, industry, aviation, medicine, major businesses, etc. The Third World no longer only supplies cheap labor – maids, bricklayers, cleaners – we still supply this category of much needed workers, but also medical doctors, IT czars, designers, aircraft engineers, 747 pilots, *summa cum laude* academics, etc. It is similar in Sydney, which has become a regional financial center.

Not all will succeed; some born or who grew up in their parents' adopted countries never adapted; some suffered abuse, discrimination, and grew up angry, easy prey of unscrupulous elements, and began to experiment with drugs and alcohol. Some others are lured in particular to mosques via social media, into extremism and violence.

Modern Europe, particularly post-World War II Europe, living in peace and prosperity, has been a region of destination, of dreams and utopia, of hope and promise for millions from the impoverished colonies.

I want to highlight now how labor migration can contribute to development of a developing country and to the already developed country, using my own country as the example.

Labor migration has the real potential to drive national development in Timor-Leste if properly supported and harnessed by the State to ensure protection of Timorese abroad and helping to ensure funds sent home are put to good use.

As Foreign Minister in 2002–06, I began to explore the possibility of developing with ROK a labor agreement. After some years, we began to send the first batch of Timorese to work in [South, or Republic of] Korea. I went to the airport to bid farewell and say words of advice to the first batch of departing young workers. We now have about 2,000 Timorese working in ROK, and the Korean Government has allocated to Timor-Leste a quota of 10,000 workers for work in ROK.

Back then, as Foreign Minister I attempted to explore a similar program with Australia. I wrote to, and spoke with, then Foreign Minister Downer, wrote to the no-nonsense Minister of Immigration Amanda Vanstone to have young Timorese doing seasonal work in Australia, and talked to anybody who would listen. Years of lobbying by many, including employers in Australia, bore fruit, with a limited number of guest workers from Timor-Leste now finally allowed into Australia.

I propose that Australia consider granting guest worker-type visas to up to 10,000 young Timorese for longer work contracts, of six to nine months' duration.

In both cases, with ROK and Australia, my advocacy of this scheme rested on a number of tangible and intangible principles and goals:

- The urgent need to relieve the unemployment, social pressure in Timor-Leste
- Generate income for the families back home with the remittances which, in turn, would improve the lives of many in Timorese extended families
- The work experience abroad would transform our youth, acquiring new skills and work habits – discipline and hard work
- Through them, we develop further people-to-people relationships
- The host countries get additional labor that they need

There are 16,000 Timorese living, studying, and working in the UK, a significant number in the chicken-packaging industry in Northern Ireland, some 4,000 in the Oxford area, doing hard work in factories, restaurants, hospitals, and colleges as cleaners. They earn from £750 to £1,300 a month and send much of the money home.

When I was in Oxford a year ago for some public lectures, I met with a number of them and heard their heart-wrenching stories of hard work, resilience, and generosity. I felt small, humbled by their experiences.

In Australia, Europe, the US, or anywhere in the world, there must be very scrupulous application of the international treaties and national laws protecting migrant workers and refugees, their safety in the work place and in the communities they live.

We know of too many abominable cases of ill treatment of migrant workers in Hong Kong, Qatar, Saudi Arabia, to name but a few of the more notorious ones, and some indeed in our region. Unfortunately, it has happened in Australia as well, but has been exposed, workers have been awarded monies owed to them, and prosecutions are ensuing.

These are all fundamental questions on migration – safe migration, protection of migrant rights, and taking stock to harness the potential of migration for national and global development.

So, brothers and sisters in Australia, brothers and sisters in Government and Parliament, both at the Federal and State levels, my sister Pauline Hanson (yes, she is my sister in God): rethink old fears and prejudices. I am sure you have had a good look at the record of generations of refugees and migrants in this country, and you have seen how they have contributed to the comfort, prosperity, and safety of today's Australia, and how a vast majority are loyal Australians serving with distinction in the Defence forces, customs and immigration, and police.

I didn't like watching on TV how Mrs Pauline Hanson was recently cursed and chased away from some café or public place in Queensland. I would have invited Mrs Hanson in, offered her coffee, and politely engaged her in conversation.

Australia need not fear – Australia does need more people, educated people, a more inclusive and egalitarian society. Welcome the refugees fleeing wars and extreme poverty; educate their children and youth; give a chance to their parents – some might be educated; give a chance to improve on their education and experience. Others might not have education and experience relevant for the needs of Australia. Surely you can offer appropriate retraining programs that are in need in Australia that would make them more employable.

Australia is better than the fabled El Dorado because it is real – gold and fortunes were found here, and the greatest gold of all found here is freedom, dignity, the rule of law, peace, and security.

You live in a privileged, affluent country, an increasingly more open and tolerant one. Australia has changed for the better, much better; much has to change further to be an abode of safety and peace for all its peoples, for the poor and the unwanted fleeing wars and deprivation.

You are all in my daily prayers to the Almighty and the Merciful, the Wisest of all, and I plead with Him to bless you all with bountiful health and endless wisdom.

A Conversation on Peace

Siem Reap, Cambodia, 4 August 2017

Nobel Peace laureate José Ramos-Horta was the guest speaker at the Cambodia's Center for Peace and Conflict Studies. His talk became a tour à vol d'oiseau on the evolution of peace, conflict, and security in the last decades drawing from his more than 40 years of activism and peace building. A dialogue with the public followed. Some of the author's remarks and dialogue are highlighted here.

On my way here, as I was reflecting on this meeting and my trip to Myanmar in the next few days, and thinking to myself, *God, do we still have to pursue all kinds of armed struggle in this 21st century of ours – as legitimate and as justified as they may be – in order to achieve a political goal?* Because, in the end it's for a political goal. We don't fight for a military goal, for the sake of it. It's a political goal.

Of course, there are responsibilities on all sides. Whatever the nature of the struggle, of the conflict, the solution rests on all sides, not just on the people who opted for the armed struggle. People just do not dream up one day, like, "Let's have an armed struggle." Often, people are forced into a corner.

Some resist the temptation of picking up arms – ask Mahatma Gandhi. Others don't think twice. Even Mandela, who was elevated to sainthood in his lifetime. The ANC pursued armed struggle until the very end of apartheid.

I had the privilege of meeting with Mandela several times after he left prison and I have the greatest respect for him as an extraordinary human being. It doesn't diminish my respect for him that he opted for armed struggle against the apartheid to pursue freedom for the majority in South Africa.

Timor-Leste: Peace and governance

Xanana Gusmão, Timor-Leste's charismatic leader, shows real statesmanship. His attitude is a lesson to many leaders around the world, in many countries who are creating problems right now, refusing to show dignity and integrity, pride, commitment to democracy by not accepting the results when they lose.

Let me start by sharing a little bit with you about Timor-Leste. Just before entering this room I have been on the phone and in WhatsApp and email contact with my country, because we just had elections, on 22 July 2017. They have been absolutely peaceful, despite three major parties and major personalities competing. I wouldn't expect violence, but tension might be high. Not really, though.

Normally, if you have a debate of this nature, tensions are to be expected, and if there is no tension something must be wrong. Everybody must be in agreement and everybody *cannot* agree, as we know we still have problems and challenges in our country. We have corruption, mismanagement, we have waste … we have done a lot of good things, but even the Vatican, even the Pope, who is known to be infallible, have had to correct a lot of things over the centuries.

So, I thought we would have a quiet election, but in the end we didn't have even the normal political tension. Parties campaigned, flags proliferated; rich parties, poor parties, rich people, poor people – they all competed. Of course, not on the same level playing field, as one or two of the competing parties have much more money than the rest combined.

Our democracy is becoming an Asian-typical democracy, meaning a money democracy. Very little differs … except that we learn very fast. Still, when people ask me about a measure of democracy, I say, "In my country, in a developing country, the main criteria for me is that no one gets killed because of some damn election."

To everyone's surprise, particularly to the surprise of the main loser, a great and charismatic leader, Xanana Gusmão's party lost the election. He reminds me a lot of Sukarno, the founding father of Indonesia, and is sometimes compared to Mandela. He was a prisoner, very forgiving, and came to lead our national reconciliation process. Like Sukarno, he is a great orator.

Xanana lost the election and everybody was in suspense for like a week, because he had hidden himself in his home in the hills. I was asked to comment why Xanana was absent. I said, "He is reflecting on the election result, first; and second, of course, on its effects."

His party just met today and he announced that he takes full responsibility for the defeat and resigned from the party's leadership. He will stay on, but resigned his leadership and he is telling his party not to join in any coalition.

Xanana shows real statesmanship. His attitude is a lesson to many leaders around the world, in many countries who are creating problems right now, refusing to show dignity and integrity, pride, commitment to democracy, by not accepting the results when they lose.

For Timor-Leste, a 15-year-old democracy, it is remarkable. As no party won an overall majority, the winning party, FRETILIN, won by one seat, by around 1200 votes. It is an extraordinary measure of democracy that a party can win by only a few hundred votes and yet the second party didn't contest the result.

We have very strong established procedures, electronic tallying and hundreds of foreign and international observers around. Any claimant can go to our equivalent to the Supreme Court. Yet no one lodged a complaint and everyone accepted the result. So, we will see FRETILIN trying to forge a coalition government.

We have recovered from the past of violence and destruction in 1999/2000. The country was thoroughly destroyed. Some of you might have read or seen pictures or the film about it. Anyone who was in Timor-Leste in 1999/2000, in the first few years of independence, and witnessed the destruction would be impressed, surprised, if going back there now. We now have electricity 24 hours a day for more than 80 percent of the country. We have new power lines and also fiber optics wiring all over the country. If you travel there right now you will see everywhere either brand new roads or roads under construction. Construction has just started of a new US$400 million port to the west of Díli, the capital, contracted to a French company.

Almost 100 percent of children of school age are properly enrolled, even though this doesn't mean we have achieved high quality schools and education. School infrastructure has expanded enormously, but we have serious problems with the quality of teachers and we don't have enough of them because of the explosion in pupils' enrollment. Also, providing clean water to every school in the country is still a challenge.

We have a school nutrition program and every child in the country is supposed to get one hot meal a day, consisting of rice, beans, vegetables, and in some cases vitamin supplements. But you can imagine the country's challenges without proper roads which we are only building now. Most of the roads are 100 percent financed by our own national budget, not from international borrowing or funding. 80 percent of the expenditure in road building comes from our sovereign Petroleum Fund. Our Petroleum Fund is considered the best managed in Asia, the third best in the world.

In most mineral rich countries, governments manage revenues from oil and gas, diamonds, gold, and so on. Not so in the case of Timor-Leste. We chose to do something else, similar to the Norwegians. Norway created a Petroleum Fund and all the revenue from oil exports go to that fund. The fund then invests in what they call a sovereign fund.

In the case of Norway, 40 percent of the assets of the Fund are US Treasury bonds and 60 per cent diversified portfolios of securities, around the world. In our case, we began with investing 100 percent of our petroleum resources in US Treasury bonds. Only after 2009 a new law approved by our national parliament enabled us to diversify, and now 60 percent are invested in US Treasury bonds and 40 percent in diversified portfolios. We have investments in more than a thousand portfolios around the world.

In less than 10 years, we have accumulated about $16.5 billion. We have very modest oil and gas reserves, nothing like Kuwait or Qatar; rather a bit closer to Brunei. Our oil is similar to the Saudi oil, which is very light crude, easier and cheaper to refine, unlike the Kuwait oil, very expensive to refine.

So, we have used our oil resources very wisely. Timor-Leste's government doesn't have direct access to the Petroleum Fund, as revenues go directly from the point of sale to the Petroleum Fund administered by the President of the Central Bank and a board that includes the former Minister of Finance, the former Prime Minister, the former President, etc. The board is accountable to the National Parliament and the government is allowed to use only what is considered to be "sustainable income" of the Fund as evaluated by the President of the Central Bank, who officially writes to the parliament every year saying, "'Such and such' is the sustainable income that you can use."

So, our country is doing well, although corruption is an issue. Our courts are fighting back and they are very harsh – a bit beyond proportion, even. A Secretary of State of Public Works was sent to jail to serve a three-year sentence. A former Minister of Education, a great guy by the way, appealed against his seven-year sentence. But the accusations were proven and the Court of Appeals reaffirmed the District Court verdict. He was handcuffed and taken to prison.

A former Minister of Finance was also given seven years, but for an irregularity, not that she stole money. US$800,000 were used to purchase hospital beds and the beds are being used in our ICU, but her husband was part owner of the company the beds were purchased from and that's against our laws. I have to tell you that I feel bad for these cases because justice has to be fair, proportional.

This is in a nutshell to tell you where we are after 15 years of independence after so much destruction – and with a lot of international help from many development partners, in particular Australia, which is our major donor of official development assistance.

Reconciliation and good neighbors

Timor-Leste was a victim of Indonesian aggression and occupation. And yet the two countries today have the best possible relationship of any two countries in South East Asia or in Asia.

Australia remains our biggest donor, followed probably by the European Union, followed by Japan. China's also there, but comes way down the list.

The Australian media from time to time write articles discussing the "growing Chinese influence in Timor-Leste." Total nonsense. But I told them, "Listen, I'm not even upset. Care to know why? Because of your misleading articles, the Americans are paying more attention to East Timor. So please keep writing that the Chinese are taking over so that we have more help from Washington."

The US Naval Secretary came to Timor-Leste, and Hillary Clinton came to Timor-Leste. We have in Timor a good-sized American US Peace Corps. I lobbied to bring them to Timor. They do fantastic work with our communities. We also have a small US Navy detachment of army engineers who also do great work.

We have more or less zero conflict with anyone and in the region. Timor-Leste is predominantly Catholic, 98 percent active, devout Catholics, from young children to older people. When you go to Australia, or Europe you see only elderly people in Church services. In Timor-Leste you see children of all ages, youth, adults, elderly – everybody.

Indonesia is the largest Muslim-majority country. It's not a Muslim country in the sense that they don't have a state religion, unlike Malaysia, but it is a 250 million Muslim-majority nation. Timor-Leste was a victim of Indonesian aggression and occupation. And yet the two countries today have the best possible relationship of any two countries in South East Asia, or in Asia. You can compare Indonesia's relationship with Malaysia or with Singapore – there are some tensions, some rivalries. Thailand and Cambodia, Cambodia and Vietnam, Vietnam and China, Japan and China, Korea and Japan, India and Pakistan, Bangladesh and Pakistan, etc. You have tensions in all of these.

But Timor-Leste and Indonesia have an exceptional relationship and that has to do with our leadership. Upon independence we said: Let's put the past where it belongs. We honored the victims; we honored those who fought and died, those who suffered and those who were victims of abuses.

But as a country and as a people, Indonesia itself was a victim of the Cold War. During those years, starting with the Bolshevik Revolution that had an impact around the world, people took sides. There were fears, prejudices, and perceptions, wrong, misinformed, or informed. In the process, millions died around the world and Indonesia suffered as a result of the Cold War. Nineteen sixty-five/sixty-six witnessed the worst massacre in the history of Indonesia. Between half a million and a million are estimated to have been killed during the six-month period when the Suharto regime took over.

And then came the invasion of Timor-Leste. Many of our people died, but our leadership – not only Xanana Gusmão but Nicolau Lobato, a great national leader before him – said from day one in 1975: "We are not fighting the Indonesians as a people. We are not fighting against anyone. We are fighting for freedom, for independence."

In 24 years of a struggle, not a single one of Indonesian military personnel captured in the field was killed. Those who were captured alive were returned after a few months, even though the Indonesians never returned our people.

Timorese resistance fighters, activists, also never touched a single Indonesian civilian life. Not one.

We never demonized the Indonesians as a people, never mixed religion with the fight.

Most fights are political. If you fight for democracy in Iran, you are not fighting for the Shias, or Sunnis, or whatever interpretation of Islam. You are fighting for political power. And why should people of one interpretation of Islam or another die because of that?

I always said that Suharto of Indonesia, the Indonesian dictator from 1965 to 1998, never discriminated when it came to violence. Whether you were Muslim, Hindu, Buddhist, he didn't care as long as you challenged him. In Indonesia, when it came to violence by Suharto, it was equal opportunity for everybody. Even if we were the most devout Muslims in the world he would still have invaded, and they would repress you if you challenged him. Ask the Acehnese. Aceh, the most Islamic province in Indonesia, in the past they were much more victimized than Timor-Leste in terms of violence.

Justice is not always closure

We were not freed on our own. We fought in many different ways, but we would not have been freed if it were not also for the changes in Indonesia, when Indonesian students went to the streets and brought down the regime, paving the way for dialogue (with the Timorese Resistence) and independence.

We have resisted pressure from friends – the Amnesty International, members of the US Congress, members of the European Parliament – to push for an international tribunal [on war crimes committed during Indonesia's 24-year occupation of Timor-Leste]. We said no, we didn't want an international tribunal.

The Indonesian dictatorship fell in 1998, and there began a very difficult, painful transition to democracy. We must assist [that process], and one way to assist was to understand the difficulties of the transition to democracy in Indonesia. Bringing in an outside element, an international tribunal, would have ignited even more polarization in Indonesia, and would have endangered or completely undermined any effort on our side to normalize the relationship with Indonesia.

The Indonesian side, they responded in kind. They saw that the Timorese understood their challenges and so they turned around and embraced us. The Indonesians didn't behave like some other people or leaders who, when they lose, get very vindictive, and start creating problems for you. No. When the Indonesians realized – because they didn't know us much, in the past we were fighting in opposing trenches – but then in 1999/2000 they started realizing who we were and they walked halfway to meet us.

The referendum happened in August 1999 and the Indonesian military vacated the territory in September. The country was still burning. In early October, Xanana Gusmão and myself were in Indonesia, meeting with the Indonesian military. I remember sitting there, our small delegation facing, on the other side of the table, some 30 military personnel in green uniform, Indonesian generals and so on. They all carried their name tags and I remembered looking at their names, and I recognized all those names from the past. And there we were, meeting with them.

The Indonesian president, Gus Dur, a great human being, a great Muslim leader, was very conciliatory. He came to Timor even before independence, in January 2000. Then Ibu Mega, Megawati Sukarnoputri, more nationalistic, more reluctant in relation to Timor-Leste – she also came for our independence celebration. Then Susilo Bambang Yudhoyono came, three times. And just a few days ago he has been again in Díli, for a regional meeting. President Joko Widodo came and visited our hero's cemetery where Timorese fighters are buried. He also went to visit the Indonesian cemetery in Díli, which is very well kept. We didn't touch the Indonesian military cemetery. (...)

QUESTION: You talked about the sort of amnesty of not having a tribunal between Indonesia and Timor. What's your opinion on the Khmer Rouge Tribunal?

José Ramos-Horta: After more than seven years and at least US$250 million spent, the tribunal[71] has produced how many convictions? The same [can be said of] many other international tribunals. Not because the prosecutors and judges are not doing their job, but because it is enormously complex.

In my own country, we rejected completely the notion, partly, as I mentioned, because we understand Indonesia. And for us the greatest gift, the greatest act of justice done to Timor-Leste, is that we are free today. We were not freed on our own. We fought in many different ways, but we would not have been freed if it were not also for the changes in Indonesia, when Indonesian students went to the streets and brought down the regime, paving the way for dialogue and independence.

Countries like the US were also accomplices of Indonesia in 1975. Then, at that crucial time, in 1999, Bill Clinton played a critical role. Actually, after he took office in 1993, United States policies began to change, and in 1999, if it were not for Bill Clinton I don't know whether we would have got the outcome we did. Overall, my point is that after having failed Timor, the international community redeemed itself.

We also recognize that many of our own people were involved in crimes; it's not only Indonesia.

As I said, we don't know of Indonesian civilians killed during the war, but there were Timorese killed during the civil war before independence, due to rivalries and suspicion, particularly in the first year or two. Those who did the killing are there, in Timor, some even in government, some even in the parliament. We know. So, are we going to have a special tribunal just for Indonesia? As Xanana himself once said, "Are we going to be that hypocritical and not start with ourselves? Who can judge whom? So, better to talk."

In the case of Cambodia, who am I to tell my brothers and sisters in Cambodia, particularly the victims, what would be the best? But I would say the following, that I have said a number of times: Live on. Extricate

---

71   The Court is officially named Extraordinary Chambers in the Courts of Cambodia, and was created to try crimes committed during Cambodia's Khmer Rouge regime (1975-1979).

yourself from the pain of the past. Do not allow yourself to continue to be a hostage of your own past, your own suffering, because that way you are not living. Find ways with help, as individuals, as communities, as societies, to live on.

Honor the victims, write and read histories so that no such tragedies of the past ever happen again, but don't allow yourself to be consumed by the suffering. If you have lost people and you keep thinking about it every day, you lose all your creativity, your initiatives; you become numb, you become angry. So, the perpetrators win again. They still dominate you.

So, that's my philosophy, and that's what I tell people, you know.

Cambodia, for all of its imperfections, has come a long way. I'm told by friends here that criminality is very low, almost non-existent. Can you imagine that, after so many years of violence? It's remarkable that you have a country that went through this incredible violence that has been able to build such a peaceful society. And it's a tribute to Cambodians and a tribute to the government.

So, my point is, first things first. If it's possible to go together, hand in hand, so much the better. Along the way democracy will be perfected, justice will be perfected. In the meantime, don't allow history to dominate you.

Unpredictability and high expectations

The first time in my life I met an Armenian was in the US in the small, prestigious Wesleyan University, in 1976. I remember this Armenian historian saying, "You know, my brother, my country will never be free. But yours I hope will be."

I have a book coming out in Sydney[72] – it will be released in many cities – a book mostly of speeches and articles I wrote during my time in office and since. I'm writing an introduction to the book, and a reflection on the challenges that the world faces.

Of course, some of you, and probably many around the world, have a very pessimistic view of where we are. Twenty years ago, at the end of the

---

72   The author refers to the present volume, which was being prepared at the time of his talk at the Center for Peace and Conflict Studies in Siem Reap, Cambodia, in August 2017.

Cold War, there was incredible optimism with the end of the Cold War and soon after apartheid ended. The Eastern/Central Europe Baltic States were freed. It was just unthinkable that Baltic States could be free.

I remember, the first time in my life I met an Armenian person was in the US, in a small, well-known prestigious university called Wesleyan University. I went there in 1976. I met this historian from Armenia and remember him saying, "You know, my brother, my country will never be free. But yours, I hope, will be."

Then sometime later I became good friends with American ambassador Melissa Wells. When younger, she was a synchronized swimmer in the Olympics. Later she became US ambassador (to the UN) in New York. She told me, "Jose, my country will never be free." She was referring to Lithuania, from where she came to the US as a kid, age six. Well, 20 years later, Lithuania was free.

So, the unthinkable happened. Optimism spread to Asia. Before then it was only the Philippines that had freed itself. South Korea was still under the military. And then you had Thailand and all of that.

So, I look at the bigger picture, where we were 50 years ago, 30 years ago, and where we are today. Of course, with the change there are setbacks, developments beyond anyone's control, that are not in our plan and no wise academic analyses foresee. Totally unpredictable.

The Rise of Extremism

This is no 'clash of civilisations', this is a fight within Islam. It has been going on for centuries, accelerating and accentuated because of the ready availability of weapons and communications. And it is no different from the violence that plagued the Christian world for Centuries.

Then you have the rise of extremism and violence. We hear more today about ISIS, and before ISIS, Al-Qaeda. Compared with ISIS, Al-Qaeda are moderate. Even bin Laden was shocked with the extremism of Zarqawi, the guy who was operating in Iraq. Look at the number of people killed through this violence – millions more Muslims of different interpretations of Islam died in the last many years than Europeans or Americans or any people of other ethnicity or religion.

What does it all mean? My argument against some, Huntington[73] and others: this is no "clash of civilizations." This is a fight within Islam that has been going on for centuries, accelerating and accentuated because of the ready availability of weapons and communications. This has been in existence since early times, and is no different from the violence that plagued the Christian world for centuries. And where will this end? Well, there is no cut-off date that it will end in such-and-such time. Unfortunately many people will die.

Three or four years ago in Geneva, I was giving a speech together with the former President of Finland, Martti Ahtisaari. We had several hundred people there in the Palais des Nations and someone asked me about Syria. I could have given one of those cliché diplomatic answers, but I told the audience, "I am sorry, I am not going to give you a politically correct answer, a promising, hopeful answer. The war in Syria will go on for a long, long time. Do not forget the Iraq war, initiated by Saddam Hussein when he invaded Iran. It went on for eight years. Chemical and biological weapons were used. More than a million people died on the two sides, primarily on the Iranian side. Kurds were gassed. The war ended only when the two sides, exhausted by the war, decided to sit down. But it was easier then because these were two states. As crazy as the leadership may have been, these were organized states. So, when the leaders decided to end the war, it ended.

Shattered Syria

Syria, it is no longer an organized state and has become a huge battlefield where many interests – regional interests, rival interests, extra-regional interests, plus different interpretations of Islam – are at play. On the one hand, you have a portion of the state that is organized, and then you have more than a hundred armed groups. Who are you going to negotiate with? In the middle of it you have some religious and ethnic minorities who are caught up. The conflict will go on for a long time.

Three or four years ago everybody blamed Russia and China.[74] Really? Russia and China are the main problems of Syria? Partly, maybe. But

---

73 US political scientist Samuel Huntington suggested in his book *The Clash of Civilizations?* that, in the future, wars would be fought between cultures instead of countries, and that the most significant threat posed to world peace would be Islamic extremism.
74 Reference to the refusal to support a UN intervention in Syria.

in the end, we in the UN may one day thank Russia and China for not allowing the UN to be involved. In fact, why did China and Russia veto the resolution on Syria? I remember the Security Council meeting on Libya a few years earlier. There was talk about Benghazi, that there would be happening a bloodbath there, the killing of civilians by Libyan Air Force, and the Security Council must authorize a mission to create a no-fly zone to stop the Libyan Air Force from going to Benghazi to bomb the people, as Benghazi was a hotbed of the opposition.

Russia and China naively signed on the resolution. And what did it become? No longer a humanitarian mission but a regime-change mission. They bombed the hell out of Gaddafi. A few weeks earlier Gaddafi had said, "After me, you will see what will happen." We have seen now what happened in Libya.

So, the Russians and Chinese said, "You are not going to use the Security Council again to justify your regime-change policy." And they were the same states' members, the US, France, and the UK, gung-ho on Libya [who] wanted to be gung-ho on Syria. The Russians said no. Are the Russians innocent? I'm not saying that. The Chinese, maybe, are the ones more innocent, as they are not directly involved.

Demography is unstoppable, leadership is needed

There is this Humanity [whose humane ethos] cuts across the world and across religions and cultures and this is what gives me hope – with no illusion that it's going to be simple.

Only a year ago the OSCE, the Organization for Security and Co-operation in Europe, invited me [to speak at their annual conference]. The OSCE is a multilateral body made up of some 60 countries, from the US to Canada to all of Europe, Russia, Ukraine, and all the way to Mongolia. As the keynote speaker in that particular year, they asked me to speak on anything I wanted. As usually the Europeans and Americans are the ones who lecture us, giving us speeches about the challenges in the world, I told them, "For once, let me be the one who talks [to you] about your problems."

One of the things I focused on was the movement of people, refugees and immigration. We have witnessed movements of people for hundreds of years. Some countries that exist today are the direct result of those movements, with incoming people replacing others that were there [who had] arrived hundreds of years ago.

Europeans went to the Americas – North, Central, and South – to Australia and New Zealand, because of religious wars in Europe, because of poverty or forced labor. Now we are witnessing demographic changes similar to those millions of people dislocating from Africa and Asia to Europe, and changing the demographics of Europe. This is inexorable, unstoppable, and in many ways it's natural and not necessarily negative. We will see a more colorful Europe, very multicultural... Or will all become one single culture again? Who knows? In this process will be a lot of changes, upheaval, and prejudice. The responsibility lies with the people of Europe, and with the leaders in Europe, to inspire and guide and show that people can live together, can co-exist.

During the London blaze,[75] Muslim residents rescued many of their neighbors from the tower. I have just heard from friends that in the Philippines, when an ISIS-affiliated group or ISIS sympathizers took over the city of Marawi, Filipino Muslims rescued a lot of Christians trapped in the city's buildings. Two years ago, in Kenya, when scores of people were killed by a large scale Al Shabab's[76] attack to [the Garissa] university, Kenyan Muslims protected and sheltered Christian students.

So, there is this Humanity [whose humane ethos] cuts across the world and across religions and cultures, and this is what gives me hope – with no illusion that it's going to be simple.

Climate challenges

You talked a lot about human migration and integration, and I'm just curious – what is your take on how global climate change and rising sea levels, especially in a coastal island country – how do you perceive that that might impact the future of human migration and conflict in your region?

---

75 Reference to the destruction by an accidental fire of Grenfell Tower, a 24-storey social housing tower in the Borough of Kensington and Chelsea on 14 June 2017, which caused more than 80 deaths among its residents, according to official London Metropolitan Police statements.

76 A Southern Somalia extremist group that also occasionally operates in the neighbouring Northern territory in Kenya. During Al-Shabab's attack in Garissa on 2 April 2015, 148 people were killed and 79 injured, mainly students and university personnel.

JRH: Allow me to make a comment in a most politically incorrect way. In any international conference, everyone from the Third World will blame the West, and if you do this you will have more than 100 countries applauding, the Africans, the Asians, everybody.

Of course, we all know the role the industrialized countries played over more than 100 years, and what they did. But as I have said, we benefited from the development of science, of medicine too. We live much longer thanks to the discoveries by Western scientists and medicine, before and after World War II.

I rather prefer to focus on our own responsibilities. India is a country of 1.2 billion people, even if they were not having this current industrialization -- you know, really desperate to catch up, and of course they have done remarkably well... Still, 1.2 billion people extracting water, sitting on the land, extracting from the land just to feed yourselves, every day. How much water is consumed, and how much water is poisoned or destroyed every day? And in China? Bangladesh? Indonesia? The Philippines? And in my own little country, Timor-Leste?

We are 1.3 million. You travel in my country, and who does the most littering? The young people.

Our government should have banned the import of plastic. I have been urging this for a long time. Hopefully, with a new government, one of their first actions [will be] to stop the import of non-reusable plastics. As we drive on the roadside, we see many of our people sitting with bundles of firewood. They make some easy money: walk a few meters into the bush, nicely cut some trees in pieces, and come to sit on the roadside to sell firewood. So, we are responsible. Even in my little country, we are responsible.

When we were preparing the Copenhagen Convention,[77] Kofi Annan invited me to speak in Geneva [at the Climate Conference][78] and I remember listening to non-Government organizations making bold predictions and commitments, including many from Asia: *We are going to achieve this, we are going to do that.* I recall telling them, "Can you

---

77   The United Nations Framework on Climate Change Convention, which met at Copenhagen from 7 to 18 December 2009.
78   The World Climate Conference-3, held in Geneva, Switzerland, from 31 August to 4 September 2009, focusing on climate information and predictions in preparation for the decision-making process later in the year at Copenhagen.

calm down? Let me tell you: there will be no agreement in Copenhagen. [US President Barack] Obama will not have the mandate from the US Senate." At the time a former rising star on Climate Change, former prime minister of Australia Kevin Rudd, had just been dealt a blow in the Australian Senate [which, in August 2009, rejected newly proposed climate-related carbon trade laws]. I asked, "Where will the money come from for financing on adaptation, mitigation, all of that?"

After the 2008/2009 financial crisis, the countries that traditionally provide the bulk of the Official Development Assistance all but obliterated the ODA with very few exceptions. For over 20 years, the UN had recommended that each OECD country increase their allocation of aid to 0.7 percent of their GDP.[79] That would amass enough money to improve education, water, sanitation, food security, etc., in the Third World. But only very few countries had reached this level after more than 20 years, and almost all of them small ones: Norway, Sweden, Denmark, Finland, and the Netherlands. One great exception has been the UK, the only G7 country which did increase ODA to 0.7 percent, under Prime Minister David Cameron, even in the midst of a financial crisis.

So, in Geneva, I said, "We in developing countries, let's stop always engaging in a blame game. Let's focus on [what we can do in] our own country." What should we be doing in Timor-Leste? A host of things of course, but I remember, as I was the President of my country at the time, I mobilized the President's Office staff from eight to 11 every Friday morning to clean up the beaches in Díli. I told people, "I am not doing this for the tourists. I am doing this for you, for your children, so that we have less malaria, less dengue, less cholera, less diarrhea. So that we spend less money on medications and more money can go to education."

I also mobilized people to plant trees. Thousands were planted, but the resulting success was not that great because, in the end, pigs and goats were the most satisfied with the tree planting initiative.

But [global warming] is a real problem in low-level countries. Kiribati, I understand, is buying or considering buying land in Fiji and elsewhere to eventually transfer their people to. There are over 100,000 inhabitants in Kiribati. Also, the Maldives are looking at such contingency plans.

---

79 Gross domestic product.

The new president of the United States could mean a serious setback [to the international effort to tackle the climate challenge], after decades of negotiations. But, fortunately, the Europeans are united and challenging the US.

Suu Ky: The Best Hope for Myanmar

Myanmar really has to deal with a colonial legacy compounded by 50 years of dictatorship. I also have a particular concern about the Rohingya and understand, the roots, the complexity of it. Still, the Rohingya are one million human beings, regardless where they may have come from. But the reality is also the context of a vast majority of people very resistant to any accommodation or acceptance of the Rohingya. That's the reality you have to deal with.

QUESTION: Your Excellency mentioned that you will be visiting to Myanmar in the next few days' time. What is your purpose of visiting there? That's all I wanted to know.

JRH: I'm not very familiar with the details of the complexities of the problems (in Myanmar). It was great when Suu Kyi was finally released and generated extraordinary expectations, an incredible international honeymoon with Suu Kyi: the lady would be doing miracles.

The miracles have not happened, at least not as liberals and everybody else abroad expected. And she has been under fire.

Obviously, Suu Kyi inherited a situation that has been building up for 40 years. Many of us in Third World countries have some European legacy and, frankly, when heard my African brothers blaming the Europeans, the Berlin Conference, I used to say, "God, the Berlin Conference happened in the 1800s! We are talking about the twenty-first century and still blaming the Berlin Conference." But when you are actually there and you look at the map of Africa, carved up by a bunch of people smoking cigars in Berlin ... you look at The Gambia, an English-speaking little piece of territory squeezed into Senegal surrounded by French-speaking countries. You look at Lesotho, a landlocked kingdom inside the Republic of South Africa. Not landlocked by four or five countries but landlocked in South Africa. I could go on and on. Like the Gulf countries. Anywhere and everywhere, whenever there was oil, the British decided to have an independent kingdom there.

So, Myanmar really has to deal with a colonial legacy compounded by 50 years of dictatorship.

I'm not going to Myanmar on any fact-finding mission. I'm Vice-President of the Asian Peace and Reconciliation Council, made up of many former Presidents, Prime Ministers, and Ministers from the Asia region, and we are going to meet with Suu Kyi and others and try to see whether there is any way we can help.

I also have a particular concern about the Rohingya situation. I understand the roots, the complexity of it. But still, they are one million human beings, regardless of where they may have come from. But the reality is also the context of a vast majority of people very resistant to any accommodation or acceptance of the Rohingya. That's the reality we have to deal with. No one will be able to impose the Rohingya on the rest of the country in the sense of telling the people, "You have to accept them and embrace them."

We have to find ways to educate the people, initiate a process – that will be very long – so that the Rohingya can be welcomed in the end. To simply blame Suu Kyi … just look at [Myanmar's] constitution adopted in 2008 and realize what are her [constitutional powers], who else is in charge, and who has more power. I think she couldn't do much at the moment, even if she had more power. She has to be extraordinarily prudent, as she has been. And for being so, she has been criticized.

Anyone who wants to help Burma, help Myanmar, has to really try to help her. She is the best hope for Myanmar's people and for the country. She is the best hope for the Rohingyas too. And that is a heavy responsibility.

A few years ago, in 2006, we had a political crisis in my own country. We had a breakdown of law and order, but people were traumatized by past violence, when this situation happened. And a great *Los Angeles Times* reporter came to Timor, all the way from LA, and wrote a long feature that said, "Ramos-Horta, the last hope of Timor-Leste." God, when I read that title – it was very sympathetic, but the situation was not like one of lost hope, where I had become "the last hope." That's when I felt a burden: *Do I have this responsibility?*

You can imagine the pressure Suu Kyi is under. Sometimes I wonder who she is with, who advises her, who is loyal to her. Myanmar is a country of 50 million people. My country is a bit over a million and we are not doing a great job. We are doing reasonably well, but I am not in a position to judge. So, we really need to put things into perspective. And that's why I couldn't give you a really great answer. But this was from the heart.

An Exchange
on Torture

Barack Obama and fellow Laureates

27 October 2014

President Barack Obama
The White House
1600 Pennsylvania Avenue NW
Washington, DC 20500

Dear Mr. President,

The open admission by the President of the United States that the country engaged in torture is a first step in the US coming to terms with a grim chapter in its history. The subsequent release of the Senate Select Committee on Intelligence summary report will be an opportunity for the country and the world to see, in at least some detail, the extent to which their government and its representatives authorized, ordered and inflicted torture on their fellow human beings.

We are encouraged by Senator Dianne Feinstein's recognition that "the creation of long-term, clandestine 'black sites' and the use of so-called 'enhanced-interrogation techniques' were terrible mistakes," as well as the Senate Committee's insistence that the report be truthful and not unnecessarily obscure the facts. They are important reminders that the justification of the torture of another human being is not a unanimous opinion in Washington, or among Americans as a whole.

We have reason to feel strongly about torture. Many of us among the Nobel Peace Prize laureates have seen firsthand the effects of the use of torture in our own countries. Some are torture survivors ourselves. Many have also been involved in the process of recovery, of helping to walk our countries and our regions out of the shadows of their own periods of conflict and abuse.

It is with this experience that we stand firmly with those Americans who are asking the US to bring its use of torture into the light of day, and for the United States to take the necessary steps to emerge from this dark period of its history, never to return.

The questions surrounding the use of torture are not as simple as how one should treat a suspected terrorist, or whether the highly dubious claim that torture produces "better" information than standard interrogation can justify its practice. Torture is, and always has been, justified in the minds of those who order it.

But the damage done by inflicting torture on a fellow human being cannot be so simplified. Nor is the harm done one-sided. Yes, the victims experience extreme physical and mental trauma, in some cases even losing their lives. But those inflicting the torture, as well as those ordering it, are nearly irreparably degraded by the practice. As torture continues to haunt the waking hours of its victims long after the conflict has passed, so it will continue to haunt its perpetrators.

When a nation's leaders condone and even order torture, that nation has lost its way. One need only look to the regimes where torture became a systematic practice – from Imperial Japan and Nazi Germany to the French in Algeria, South Vietnam, the Khmer Rouge and others – to see the ultimate fate of a regime so divorced from their own humanity.

The practices of torture, rendition and imprisonment without due process by the United States have even greater ramifications. The United States, born of the concept of the inherent equality of all before the law, has been since its inception a hallmark that would be emulated by countries and entire regions of the world. For more than two centuries, it has been the enlightened ideals of America's founders that changed civilization on Earth for the better, and made the US a giant among nations.

The conduct of the United States in the treatment of prisoners through two World Wars, upholding the tenets of the Geneva Convention while its own soldiers suffered greatly from violations at the hands of its enemies, again set a standard of treatment of prisoners that was emulated by other countries and regions.

These are the Americans we know. And believing that most Americans still share these ideals, these are the Americans we speak to.

In recent decades, by accepting the flagrant use of torture and other violations of international law in the name of combating terrorism, American leaders have eroded the very freedoms and rights that generations of their young gave their

Words of Hope in Troubled Times

lives to defend. They have again set an example that will be followed by others; only now, it is one that will be used to justify the use of torture by regimes around the world, including against American soldiers in foreign lands. In losing their way, they have made us all vulnerable.

From around the world, we will watch in the coming weeks as the release of the Senate findings on the United States torture program brings the country to a crossroads. It remains to be seen whether the United States will turn a blind eye to the effects of its actions on its own people and on the rest of the world, or if it will take the necessary steps to recover the standards on which the country was founded, and to once again adhere to the international conventions it helped to bring into being.

It is our hope that the United States will take the latter path, and we jointly suggest that the steps include:

- *Full disclosure to the American people of the extent and use of torture and rendition by American soldiers, operatives, and contractors, as well as the authorization of torture and rendition by American officials.*

- *Full verification of the closure and dismantling of 'black sites" abroad for the use of torture and interrogation.*

- *Clear planning and implementation for the closure of Guantanamo prison, putting an end to indefinite detention without due process.*

- *Adoption of firm policy and oversight restating and upholding international law relating to conflict, including the Geneva Convention and the UN Convention against Torture, realigning the nation to the ideals and beliefs of their founders – the ideals that made the United States a standard to be emulated.*

Respectfully,
Archbishop Desmond Tutu, South Africa, Nobel Peace Prize laureate, 1984
President José Ramos-Horta, Timor-Leste, Nobel Peace Prize laureate, 1996
Mohammad El Baradei, Egypt, Nobel Peace Prize laureate, 2005
Leymah Gbowee, Liberia, Nobel Peace Prize laureate, 2011
Muhammad Yunus, Bangladesh, Nobel Peace Prize laureate, 2006

Oscar Arias Sanchez, Costa Rica, Nobel Peace Prize laureate, 1987
John Hume, Northern Ireland, Nobel Peace Prize laureate, 1998
F.W. De Klerk, South Africa, Nobel Peace Prize laureate, 1993
Jody Williams, USA, Nobel Peace Prize laureate, 1997
Bishop Carlos X. Belo, Timor-Leste, Nobel Peace Prize laureate, 1996
Betty Williams, Northern Ireland, Nobel Peace Prize laureate, 1976
Adolfo Perez Esquivel, Argentina, Nobel Peace Prize laureate, 1980

The Reply: From President Barack Obama

23 February 2015

Dear Dr. Ramos-Horta

Thank you for sharing your views on the issue of torture. I deeply value the insights you and your fellow Nobel Peace Prize laureates provided in your letter, some of which are derived from harrowing personal experiences. I am sending this response to the other signatories of your letter as well.

This issue is linked to our deepest values as a nation. It is one of the reasons why, from the beginning of my administration, I have made the human treatment of detainees a core requirement of our national security policy. It is also why you have seen my administration recognize instances in which the United States has fallen short of those standards and our own values.

At the foundation of this policy is the bedrock rule that torture and cruel, inhuman, and degrading treatment or punishment are categorically prohibited always and everywhere, violate US and International Law, and offend human dignity. Torture is contrary to the founding documents of our country and to the universal values to which we hold ourselves and the international community.

One of my first acts in office was to sign an executive order ending the Central Intelligence Agency's (CIA) Detention and Interrogation Program. As I directed in that executive order, consistent with the Convention Against Torture and Common Article 3 of the 1949 Geneva Convention, any individual detailed in armed conflict by the United States shall in all circumstances be treated humanely and shall not be subject to torture, cruel treatment, or outrages upon personal dignity (including humiliating and degrading treatment). The order also directed the closure of any detention facilities operated by the CIA and prohibited the operation of any such facilities in the future.

More recently, in our presentation to the committee against torture in November, the US delegation underscored that all US personnel are legally prohibited under international and domestic law from engaging in torture or cruel, inhuman, or degrading treatment or punishment at all times and in all places. Torture and cruel, inhuman, or degrading treatment are categorically prohibited, both in peacetime and during times of armed conflict. The delegation made clear that there are no gaps, either in the legal prohibitions against these acts by US personnel, or in the US commitment to the values enshrined in the convention against torture. Moreover, the United States pledged to continue working with its partners in the international community toward the achievement of the convention's ultimate objective: a world without torture. The United States also articulated a number of changes and clarifications to our interpretation of the convention, including that certain key provisions apply in places outside the United States that the United States Government controls as a governmental authority, and that a time of war does not suspend the operation of the convention, which continues to apply even when a state is engaged in armed conflict.

At the same time, we do not claim to be perfect, and I have been very clear that our response to the attacks of 11 September 2001, although our nation did many things right, some of our actions were contrary to our values. The report of the Senate Select Committee on Intelligence on the CIA's former Detention and Interrogation Program reinforced my view that these harsh methods were not only inconsistent with our values as a nation but did not serve our broader national security interests. I consistently supported the declassification of the executive summary, findings, and conclusions of the committee report, as I firmly believe that public scrutiny, debate, and transparency regarding this program will help ensure these methods will never again be used.

The true test of a society committed to the promotion of universal values and fundamental freedoms is not that it never makes mistakes, but that it takes responsibility for those mistakes and corrects them. US national security agencies now have perhaps the most explicit and robust safeguards against torture and cruelty and requirements to ensure human treatment in the world. We are also pressing ahead with other efforts to ensure our national security policies and practices conform to our values.

One of these efforts, which you raised in your letter, is the closure of the detention facility at Guantanamo Bay, which my administration has been working tirelessly to close. The continued operation of this facility undermines America's standing in the world and weakens our national security. Since I took office, we have transferred over 100 detainees, including 20 in 2014, and we will continue to press ahead with detainee transfers. But we continue to face restrictions imposed by the Congress that impede our ability to close the facility, and I continue to call on the Congress to remove them. Closing the facility is a national imperative, and I will make every effort I can to finish the job so that we can bring that chapter of American history to an end.

The United States can and should be a model for others on these important issues, and I thank you for holding us to the same high standard to which we hold ourselves.

Sincerely,
Barack Obama

Building Peace in East Timor

Words of Hope in Troubled Times

At the National Parliament in Díli Following a Brutal Assassination Attempt

God Wanted Me to Live On

23 April 2008[80]

When I took office, our country was sliding into a civil war, our people profoundly traumatized. Tens of thousands were displaced from their homes, disoriented, broken. In dealing with the complex and volatile situation, I always chose the path of patient dialogue and compassion. I saw all as children of the same God and the same nation.

I return today to this House of Timorese Democracy after the sad and tragic events of 11 February. Without divine intervention and the wisdom and care of the doctors and nurses in Díli and Darwin, I would not be among you today. God wanted me to live on.

This year marks the 40th anniversary of the assassination of Martin Luther King, a man of dialogue and tolerance, Nobel Peace Prize laureate, and generous and inspiring fighter for the emancipation of black Americans and the oppressed the world over. Martin Luther King, Mahatma Gandhi, Olof Palme, John F. Kennedy, Robert F. Kennedy, Patrice Lumumba, Kwame Nkrumah, Amílcar Cabral are some of the twentieth century's great figures who did not survive the killers' bullets. God called them, depriving Humanity of their moral greatness and intellectual, inspiring force. Still, they bequeathed to Humanity great lessons that inspire us to this day. Their legacy is eternal and inspires us day by day.

I survived the two bullets fired at me from less than 20 yards away. I am small compared to the greatness of those martyrs who have always been my inspiration. And I ask why God wanted me to live but deprived

---

80   This message to the National Parliament was personally delivered upon President José Ramos-Horta's returning after being in emergency care in the Royal Darwin Hospital and recovering in the Northern Territory's capital from 11th February to 17th April 2008, following the brutal assassination attempt on his life by two members of a rogue group of army deserters on 11 February 2008.

us of these great men. Only God knows. Shrapnel of the bullets that hit me stopped only a few millimeters from the spinal cord and within inches of my heart and lung. No vital organ was affected. God wanted me to continue to use all my modest abilities to continue my modest work for the sake of our great people and for the sake of Humanity.

An Australian nun friend told me that she and other sisters prayed to God to save me, saying, "God, You do not need him in heaven. We need him on earth." And God heard this request.

On 11 February, I was on the border between life and death. At that moment, I seemed to see and feel a group of men trying to stifle me. Just as Christ asked the Father when He was crucified, "Father, why have You forsaken me," I asked, "May You at least tell me what wrong have I done?" At that moment, I heard a very clear voice, a voice that I will never forget, saying to my executioners, "Let him go; he did no harm to anyone." Shortly afterwards, my executioners disappeared and I felt a sense of lightness, the feeling of still being alive.

I believe it was a voice of command, the voice of God. I was also saved by the *matebians* and *lia nains* that I know throughout Timor-Leste prayed for me and protected me. That is why I am here again, before you, in this sacred Land of ours, among the people who have suffered so much and who have suffered through my suffering.

The prayers, the vigils, the sacred rituals that have the force of thousands of years of tradition, and the welcome reception that was extended to me on 17 April, reflect the greatness of your heart, of your goodness, and the greatness of our people. I did not know I deserved so much, I, who am a sinner. The prayers and all the attentions I have received from people all over the world, large and small, powerful and weak, rich and poor, of all cultures and religions, deeply touch me and teach me to be more humble, patient, and tolerant.

I thank the honorable Members from all the benches who have telephoned me, sent messages, or went to Darwin to convey their support. I congratulate the President of the National Parliament, Fernando La Sama de Araújo, for the serenity and balance with which he assumed his responsibilities as acting President of the Republic.

And I especially thank the Timorese people for their expressions of support and messages, which I continue to receive every day. I thank the entire population for their support and concern for my health and for the future of our sacred land, Timor-Leste. I bow to our poor and humble people who possess almost nothing, but through their generous hearts, give away everything they have.

I would also like to thank the staff of Aspen Medical Clinic in Díli and the Australian military who have given their blood to help stabilize my health in the first hours after I was injured. The intervention of the doctors and other specialists at the Aspen Medical Clinic was crucial for me to reach Darwin alive and to be here today speaking before this National Parliament.

I also thank the professionals at the Royal Darwin Hospital for the dedication with which they treated me. I was treated with special attention and care by everyone in that hospital, from the cleaning staff to the team of nurses and doctors who operated on me, headed by Professor Phil Carson. I can't but thank the agents of the Australian Federal Police and the Northern Territory Police who accompanied my stay in Darwin. To the Australian government and people, my eternal recognition. Prime Minister Kevin Rudd as well as the entire Australian people have shown true friendship and solidarity, not only to me but also to all the Timorese people.

To my family, my suffering mother, my son, siblings, uncles, nephews, cousins in Timor-Leste, Australia, and Portugal, who cried, suffered, and watched over me, spending nights at my bedside, always attentive to my calls, I am eternally grateful.

I now turn to the question of Mr Alfredo Reinado and the so-called "petitioners." My commitment to finding a peaceful solution to the case of Mr Alfredo Reinado is well known by all. Unfortunately, their response to all efforts for dialogue and peace was the one you also know. Over the course of a year and a half, I have explored all possible ways to resolve these two issues through dialogue, never hesitating in reaching as far as I could to listen to Mr Alfredo Reinado and Mr Gastão Salsinha.

On 11 February, I had no meeting with Mr Alfredo Reinado. I did not schedule any meetings with Mr Alfredo Reinado at my residence. The meetings we had were always out of Díli and were never secret. Over almost two years of efforts to solve this case, as in many others cases, I have always opted for transparency, always informed my leadership colleagues. Whenever meetings were held, my leadership colleagues were always briefed by me, including former Prime Minister Mari Alkatiri and the High-Level Forum. I would not have scheduled a meeting at my house without having consulted and informed the President of the National Parliament and the Prime Minister.

On 11 February, I left home at 6 a.m. and jogged to the Christ-King, at a fast pace, in my usual morning exercise. I was accompanied by two members of the F-FDTL. On the way back, around 6:50, I heard shots. I continued my exercise and about five minutes later I heard a second burst of gunfire. At that point, I noticed that the shots came from the area of my residence. I kept walking and came across an acquaintance who told me there were ISF exercises in the area of my house. I was puzzled that I did not know about such exercises of which I should have been informed. I continued towards my house and saw at some distance before me an F-FDTL car lying in a ditch, not far from the main gate of the house. There was no one visible, let alone ISF members. I felt worried about the safety of the children and other people in my house and hurried on.

But then one of the F-FDTL members who accompanied me alerted me to the presence of an armed man a dozen meters away, near the residence's main gate. I could see this man clearly; he was in a military uniform, which I knew was from the group of Mr Alfredo Reinado. He pointed his gun at me. I turned around with the intention of running away, but then he fired, hitting me on the back, on the right side. I hit the road and the two F-FDTL troops rushed over to me, trying to come to my aid.

On my way home, before I was hit, I called General Taur Matan Ruak to inform him that there was gunfire in the area of my residence. General Taur immediately mobilized men under his command to close the exits of Díli from the side of Hera and Fatuahi and went to Campo Fénix to ask for help from the ISF commander. From there he went to the GNR Command and was somewhat reassured when he realized that the GNR was already acting. After I was injured, I asked the military men that accompanied me to take my phone out of my pocket and I called my own Chief of Staff, whom I asked to inform UNPOL and the ISF that I had been hit.

Showing their complete lack of respect for the Head of State, Mr Alfredo Reinado and his group forced themselves into my residence, disarmed elements of the personal security of the President of the Republic, and illegally appropriated more weapons. This is not the behavior from anyone who comes for dialogue. The F-FDTL member who hit Mr Reinado and his bodyguard fulfilled his duty in the face of a criminal act severely punishable in any country in the world. One of the assailants waited for my return and fired, coldly, without warning, against me. This was an extremely serious act – the deliberate assault on an unarmed person and democratically elected head of state.

I calmly await the result of the investigation that is underway and reiterate my confidence in the Attorney General. For the progress that has been already achieved I congratulate him and his entire team who enjoy the excellent support of the Australian Federal Police, the POLRI, and of FBI agents. The POLRI, acting under the authority of the President of the Republic of Indonesia, has already apprehended three accomplices of Mr Reinado who illegally entered Indonesia shortly after the criminal attack of 11 February.

Incidentally, Mr Gastão Salsinha, by becoming an accomplice of Mr Alfredo Reinado, lost all legitimacy or reason to make demands and address the Head of State. Mr Salsinha must surrender immediately, surrender all weapons, and face justice. The operation of the Joint Command must continue, with a view to recovering all weapons and detaining all the armed elements that act in complicity with Mr Salsinha. This man does not represent the petitioners who chose to register, and does not deserve the title of Lieutenant of the Armed Forces. His behavior is improper of a military officer. He who wears a uniform knows that he has a high responsibility. In the case of a military officer he has the high responsibility to protect the good name of the institution to which he belongs, the integrity of the State institutions and the organs of national sovereignty.

For almost two years, not only when I was the Foreign Minister but also later, as Prime Minister, and now as President of the Republic, I provided Mr Gastão Salsinha with many opportunities to lay down his weapons. I have always appealed with insistence to him and the so-called "petitioners" to never resort to violence. In July 2007, with the intermediation of the former [Parliament] Member Leandro Isaac and the Attorney General, I met with Amaro da Costa Susar and Felisberto Garcia Pinto in Alas, having had a dialogue with both. They handed over a gun and promised they would give themselves up with more weapons a few days later. Mr Susar changed his mind and joined Mr Reinado again.

Mr Garcia showed greater maturity and seriousness and came to Díli, presenting himself to the PNTL Command and then to the Presidency of the Republic, with a weapon. As a manifestation of good faith and trust, I immediately integrated Mr Garcia into my personal security team.

The Commission of Notables, created in April 2006 by the then Prime Minister Dr Mari Alkatiri, was composed of Timorese personalities representing the government, the National Parliament, and civil society, as the "petitioners" requested. I, myself, listened to Mr Gastão Salsinha's[81] opinion at a meeting held at my residence on 27 April 2006. He was pleased with the names mentioned. However, after the formation of the Commission, Mr Gastão Salsinha not only did not want to cooperate himself but also directed his men not to cooperate, revealing bad faith.

During my brief term as Prime Minister I had several meetings with General Taur Matan Ruak and all senior officials to find a fair and dignified solution to the "petitioners" issue. I have always said that it would not be possible to modernize our Armed Forces and implement the model recommended in the 20/20 program for the Forces without having resolved the question of the petitioners. General Taur Matan Ruak and the senior officers of his staff who have fought for 24 years – thanks to whom we are now a free and independent country – and who have survived, thanks to the support of the small and poor people, are men of golden hearts.

When we face a conflict or situations where the parties are not in agreement, we seek to resolve the conflict through dialogue, and this process of dialogue can only produce a positive outcome for all parties if each is acting in good faith and ready to put national interests above all else. The military leadership endorsed my proposal, which the current AMP[82] executive is carrying out.

My proposal is summarized as follows:

1. There will be no block readmission of all "petitioners."
2. There will be a new recruitment process based on the Mandatory Military Service Act that the Second Constitutional Government

---

81 Allusion to one self-styled leader of a rebel breakaway group expelled from Timor-Leste's military during the 2006-08 political and security crisis with which the address deals at length.

82 The Portuguese acronym AMP (from *Aliança para a Maioria Parlamentar*, or Alliance for a Parliamentary Majority) refers to the multiparty coalition supporting Timor-Leste's 4th Constitutional Government (2007-2012).

sent to the National Parliament and which was approved and promulgated in 2006.

3. "Petitioners" wishing to return to the F-FDTL ranks will have to submit to a new recruitment procedure, with no guarantee that the applicant will be admitted.

4. "Petitioners" who prefer to opt for civilian life are eligible to receive a monetary incentive equivalent to three years of their salary.

I heard Mr Gastão Salsinha's opinion on my proposal on two occasions, through Mr Augusto Júnior of the MUNJ. According to Mr Júnior, Mr Salsinha was, in fact, very enthusiastic about my proposal. Although Mr Alfredo Reinado was not part of the "petitioners" group, according to Mr Júnior he also agreed with my proposal.

However, when I met with Mr Alfredo Reinado and Mr Gastão Salsinha in Maubisse, in early January of this year, they both denied ever agreeing to the proposal.

I would like to remind the Members [of this Parliament] and all the people that at the beginning of the crisis in April–May 2006, Mr Alfredo Reinado told me and the Press that he was not a "petitioner" and that his case was different – separate. Only Major Tara has allied himself with the petitioners, defending his interests. Mr Reinado began to change his position in late 2006, self-proclaiming himself the leader of the petitioners.

Why did he change position? He changed because he was advised by his many Timorese and non-East Timorese advisers who told him that by seizing the petitioners' cause, he would have more bargaining power with the Government and the F-FDTL. I had several meetings with Mr Alfredo Reinado and Mr Gastão Salsinha in 2006 and 2007. I noticed that lately they had more resources, evidence that Timorese and non-Timorese elements supported them with the acquisition of new uniforms, communication devices, mobile phones, cars, fuel, etc. Certain Timorese and international press agencies ran to the feet of Mr Reinado and inflated his ego. They made him a "hero." There were East Timorese NGOs and individuals who fed Mr Reinado's ego, instead of contributing to a peaceful solution, and made him become increasingly irrational and arrogant.

I do regret the death of Mr Alfredo Reinado, just as I regret the death of any human being, and even an animal when that animal is killed for no reason or apparent reason. We do not kill an animal for pleasure. We kill to feed ourselves, as animals seek food and sometimes use their brute force. Too many East Timorese lives were mowed down by violence over more than three decades.

In the penultimate meeting I had alone with Mr Reinado, in the Ermera region, I said the following words to my brother. I repeat my words because they were words well thought out and felt by me:

"Alfredo, what is your cause after all? I can understand that someone – you – take up arms when you face a tyranny that oppresses the people and does not want dialogue. I am the Head of State of a free, democratic country. I'm right here in front of you. Come down with me to Díli, go back to your institution, we'll talk to your F-FDTL comrades in arms. Alfredo, how long are you staying in the mountains? Who are you fighting against? Am I your enemy? You have a wife and children. Go back to your family. Take care of them. You like guns, but any day you die with them. He who plays with the fire can hurt himself."

Mr Alfredo Reinado answered, worked up: "I am not afraid of dying ... I do not think of my family. I think of the people." To this rhetoric I replied: "That's false – it's demagoguery. If you say you do not think about your family, then you have no feelings towards anyone. Those who do not think about their spouses and children, parents and siblings, cannot have feelings for others."

On 11 February, Alfredo Reinado died a death without glory; he did not die the death of a hero, a martyr. He died the death without a cause; he died for the weapons of which he was very proud.

As everyone knows, I was criticized for defending and ordering the non-use of force to make the arrest warrant prevail over Mr Reinado. My decision was not unilateral. It was widely discussed at the High-Level Forum and supported as a State decision to be followed by international forces. This was a wise, sensible decision.

In 2007, when the use of force was chosen as a means of law enforcing, five people lost their lives and the fugitive escaped. Abandoning the dialogue once again to make use of force contradicts the spirit and the letter of our Constitution where, in letter and spirit, the primacy of life and the non-use of force are enshrined as opposed to the use of violence as means to solve eminently political cases.

Even the worst criminal escaping from justice deserves to have his sacred right to life respected. This is the reason, the only reason, why I, as Head of State, opted for a process of dialogue with Alfredo Reinado and Gastão Salsinha to prevent further bloodshed and loss of life in a society that has seen too much blood gushing and lives lost to violence.

I am not a utopian pacifist. I am a realistic and pragmatic pacifist who believes in the way of dialogue, but I do not blindly believe in dialogue when it is known that the other side wants to impose itself through arms.

After decades of violence, independent Timor-Leste wants to open a new page in the history of national construction, in our economic development, and in improving the living conditions of the small people, a new page that represents a better life for the children, the women, and the men of our land who put their hope in the fruits of independence. We must all lead by example. That is why I call on the government, in a permanent dialogue, to involve the most voted party in building consensus and solutions to the challenges facing the country: the case of the petitioners, the displaced, the reform of the Public Administration – particularly in the areas of Justice, Defense, and Security, and decentralized administration.

Displaced people should be encouraged to quickly return to their communities, as the current security situation allows them to face the future with renewed confidence. We will renew the dialogue within the neighborhoods to the effect that the reinsertion of the IDPs [internally displaced persons] proceeds in the most dignified and peaceful way possible. This problem is closely intertwined with the issue of land, property, and housing, and the opportunities for each resident to feel he is not abandoned and forgotten by the leaders. The State has the financial means to ensure that, in the medium term, every single Timorese family who, today, lives in precarious conditions can have a simple but dignified home.

The challenges we face include major national causes. To remain divided, each in his trench, warring, would do nothing to help overcome the crisis. We must be able to generate solutions for political and institutional inclusion.

Before 11 February, starting with a proposal presented by FRETILIN, we initiated dialogue with a view to creating mechanisms for inclusion and participation. I want to deepen this dialogue, which is of structural importance for our future, to enhance the role of the representative political forces in the democratic system. There is already some legal basis to this effect that needs to be developed. The Law 07/2007 provides for the creation of Offices for former holders of Organs of Sovereignty. At this stage, our country needs all skills and competencies to be harnessed and valued for the development of our common national goals – such as the consolidation of the democratic rule of law and the eradication of poverty.

I therefore urge all former holders of high office to participate in the national effort to consolidate the state institutions and the democratic system. I especially call on our ex-Prime Minister, Dr Mari Alkatiri, friend and companion of so many years, to contribute by making his office as ex-high official an office supporting the tasks of political, economic, social, and institutional development. Such an objective probably requires more resources than those provided for in the existing legislation. But if this idea is accepted, the former Prime Minister can put forward clear proposals on the needs of a cabinet of this nature. I am committed to contribute to the effect that the Government and Parliament take legislative action welcoming such proposals.

As Head of State, I will soon invite former heads of Organs of Sovereignty to represent me in missions of national interest outside the country which have their acceptance. They will thus be able to make a renewed contribution to the satisfaction of national goals and to the visibility and affirmation of the image of an independent and united Timor-Leste. It is important to use the experience and knowledge of all Timorese at the service of common national goals.

I am interested in resuming and developing the dialogues begun at my residence between the Government, represented by the Prime Minister; the AMP, represented by the President of the National Parliament; and all the opposition parties – FRETILIN; the National Unity of Timorese Resistance (UNDERTIM); Association of Timorese Heroes (KOTA) party, and the People's Party of Timor (PPT). The two rounds of dialogue that have taken place so far proceeded in a positive atmosphere and I congratulate everyone for the mature and constructive ways of the dialogue. Conditions can develop to reach an understanding between the AMP Government and the other political forces that sit in this National Parliament, including the most voted party, and without neglecting the other parties represented here.

Despite differences, which are natural in politics, I believe that the national leadership's first and foremost common concern is the construction of peace and development in our country.

Brothers in the Timorese political leadership, we must never forget – indeed must always keep in our minds – the mistakes and the lessons of the past. In 1975, there were interferences and manipulations from abroad in the internal situation of our country. Some of us fell into the trap prepared against us by outside interests and entangled ourselves in the first civil war in the history of this country. In 2006, extraneous elements fostered the division between the PNTL and the F-FDTL. Immediately following the assassination attempt against me and the Prime Minister, there were mutual accusations among Timorese leaders, without pausing to consider whether once again elements foreign to this country would be implicated in these heinous crimes.

The ongoing investigation, led by the Attorney General, Dr Longuinhos Monteiro, and supported by the Australian Federal Police, is revealing data confirming that there were elements foreign to our country involved, for at least a year, in supplying Mr Alfredo Reinado with financial means, communications equipment, and uniforms. Soon after the attacks against me and the Prime Minister, some Timorese elements of Australian nationality fled to Australia. Other Timorese implicated in the crimes of 11 February fled to Indonesia.

I want to express here my sincere appreciation to the President of the Republic of Indonesia, Susilo Bambang Yudhoyono, who warned me about the involvement of certain elements and ordered immediately that the Indonesian Police support our investigation.

High-ranking members of the Indonesian Police have been in Díli and are giving their full support to the Attorney General. Indonesia is a country of almost 250 million people and it is almost impossible for border authorities to control the movement of every single person circulating in and out the country.

In 2007 Mr Alfredo Reinado used false documents to enter the Indonesian territory and was interviewed in Jakarta by Metro TV. On the eve of the attacks against me and the Prime Minister, dozens of telephone calls were made by Mr Reinado and Mr Salsinha to Indonesia and Australia. I have full confidence in the Indonesian State, and, in particular, in President Susilo Bambang Yudhoyono, and I have full confidence in the Australian leaders, and, in particular, in Prime Minister Kevin Rudd.

As Timor-Leste, since independence, has never allowed elements hostile to Indonesia to use our territory to destabilize our neighboring country, we also believe that Indonesia will not allow any elements, whether they are East Timorese or non-East Timorese, to use Indonesian territory – taking advantage of the freedom and openness in Indonesia – to foment instability in our country.

I would like, yet once more, to point out the exemplary conduct of the Joint Command's staff at all levels, who were able to induce the surrender of 26 elements and the handover of their weapons almost without a shot being fired. To General Taur Matan Ruak, and through him to all the senior officers and staff of the Forces, a word of congratulations from the Supreme Commander of the Armed Forces. For the PNTL, through its interim commander Afonso de Jesus, also a word of congratulations to all police officers. I appeal to both forces so that misunderstandings and deceptive divisions can no longer take place between them. The F-FDTL and the PNTL are national forces that have the duty to defend the homeland and all the people. They shall not fall into traps of those who want to divide them to destabilize our nation. The State will invest in the best preparation of the forces. F-FDTL and PNTL will have more training and better material resources to carry out their duties with dignity and professionalism.

To the petitioners, as well as to those members of Mr Alfredo Reinado's group who surrendered, I guarantee that they won't be persecuted or discriminated against. They will be treated with all respect, concerning both their personal dignity and physical integrity in accordance with the law and as guaranteed by our Constitution. I know that the overwhelming majority of the petitioners were manipulated into leaving the Armed Forces.

As Head of State and Supreme Commander of the Armed Forces, I also wish to reiterate, before the dignified National Parliament, and before the people of Timor-Leste, that the late Mr Alfredo Reinado and Mr Gastão Salsinha deserve my most firm condemnation. The condemnation is all the greater as they, being officers of the Armed Forces, had the duty and obligation before the whole Nation of loyalty, discipline, and obedience to their commanding officers. The duty of an officer of the Armed Forces, as of the police, is one of loyalty to one's country and of respect for the State, which they must protect and defend. A military officer has a duty to contribute to the solution of the institution's problems and to direct the men under his command in pursuit of the objectives of the institution and the country. To promote riots or insurrections against the State and the Armed Forces is unacceptable behavior from military men. The return to the Armed Forces of any of these two elements is unacceptable and could never have my support.

Within five years General Taur Matan Ruak and other great officers of our Forces who came from the armed struggle will undergo the reform they deserve. The state is indebted to them for more than 30 years of patriotism, dedication, and self-denial. They gave everything to the people and to the Motherland, and our free, democratic State must do everything to honor them and recognize their right to take a rest and retire.

But I ask: Who will replace them? Officers like Mr Reinado and Salsinha? My answer is a categorical NO, because they betrayed both the institution and their comrades in arms.

They who, despite all the failings and shortcomings that may afflict the Armed Forces, have remained faithful to this institution born out of the blood of our people and of so many of people's heroes, those are the ones meeting one of the requirements to replace those who retire due to their age and decades of sacrifice.

But, on the other hand, I appeal to the Prime Minister and Minister of Defence and Security, the General Chief of Staff of the Forces, and the Police command to deal firmly with the problems of the Armed Forces and the police. The Forces suffer of lack of incentives for their staff, lack of training, lack of infrastructure, logistics, and communications.

The men and women of the two institutions, whom we demand to uphold the law, order, and integrity of the country, must be treated in accordance to what they are asked to do and have the corresponding resources. The country's demands from both institutions are greater than the ones demanded from other State institutions. The Ministry of Defence and the command of the Armed Forces must be firm in addressing the institutional problems that persist, namely those concerning discipline, mismanagement of resources, and misuse of state assets.

Beyond security, Timor-Leste faces other important challenges. The most urgent among them is the consideration of the financial means available to combat poverty.

As a member of the First Constitutional Government, I am proud of the Law of the Petroleum Fund and the mechanism of its functioning. At the time, it was a smart, serious, and transparent solution. But circumstances have changed. Now, the Petroleum Fund now only benefits the United States Treasury, for very low capital returns. At current levels, these returns, coupled with the devaluation of the dollar, which reduced its purchasing power by 50%, have already caused us to lose hundreds of millions of dollars.

The great world financial and food crisis we are going through, with rising prices of fuels and food staples, is affecting millions of people around the world, and in East Timor threatens to exacerbate poverty if nothing is done to change this situation.

The government should start a dialogue with its opposition counterparts to the effect of changing the Law of the Petroleum Fund as consensually as possible. It is advantageous for the country to draw from the resources of knowledge and experience of the opposition leader, Dr Mari Alkatiri, and of other respected former members of the Government, such as Eng. Estanislau da Silva, Dr Ana Pessoa, Dr José Teixeira. They are Timorese patriots with deep knowledge of the petroleum dossier and also feel the pain of the poor.

The reform of the Petroleum Fund is indispensable in order to equip our state to face its greater priorities: fighting poverty and promoting a sustainable development process with job creation for our young people. The fight against poverty and the strengthening of national and social cohesion are two sides of the same duty of the Timorese State – to promote the development of our society and to consolidate our institutions.

In conclusion, I would like to throw a challenge to all political forces for dialogue and understanding. I am convinced that it is possible to build peace around the country's most important priorities and cultivate an atmosphere of political understanding intent on chasing poverty away from us. Believing in ourselves, in the best that each one has within us, is the real challenge.

To celebrate faith and renew the hope in the Timorese, the Presidency of the Republic will decree on May 20 a broad pardon benefiting all those sentenced to prison terms who have good prison behavior.

Rogério Lobato[83] will be one among the more than 80 beneficiaries of the presidential pardon. Knowing to forgive is a virtue that we need to cultivate in our hearts, as well as being humble and listening to the feelings of our brothers and sisters. Let us consecrate the day of the Restoration of our National Independence as the Day of Forgiveness and Mercy among the Timorese. The Presidency of the Republic counts on everyone for the reconstruction of Peace and the Development for our beloved homeland Timor-Leste.

I have learned the value of pain and anguish. I have felt the cruel vulnerability of human existence. This experience leads me to share the vulnerability of my people in a humane manner. But events have also confirmed beyond doubt that the state is able to function in a time of crisis. We are not a failed state.

After 11 February, nothing is the same. We have turned a page in the history of Timor-Leste. God did not divide the Red Sea before the Israelites until the water reached their noses. We are at the crossroads where, as God's people, we are called to choose between a hard victory or a simple defeat. In the Bible there is an injunction to choose life instead of death. God said to Moses, "I give you a choice between life and death, blessing and sin; hence choose life."

The prophet Jeremiah reminds us that God's will is for "good deeds, righteousness and steadfastness on earth," Jeremiah 9:24. And the prophet Isaiah said: "Learn to do good, defend justice, help the oppressed, protect the rights of the orphans, defend the cause of the widows," Isaiah 1:17.

We have our land owing to the sacrifice of many who gave their lives, and many others who are still scarred today by the war and torture. We have a land that is ours to love and protect by the grace of God. We have a place on the world stage as the first State created in this millennium. We have a country built on the high principles of Human Rights and international law. But we were on the verge of destroying it, due to the

---

83 Rogério Lobato was Minister whose brief included the National Police in 2006 at the flare-up of the crisis. He was later tried and convicted by a Timorese court of authorizing the unlawful issuing of some firearms to civilians.

attacks of 11 February against not only two important institutions of the Nation but also against the people who struggle day by day to free themselves out of the poverty, lacking in food, weakened, unemployed.

We have recovered the promised land of the Maubere people through a liberation struggle that cost the lives of many brothers. But since then, we lost our way through violence that has cost the lives of many who had survived the atrocities of occupation. We, who have been chosen by the people to build a democratic nation with respect to Human Dignity and Human Rights, are concerned about the power of the parties rather than the power of the people. If we today revisit our ideals, the ideals that inspired our struggle for independence and freedom, we are again called upon to resist destructive forces. To earn the freedom that became ours with the birth of this nation, we must, every day, resist the internal powers that destroy or devalue the great victory.

We must engage and resist any tendency: to abuse power; to devalue instead of building; for corruption at high levels; to a culture of violence; to attempts to place the interests of the parties above the common values of the people and the Nation; to the culture of impunity that forgets the victims' need for truth and justice; to a spirit of pessimism or even cynicism; to accept the status quo instead of striving for higher values, such as reconciliation and peace. We must resist the defeatist spirit.

May God the Almighty and Kind-hearted bless us.

Timor-Leste has Rebounded Stronger from a Period of Instability

Díli, 12 June 2011

Timor-Leste in recent years has been remarkably free of tension, without ethnic or religious conflicts, organized crime, or armed insurgency. The UNDP Human Development Index shows we moved ahead of countries in our region and beyond.

Since the restoration of independence nine years ago, Timor-Leste has made a long way towards stability, development, peace, and the welfare of our people.

Occasional episodes of instability, though serious as they certainly were, obscured, at times unfairly, our achievements, which, I dare to say, are very significant, and probably unique in such a short time in a post-conflict society.

Key economic indicators and development benchmarks reflect the progress our society and our young institutions have made – a very long way, in a short time, from the smoldering ruins of a decade ago.

Social and economic achievements

According to the just-released UNDP Human Development Report 2011, Timor-Leste's Human Development Index value for 2010 is 0.502, placing our country in the medium human development category. In 2005, Timor-Leste's Human Development Index value was 0.428, and, at independence, was 0.375.

We have moved ahead of countries of our region like Cambodia, the People's Democratic Republic of Lao, and Myanmar, and are just behind

Vietnam in the overall measure of human development. Timor-Leste, with a ranking of 120 out of 169 countries, is above Lao PDR (122), Cambodia (124), Myanmar (132).

Timor-Leste also ranks higher than Papua New Guinea (137) and most Sub-Saharan African countries, notably Kenya (128), Nigeria (142), Angola (146), and Mozambique (165).

From 2005 to 2010, life expectancy at birth in Timor-Leste increased by more than two years and now averages 62.1 years. GNP per capita increased 228% during the same period to more than US$5000. Average annual growth has exceeded 10% for the last four years and real non-oil GDP growth remains strong as we speak, despite bad weather that prevented higher growth in the agricultural sector. According to forecasts by *The Economist*, Timor-Leste is among the nine fastest-growing economies of the world in 2011.

School enrollment jumped from a modest 63% in 2006 to 90% now for basic education, according to just released results of the 2010 National Census.

Some major population centers are now free of illiteracy, as are whole districts, totaling more than 100,00 people who have graduated from illiteracy to functioning literacy in the last two years. Illiteracy will be eliminated in Timor-Leste by 2015.

Infant mortality and child mortality under five, as well as post-birth mother mortality, have been halved. Incidences of malaria, dengue, and poverty have decreased significantly in the last four years.

According to the WHO, Timor-Leste, with less than one case of leprosy per 10,000 people, is now considered free from this centuries-old disease.

The political situation in Timor-Leste in recent years has been remarkably free of tension. On the security front, unlike the situation prevailing in parts of the Asia region, Timor-Leste does not have ethnic or religious conflicts, organized crime, or armed insurgency. Like many others countries in the early years of independence, Timor-Leste has had to confront political and social tensions, and in some instances, sporadic violence has flared up. However, we have been able to quickly overcome this crisis. As the UNDP Human Development and other indicators show, we have rebounded even stronger from the brief periods of instability.

Transparency and good governance

The London-based Extractive Industries Transparency Initiative (EITI) rates Timor-Leste the best performer in Asia, and third in the world, in terms of accountability and transparency in the management of our petroleum resources.

In the pursuit of good governance and transparency, and to get rid of the worldwide phenomenon of corruption, our National Parliament has passed the Anti-Corruption Law and we since created the Anti-Corruption Commission.

We have also strengthened the offices of the Ombudsman *(Provedor de Justiça e Direitos Humanos)* as well the investigative powers of the Prosecutor-General, whose office has been strengthened with robust investment in organization and training.

Our security institutions are now stronger. With active support from Indonesia, Australia, Malaysia, New Zealand, Portugal, the US, and other parties, we are strengthening the national police (PNTL). Training and organization are enabling PNTL to better prevent, intercept, and fight all forms of organized crime, from sex slavery to peoples smuggling, drug trafficking, and money laundering and, at the same time, preparing it to uphold citizens' rights and promote safer local communities. We are fortunate in that there is no active organized crime in Timor-Leste. But we are aware that we have to do more in this regard to consistently prevent organized crime from gaining a foothold here.

Democracy, human rights

We have a dynamic multiparty democracy with nine parties in the National Parliament. Almost 30% of the elected MPs are women. Several women hold key ministerial portfolios, among them our distinguished host today.

We have ratified all major International Human Rights Treaties and have complied with our reporting obligations. Timor-Leste, according to Reporters Without Borders, has one of the freest media in the region. Our polity stands out with its very liberal and humanist Constitution that prohibits the death penalty.

Challenges

We are proud of our achievements in the brief years since 2002, as much as we are aware of the daunting challenges still to be overcome, because most of our work from institutional fragility towards development still lies ahead.

Poverty has seen significant reduction. According to preliminary estimates by the World Bank the incidence of poverty declined from 49% in 2007 to 41% two years later. But this also means that poverty incidence is still high and remains a major challenge.

At present, Timor-Leste's economy is highly dependent on the oil sector. Efforts are underway to attract direct foreign investment and diversify the national economy.

We know that efforts for economic diversification take a very long time to bear fruit. But we also know that we have to intensify those efforts immediately. This is a top priority of our economic policy.

Meanwhile, even small steps could be a big help. Our country has one of the youngest populations in the world. We need to address the question of youth employment in innovative ways, as conventional economic policies, though important and necessary, will not create enough jobs on their own.

I would like to invite you to reflect with us on what can be done to stimulate youth economic inclusion and employment. How can Government policy help to transform our unskilled young people into, say, self-employed successful entrepreneurs?

I would like to address this question to our civil society and our development partners, because creative answers and resourceful strategies can make a real difference and contribute decisively to poverty alleviation in our country.

The Timorese people have proved resilient and resourceful in improving the livelihoods of families, as shown by the proliferation of commerce stalls and many varied family enterprises, often of minute dimension, which have boomed in recent years, since the stabilization of the security situation.

I am sure that our society and our youth will respond with enthusiasm to clever public policies directed at integrating younger generations in the national economic effort.

To tackle poverty in the long run we need to pay attention now to the health, nutrition, and education of our children and of our mothers. Child nutrition is still deficient in too many households.

Also, health and educational indicators say that we need further investment to improve the availability and quality of health services, and the quality of teaching, and of the physical environment in our schools.

Child and maternal health care outlets have to be available to every woman and every child all over the country, and vaccination rates must increase to meet some of our Development Goals.

We have yet to provide clean water and basic sanitation to every family. These are key priorities of our national Strategic Development Plan that has just been unveiled. The same applies to the goal to sharply improve the quality of education.

In the last few years, we invested heavily in teachers' training and in other measures directed at improving the quality of schooling across the country. This will remain a key priority in the next few years.

I recently proposed that local communities get more involved in the life of their schools, for instance, through involvement of the Catholic Church in management and oversight, as the Church is the largest organization of Timorese civil society and has also a solid experience in the educational sector.

Schools are important social and cultural assets that should be fully exploited by the local communities they serve. Closer involvement of parents should be promoted, as experience in many countries shows that it contributes to enhance educational achievement of children.

Quality of spending and procurement

Major government investment in infrastructure is underway. We are determined to improve the quality of investment and spending. Matching quick implementation of projects with high-quality budget spending is a challenge anywhere in the world, and more so in our country where we have a shortage of technical skills and trained human resources.

But we are confident that we will overcome the challenge of getting "a better bang for our buck," as Americans sometimes say. Steps are being taken regarding organization of procurement and oversight of procedures to ensure better quality, minimize waste, and enhance transparency.

The results we have attained, positive as they are, were only possible with your assistance and your care for Timor-Leste. We are grateful to our friends, bilateral partners, for the assistance, advice, and aid to our development effort, now as in the early years of independence. I recall a time, not so long ago, when your generosity was the main support of our national budget.

I want to mention also the key role of the UNMIT[84] [United Nations Integrated Mission in Timor-Leste], and of the UN in general, which goes back to the very early days of our national struggle, and the UNDP and all other UN agencies that assist us with their highly specialized expertise.

They give invaluable technical contributions to our public security, international crime prevention and monitoring, employment and training, education, justice, statistics, electoral procedures, children's welfare, women's welfare, public health, food security, as in many areas of state building.

I also take this meeting to reiterate our appreciation for the assistance of the World Bank and extend my warm welcome to its new head in Díli. His solid experience of many years' work in developing countries will be a welcome contribution to our current efforts to kick-start a larger private business sector, promote job creation, diversify our economy, and strengthen non-oil sectors.

The support of our friends has been and will continue to be an important asset of our country's endeavor of state building towards development and added prosperity.

But Timor-Leste and other low-income countries that have joined us in the movement known as g7+ also believe that international aid delivery can, and should, be improved and be more directed to support national priorities and local economies in low-income countries.

We do cherish your assistance and the support of international expertise to enhance the implementation of our priorities. I am sure that together we can work ways to increase the effectiveness of aid, cut wasteful over-reliance on highly paid international consultants and

---

84   United Nations Mission in Timor-Leste. Created by the Security Council Resolution 1704 (2006) and later extended in its duration, UNMIT assisted the country's government from 25 August 2006 to 31 December 2012.

Words of Hope in Troubled Times

advisers, while preventing, at the same time, wasteful clashes between national and international sets of divergent priorities whenever they arise.

Let us get to work. I look forward to a productive meeting of minds and priorities. Thank you very much.

At the opening of the Extractive Industries Transparency Initiative Conference

Transparency and Accountability: Pillars of Timor-Leste's Democracy

Díli, 25 August 2011

Transparency and accountability are the hallmarks of democratic government. We see EITI[85] as a cornerstone of our institutional framework to ensure transparency.

Thank you for being here with us today. It is a honor to host such distinguished guests. A special word of welcome for Dr Sri Mulyani. Her keynote address enriched us all. Transparency and accountability are the hallmarks of democratic government and I look forward to the debate and contributions of this conference on Timor-Leste's transparency model. I wish you a pleasant stay.

You come to Timor-Leste at a particularly exciting time and for this, too, I think, this conference is aptly named "Beyond EITI." Just two months ago Prime Minister Xanana Gusmão launched the National Strategic Development Plan 2011–30. Next year, as we celebrate the 10th anniversary of the restoration of our hard-won independence, Timor-Leste will hold scheduled Presidential and Legislative elections, after which the current UN mission in our country will end.

We look forward to developing our economy and improving the welfare of our people in an atmosphere of stability and peace, as we

---

85   The independent, international *Extractive Industries Transparency Initiative* to which Timor-Leste is an early adherent. The EITI Secretariat formally opened in Oslo in September 2007 and Timor-Leste put forward its candidacy during EITI's first board meeting in Accra, Ghana, on 22 February 2008, the same meeting where the rules for EITI's validation method were first approved. The Accra meeting accepted Timor-Leste's membership along with other candidates.

feel that our country has come a long way in a fairly short time, from a post-conflict society emerging from fragility to the demanding tasks of building solid institutions and effective public services.

Thus, it is a reason for celebration that we were granted compliance status by the board of the Extractive Industries Transparency Initiative [EITI] in July last year. At the time, we were only the third country in the world to have been granted that status and we felt particularly pleased for acceding EITI because, for us, transparency matters.

The Democratic Republic of Timor-Leste was born out of the blood and sweat of our people and we honor their sacrifices by being transparent and accountable in the service of the Nation. Transparency and good governance are always a work in progress in any country – and more so in our Nation, emerging from a long, drawn-out conflict.

We are in the process of establishing solid State institutions and financial systems. Despite the well-meaning expectations of some of our friends in countries with well-established public institutions, the truth is that we must walk before we can run. But make no mistake, we can also sprint, as we proudly found out in the Díli Marathon, when our compatriot Ms Juventina Napoleão became the first woman athlete to cross the finishing line.

I am confident that a little creativity and innovation and a fair share of hard work will help us overcome the challenges we face. Concrete steps like the Timor-Leste Transparency Portal or tomorrow's Procurement Portal come to my mind, as they can be considered ultimate tools in the pursuit of transparency.

We see EITI all along as a cornerstone of our institutional framework to ensure transparency. We are committed to proper management and safeguarding of our natural resource wealth. I recall with pride that the work on EITI started with enthusiasm by the previous FRETILIN Government and has continued with excellence and diligence under the current AMP Government, even as the two of them often say they are never in agreement.

But the celebration of EITI compliance is also important because we recognize the principle that the country's natural resource wealth belongs to the Timorese people. Our State and society are united on the principle of transparency of the State's wealth.

Colonized for centuries and occupied for 24 years, we understand the value of ownership, and one does not have to look far to be aware of the powerful role that oil, gas, and other natural resource wealth play in geopolitics. The Government is the steward of our national wealth and sees that it is used for the good of our people. I would say that EITI, whilst covering only the start of the process, has afforded us the best of beginnings.

Finally, the recognition of EITI compliance has been, for us, a cause of celebration, because the use of our natural resources wealth will have a strong bearing on the shaping of the country's future.

Back in 1999, we received a country in ruins, our national infrastructure destroyed, the fabric of our society, as a crafty woven *tais*, was deeply torn. We started rebuilding from the wreckage and rubble, our hearts heavy with sadness as much as quickened by hope.

In 2011, Timor-Leste has continued its development trajectory as highlighted by social and economic indicators. As some of you may have noticed, the recently released UNDP Human Development Report accords Timor-Leste a Human Development Index for 2010 that jumped to the value of 0.502, placing our country in the medium human development category. In 2005, Timor-Leste's Human Development Index was 0.428, and, at independence, was 0.375.

Since 2005, life expectancy at birth in Timor-Leste increased by more than two years and now averages 62.1 years. Average annual growth has exceeded 10% for the last four years and real non-oil GDP growth remains strong as we speak. According to forecasts by *The Economist*, Timor-Leste is among the nine fastest-growing economies of the world as of 2011.

School enrollment jumped from a modest 63% in 2006 to 90% for basic education, according to the 2010 National Census. More than 100,000 adults have also graduated from illiteracy to functioning literacy in the last couple of years. Illiteracy will be eliminated by 2015.

Infant mortality and child mortality under five, as well as post-birth mother mortality, have been halved. Incidences of malaria, dengue, and poverty have decreased significantly in the last four years. With less than one case of leprosy per 10,000 people, Timor-Leste is now considered by the WHO to be free from this centuries-old disease.

As we feel proud of our achievements thus far, we are mindful that we have a long way ahead of us.

Poverty has seen significant reduction, as its prevalence declined from 49% in 2007 to 41% two years later, according to estimates by the World Bank. But this means poverty is still high and remains a major challenge.

Like most of our g7+ colleagues, it is unlikely that we will meet all our Millennium Development Goals [MDGs]. The g7+ is now leading the international community towards a recognition that key Peace-building and State-building goals are necessary conditions to achieve the MDGs.

Our good economic growth figures are still primarily driven by Government spending, and in time this has to give way to solid growth driven by a strong, sustainable private sector.

Timor-Leste's National Development Plan establishes the priorities for major investments required to fully rebuild our infrastructure and develop capabilities and training of our human resources, and in the short term, these investments will have to be funded primarily from the Petroleum Fund. The effective and transparent use of the fund is, thus, critical to continue to move us along the development path.

The granting of compliance status by EITI was an occasion to celebrate within a journey that continues, day by day.

Ladies and Gentlemen: may we also celebrate this particular occasion, the first Asia-Pacific Regional Conference of the EITI. Timor-Leste is committed to being a good regional partner and this first conference in our capital city, Díli, is a symbol of our pursuit of transparency and accountability on the path to improving the welfare of our people and also a token of our willingness to learn from each other's experiences.

I have always been known to be outspoken and especially so on matters concerning the oppressed and the vulnerable. The g7+ group that Timor-Leste is now chairing represents 350 million of the most vulnerable citizens on the globe, living in fragile, conflict-affected states, many of which are resources-rich. The EITI partners – governments, enterprises, civil society non-profit organizations, and international global institutions – all stakeholders engaged in the natural resources industry – we must change the ways we do business, both to ensure the best possible deal for our peoples and a sustainable development that doesn't exclude anyone. We cannot change the past but we can certainly change the future for the better and, inspired by our female marathon winner, Juventina, I suggest that towards our common goals we sprint on our way to a better development path!

A Time of Reckoning: We Must do Much More to Extricate the Poor from the Chains of Extreme Poverty

Díli, 28 November 2011

While we should be pleased and proud of our many achievements, we should also be humble in admitting that the positive data and facts do not reveal the full picture. I have received extremely disturbing reports about mismanagement and lack of integrity in some areas and have raised these concerns with our Prime Minister.

I address you all today with deep emotion as we celebrate the 36th anniversary of our Declaration of Independence. I bow to you all. I bow to the memory of our immortal leader Nicolau Lobato, and all our brothers and sisters who gave their lives in the pursuit of our dream to live as a free people in a free country.

I greet all from north to south, from Ataúro to the southern shores, and from east to west, from Ponta Leste to Oecusse. I greet you all who live in other lands, near and far.

I greet the brothers and sisters, separated from us by past divisions and war, who still live in Atambua, Kupang, and other parts of Indonesia. I know how you long to return to the sacred land of your ancestors.

This might be my last 28th November speech as the second democratically elected President of our young and vibrant democracy.

Our people, exercising their sovereign power to decide who should be their highest magistrates – President, Prime Minister, Deputies – will go to the polling stations in March and June, 2012, to elect (or re-elect) the President and a new Parliament.

After almost 10 years since the restoration of independence, I can say that I feel happy for what we have achieved.

Most economic and social indicators show significant improvements, with extreme poverty declining by 9% since 2007; in the Health and Education sectors, with child, infant, and maternal mortality levels halved since 2007; school enrollment jumped to 90% from 63%, during the same period, and we could possibly achieve 100% school enrollment by 2013. Adult illiteracy is projected to be eliminated by the end of 2015.

Earlier this year the WHO declared Timor-Leste a territory free of leprosy for the first time in many centuries.

We have also successfully tackled one of the biggest challenges we faced in 2002 when assuming self-government: the almost nonexistence of medical doctors and other health professionals in our country.

Nine years later, last week, the first 54 Timorese students of Medicine of UNTL [National University of Timor-Leste] have graduated as fully trained doctors, having done their six-year degree in Timor-Leste.

By 2012, five hundred more Timorese doctors will graduate from UNTL to work in the districts to improve health care for our children and our grandmothers and fathers all over the country.

By 2016 we will have a thousand doctors trained at UNTL, and Timor-Leste will have one of the highest number of doctors per capita in the world, and certainly the highest in Southeast Asia.

These achievements would not have been possible without the generous solidarity of the Cuban people.

Our eternal gratitude goes to our brothers and friends from Cuba, to their leaders and people who have traveled thousands of miles across continents and oceans, reaching our shores, towns, and villages to assist us in this great humanitarian enterprise.

The creation of the UNTL's School of Health Sciences was a wise and courageous decision taken in 2004 by Prime Minister Dr Mari Alkatiri, with full support of President Xanana Gusmão, and it is a good example of the political consensus that is possible around national priorities.

It is also an example of steadiness of State Policy from the First through to the Fourth governments for the betterment of our people's livelihood and the good of our community.

And we all should feel proud for Timor-Leste's new large power plant in Hera. The first phase of this project started electricity production last night. The second phase, in Betano,[86] will be ready in 2012. This energy project, the largest ever in Timor-Leste, will produce electricity for the entire country, for every district, not only for Díli.

That is an important signal we give to the people and to businessmen and investors about our economic potential. Energy is at the heart of a modern economy and the new power plant is indispensable to promote Timor-Leste's development. But it is also a very expensive investment.

To make it successful and sustainable, everybody has to share the burden and pay a fair price for the energy. And it is only fair that people who are more privileged in our community should pay more of the burden.

While we should be pleased and proud of our many achievements, we should also be humble in admitting that these positive data and facts do not reveal the full picture.

For instance, we must ask whether services delivery in our national and referral hospitals is adequate. I must emphatically say that I have received extremely disturbing reports about mismanagement and lack of integrity in some areas. I have raised these concerns with our Prime Minister.

We must ask: what is the real benefit of these achievements for our children and their future when we know that the quality of education and of conditions in schools, like clean water, nutrition, and basic hygiene, are still far too precarious?

We could have achieved much more if we had had greater wisdom in properly addressing social and political tensions in a timely fashion.

We would have prevented the 2006 crisis that wiped out the achievements built up from 2001 to 2005.

We should have been, and must be now, much more aggressive in rooting out waste, mismanagement, and corruption at every level.

Our National Parliament must urgently approve two very important draft laws, the anti-corruption and the anti-money-laundering laws.

---

86 Six years ago, at the time of this Presidential address, Hera was a small village and port in Timor-Leste's North coast on the outskirts of Díli, and Betano a small village on Timor-Leste's South coast. Both have developed since as industrial poles, attracting new private investments.

I am sure that elected MPs want the adoption of strong anti-corruption and anti-money-laundering laws and mechanisms to prevent our country from being destroyed from within by corruption or by unscrupulous criminal elements who wish to use our country for international money laundering.

We failed in some areas; we achieved much in many areas. But our so-called development partners should also accept their share of blame for the failures.

Had they invested, from 2000 on, a much larger part of their aid in much-needed infrastructures like rural roads, electricity, schools, health clinics, agriculture, irrigation, water, and sanitation, 10 years later Timor-Leste would have achieved all the MDGs[87] proclaimed by the UN in that year.

What amazes me is how we all, Timorese and donor community included, are so slow in learning from the accumulated mistakes of past decades, and fail to improve aid and services delivery.

The donor community has not streamlined their own cumbersome, stifling procedures, which swallow up a disproportionate percentage of the aid and is an enormous burden to recipient communities.

Rather than providing direct budget support to enable and strengthen national institutions, they opted (and still opt) to work through various multilateral bodies, each with their own bureaucracies and administrative costs.

The UN system and donor community seem to have a fixation on, and are addicted to, commissioning reports with a two- to three-day drop in field missions, and then proclaim their noble recommendations.

We are overwhelmed with such copy-and-paste studies and recommendations, most of which even a six-year-old could very well do by going to the internet, downloading the reports, and just changing a few names and dates and it is done.

Nevertheless, we must scrutinize our own actions. Recently, the Prime Minister invited our national TV to carry a live broadcast of a Council of Ministers meeting, where Ministers had to explain the failures in their portfolio. This was very salutary, but not enough.

---

87 The Millennium Development Goals set by the United Nations before Timor-Leste's restoration of independence.

However, we should give due weight to what we have accomplished. The overall balance of 10 years of independence is a very positive one.

On the political front, we can be proud of our vibrant parliamentary democracy (though with too many parties) and of the fact that our National Parliament has an impressive representation of women.

I hope women's representation in our Parliament will increase from the current 29% share of the seats to at least 35% in the 2012 legislative election.

We have a free and independent media, with 250 journalists working for four daily newspapers, four weeklies, two monthlies, 30 radios stations, and two TV stations, one public, one private.

There are numerous social media outlets used by groups and individuals engaged in substantive discussion with intellectual rigor, as there are demagogic and defamatory blogs leveling personal attacks on leaders and others.

And yet there was no attempt by the Government to silence its critics. Democracy bestows the right to free speech to all, even to demagogues.

We have a vibrant democracy that derives also from the activity of a multitude of civil society groups, NGOs specializing in all areas that actively scrutinize every aspect of government policies and contribute to a peaceful and just society.

We have one of the most liberal and humanist Constitutions in the world, that prohibits life imprisonment and the death penalty.

Our Constitution enshrines the sanctity of human life and the essential goodness of human beings, as we believe that even the worst individual in the society must be given a chance to redeem and serve the community.

Our humanist Constitution imposes on us the obligation to pursue practical compassionate policies that help alleviate the daily suffering of the poor.

I have always advocated a pro-poor state budget with direct "cash transfers" to the elderly and other vulnerable groups, widows, orphans, the physically and mentally impaired, our veteran heroes, and victims.

And I am happy that our Government and Parliament share in my beliefs and have adopted policies and budgets in support of the least fortunate of our nation.

We must do more, much more, to extricate the poor from the chains of extreme poverty, but to achieve results we must carefully study, plan, and decide on priorities.

We must build better schools equipped with libraries and internet and provide every school and village with clean water and sanitation. We must improve the "one meal a day" for every schoolchild in the country as it is currently much too deficient.

If we are honest and rigorous in our planning and budget spending, we can achieve all of the above in a very short period of time and with much less money.

Maybe the Government should outsource the provision of the "one meal a day" to international NGOs like Care, Oxfam, or UN agencies like UNICEF and WFP.

On the State Budget for 2012, I refrain from commenting in detail as I have not yet received the Budget Law for promulgation. As I have 30 days to study it, I will carefully review it before the possible promulgation. What I can say now is that I am surprised by the very high total budget for 2012, an election year, with the governing coalition having literally less than six months to govern.

Good management of the country's finances requires restraint and great, great prudence.

We are a young country, but all of us still remember the financial crisis in Indonesia and in many ASEAN countries in 1997–98.

For the good of the country and of our people, we have to look at the lessons of the 1997–98 crisis in Asia and also look to the severe financial crisis that is smashing economies in the European Union and the US at present.

When in 2007 I was faced with an election result without a clear governing majority, I made every effort to bridge the divide and proposed different possible options, including a grand coalition that would include FRETILIN, the party with the most votes. I did not succeed in this endeavor, as the animosity prevailing among the parties was too intense.

It was obvious from the 2007 election result that a vast majority of our people wanted a new style of governing and new direction.

Our Constitution, Section 85(d), is clear. It says:

"It is exclusively incumbent upon the President of the Republic (...) to appoint and swear in the Prime Minister designated by the party or alliance of parties with parliamentary majority after consultation with political parties sitting in the National Parliament."

Among my prerogatives as President, one that is very important is the power to interpret and execute Section 85(d).

As President, I study the entire Constitution and do my best to clearly understand the connection between the different articles.

For instance, if Section 74 says that the President of the Republic is:

"The Head of State and the symbol and guarantor of national independence, unity of the State and of the smooth functioning of democratic institution," then I must strive at all times to promote peace and national unity. And if I fail to secure peace and stability I might be endangering our national independence, sovereignty, and territorial integrity, thus failing Section 74 of the Constitution.

In 2001, 208,531 votes supported FRETILIN and gave it a total of 57% of the votes. FRETILIN formed a government on its own as it had an absolute majority in Parliament.

In 2007, FRETILIN received 120,592 votes, significantly down from its clear majority of 2001, and accounting for 29% of total votes and 21 seats in the National Parliament. It did not win an absolute majority. But I could have invited the party leader to form a government if I had been assured that the parties in Parliament would either support or at least allow a FRETILIN-led government program and budget to pass.

The AMP had a combined 225,726 votes, which translated into a majority of 39 seats out of 65. The people elect MPs; they do not elect governments.

A party that aspires to govern must work hard to win an absolute majority. But having not acquired such a desirable majority, it still has a chance to form a "minority government." However, for this to happen it must use all its negotiating skills and political capital (if it has any!) to persuade other parties to support its Program and Budget.

As FRETILIN was not able to persuade other parties to join it in a coalition government or at least to support a FRETILIN minority government's program and budget, I had no choice but to invite Maun Bot[88] Xanana Gusmão to form the Government, as he had secured a broad-based parliamentary coalition representing an electorate of more than 225,000, with 39 seats.

The AMP promised change, a dedicated, hardworking, efficient government. They promised transparency, honesty, integrity, zero tolerance of corruption. Have they delivered on these lofty promises? The people will judge them at the ballot booth in 2012.

I remain convinced that I was faithful to, and consistent with, the relevant provisions of our Constitution and made the best decision, bearing in mind the volatile, complex, and perilous situation prevailing in our country at that time.

Apart from my absolute certainty that I acted in conformity with the Constitution, I also believed that after the 2006 political-security crisis, FRETILIN should cross the desert and reflect upon and re-examine its past policies and actions.

I know that some have learned and matured. Judging from many public diatribes, we all know that others do not seem to have learned much. They seem not to know that ours is a society that, traumatized by past violence, needs soothing words of comfort and healing and repudiates demagogy and confrontation.

We know from our history, and from the history of other countries, that confrontational, demagogic, and hateful speeches by political leaders (and, in some instances, even by religious leaders) have led to violence, as in the Balkans and Rwanda.

When I took office as Prime Minister in July 2006 and as President in May 2007, our country was sliding into a civil war, our people profoundly traumatized. Tens of thousands were displaced from their homes, disoriented, broken.

In late May 2006, as thousands of people began to flee the city, I opened up the gates of my family compound and shared the space with hundreds of men, elderly, women, and children fleeing the violence in our city.

In the following days, weeks, and months, I visited every single troubled neighborhood in our capital city at different times of the day and night. And as I lived and shared in the pain of our people, I was

---

88   *Elder brother.* It is commonly used as a term of deference in Tetum, the Timorese national language.

heartbroken and ashamed that we leaders had failed them. The dream had turned into a nightmare. "How did we arrived at such tragic situation?" I asked myself then. I don't want ever to relive those painful days.

In dealing with the complex and volatile situation I always chose the path of patient dialogue and compassion. I refuse to catalogue our people into good and bad, friend and enemy. I saw all as children of the same God and the same nation.

Some criticized my approach and demanded tougher measures, such as the use of military force. I resisted the demagogic calls for military action.

Even when I was almost mortally wounded, I pardoned those who wanted to kill me. And I have been criticized for being too lenient, and accused of fostering a culture of impunity.

My presidency has been an open one, open to the people, a presidency of the poor and disenfranchised, a presidency of compassion with wisdom.

I have made every effort to be balanced in my relationship with the political forces in our country.

The President must be the enabler of our democratic institutions, assisting in every way possible their smooth function. The President can articulate our community's concerns on waste and corruption, but he is not the Public Prosecutor and Judge.

On occasion, some brothers and sisters in the AMP accuse me of favoring FRETILIN, or of being too close to Dr Mari Alkatiri.

But my FRETILIN brothers and sisters also, on occasion, have accused me of being too close to the AMP, or of turning a blind eye to their perceived or real abuse of power and corruption.

They do not seem to understand that in this still-fragile situation, with latent tensions and wounds, the President must always try to balance the many different interests in the body politic – to be a patient bridge builder!

The past four years have been a period of relative peace and tranquility in our country. We have all contributed, directly or indirectly, to this positive atmosphere of peace and hope.

I have never failed to acknowledge FRETILIN's leadership contribution. Some in the AMP criticize me for giving too much credit to FRETILIN. But I ask my brothers and sisters in the AMP to acknowledge that if they have been able to govern for almost five years in tranquility, they owe it in part at least to the FRETILIN members in heeding their leaders' instructions not to engage in violence.

Some in the AMP believe that they, alone, resolved the problems of the IDPs, the petitioners, etc. I would prefer to say that we all contributed in many different ways.

Our Church and leaders of some minority religious groups and civil society all contributed to peace and the renewed hope among our people.

We must also show appreciation to the international community, the UN and its many agencies operating in our country, and to friendly countries like Australia and New Zealand whose taxpayers have shouldered the burden of five years of the presence of the ISF in our country.

I have just returned from a brief visit to Indonesia on the eve of the 19th ASEAN Summit. I had fruitful conversations with President Susilo Bambang Yudhoyono on our exemplary bilateral relations and on our application to join ASEAN.

I wish to state here how President Susilo Bambang Yudhoyno has been a passionate and eloquent advocate of our firm and rightful desire to achieve early ASEAN membership. And it is very heartening to see how people in Indonesia, from all walks of life, from the people in the streets to the leaders, are unanimous in warmly embracing Timor-Leste and in supporting us in every way they can.

We all know the extreme importance of regional integration and cooperation and how our country's best interests are enhanced through membership in ASEAN.

I am pleased to report that Timor-Leste may join ASEAN in a relatively short period. However, our Government must be much more proactive in adopting and implementing legislation, norms, and mechanisms to meet technical and legislative requirements for ASEAN membership.

We are part of Southeast Asia and our immediate, medium-, and long-term interests impose on us that we adapt to the region as a whole, while preserving our unique national character.

Among our many strengths I cite our cultural diversity and fluency in mastering many languages. Timorese are counted among the most polyglot nations in the world.

We have an exemplary relationship with our closest neighbor with whom we share centuries of history and a period of conflict that was extremely painful to our people. And as we continue to heal the wounds of the past, remembering and honoring our martyrs, we have been able to live on, living the present and building a future without hatred.

I commend our Maun Bot Xanana Gusmão, Francisco Guterres (Lú-Olo) and Mari Alkatiri, for their vision and courage in pursuing the path of reconciliation among our people and with Indonesia from day one of our independence when our leaders received from the then Secretary-General of the United Nations, Kofi Annan, the historical handover of sovereignty.

We wisely resisted pressure by external interests and few local elements demanding the creation of an international tribunal for Timor-Leste.

We knew then, and we know now, that such a policy would not have served the cause of Justice, Human Rights, and Peace. It would have deepened the divisions within our own society and undermined our task in nation-building, state-building, and peace-building.

But we haven't had the courage and compassion to take one step further in closing a chapter of our past. We have failed to pass an Amnesty Law covering the crimes from 1974 to 2006.

I have repeatedly appealed to parliamentary groups to consider an all-encompassing Amnesty Law so that the thousands of our people still in Indonesia may feel safe to return home.

During these meetings convened by me, everybody present expressed agreement on an Amnesty Law. And yet, there has not been a joint effort to table a draft law for discussion.

Once again I appeal to all party leaders and parliamentary groups to consider an Amnesty Law to be effected before May 2012 so that our people who are still on the red list are able to return and join us in the 10th anniversary of the restoration of our independence.

I am not proposing a non-conditional Amnesty Law. We could consider a law that demands from those indicted for past crimes that they accept their culpability, apologize, and do some community service where the crime had occurred. In cases where the crime was extremely serious, they should serve some prison time.

Besides education, health, social justice, extreme poverty, there are some other issues that I feel strongly about.

On the environment, the deforestation of our sacred mountains continues unabated. The Government has done very little in adopting strategies to plant trees and reforest our severely depleted land.

Our own people, including our youth, have shown extreme insensitivity; they have not heeded my numerous appeals to clean up our neighborhoods, towns, and villages.

We can join in the international chorus of criticisms of the industrialized countries, putting all the blame on them for climate change. But we would be more honest if we were to turn this beautiful island of ours into a fauna and flora sanctuary through simple but active reforestation and protection of our endemic plant and animal species, rivers, and corals.

The other area of concern for me is domestic violence. I bow to the grandmothers and mothers and daughters of this country who gave us birth, raised us, feed us, put us to sleep at night, bathe and clothe us, suffer with us when we are feverish with malaria, and who struggle every day to save money to send us to school. And yet our mothers who should be revered and protected from all harm are victimized every day in many homes in this country.

Our country is at peace, our streets are mostly safe, but there is no peace in many homes. Timorese homes, that should be sacred, like a Church, are desecrated by men who mentally and physically abuse our mothers and our sisters.

As President and citizen, I am happy that in a small way I have contributed to restoring peace and security to our cities. But, as President and citizen, I have failed to end domestic violence, and for this I bow and apologize to our mothers and sisters, victims of violence. We should all be ashamed when we read reports about how pervasive domestic violence is in our society.

Throughout my life I have always faced reality, no matter how harsh, in a balanced way. This is also the way I look at our country after almost 10 years of self-government. Yes, we did make mistakes. And, yes, we are still far from our hope of providing a better life for our people. But we are on the right path in building a better country and a better future for our children.

We have done more than many around us thought possible. We have done more than many countries decades after their independence. We are on the right path.

We can be hopeful, we must be persistent and we must be hardworking. All of us have the duty to strive to keep social peace, to secure stability, and to reward honesty. We and our land will succeed.

As ever, since my early years in pre-elementary school in Soibada, today I pray to God, the Almighty and the Merciful, to always bless and protect us from harm and illuminate our path to peace and happiness.

President Ramos-Horta Calls for 'Cleanest, Most Transparent and Peaceful Elections Ever'

Díli, 13 January 2012

Today our capital city is full of life; our people are enjoying the fruits of freedom, living in peace and security. Our economy continues to show fast-paced growth. Our people's lives are clearly improving. Nevertheless, we must redouble efforts to fast-track policies and implement initiatives to further assist the least fortunate and most vulnerable.

I hope you all have had a pleasant and restful holiday season with families and friends and are re-energized for the important challenges in 2012.

This year that is just beginning will be a very eventful one, filled with historical events – two democratic elections, the 10th anniversary of the Restoration of Independence, the 100th anniversary of the Manufahi Revolt led by Dom Boaventura, and the fifth centennial of the arrival on our shores of the first Portuguese adventurers.

I thank you all for accepting my invitation to attend this very special event, the formal announcement of the presidential electoral calendar.

The constitutional provisions governing democratic elections empower the President with the prerogative to set the date of the elections for the Presidency and the National Parliament.

As stipulated by the relevant provisions of the "Mother of All Laws" (Lei Inan), I have carried out extensive consultations with all stakeholders, the Executive Branch, Parliamentary Groups, leaders of political parties, and our two agencies that are entrusted to manage the elections, namely the National Electoral Commission (CNE) and the State Agency for the Administration of the Elections (STAE).

Having concluded all the required consultations, I am able today to announce that the first round of the 2012 Presidential elections will be held on 17 March (Saturday).

Should a second round be deemed necessary, it will be held in the third week of April, 2012.

I received from our National Parliament and immediately signed into law the amendment to the 2012 Presidential and Parliamentary elections' law concerning the electoral exercise by our compatriots residing overseas.[89]

The amendment defers the voting act overseas for after 2012.

This is a wise decision. We do not have yet the required resources to carry out such a complex, delicate, and costly process simultaneously in so many countries.

I am very confident that the CNE and STAE, which in the much more challenging circumstances of 2007 performed in a most transparent and professional manner, will carry out their legally mandated mission in an even more efficient manner in 2012.

I thank our friends in the international community, UNMIT and UNDP, the European Commission, our very generous bilateral friends and partners, for their support for our democratic institutions and this year's democratic exercise.

In 2007 we had extremely valuable support from UNMIT's able security personnel and logistics, namely UNPOL and the Formed Police Units.[90] We also benefited much from ISF's generous and very able support.

The fact that in 2012 we are still counting on all of them to assist us in this sovereign exercise should serve as a humbling reminder that 10 years on we are still not able to stand on our own feet. Hence, we must all redouble efforts to be truly sovereign, independent.

Our National Police, led with zeal and competence by the General Commander, Commissioner Dr Longuinhos Monteiro, and Commissioner Afonso de Jesus, in brotherly partnership with

---

89 Timor-Leste's Law no. 2/2012 of 13 January 2012.
90 UNPOL is the acronym for the United Nations Police Force. Formed Police Units (FPUs) are operational units with country-homogeneous personnel within the UNPOL. In Timor-Leste, the UNPOL included four FPUs staffed by police forces from Portugal, Malaysia, Pakistan, and Bangladesh.

UNPOL, will show, once again, that our people rightly have faith in the police institution.

I am sure that the PNTL, assisted by UNPOL, will discharge its responsibilities with professionalism and integrity.

While the F-FDTL, as clearly stipulated in our Constitution and relevant laws, is not authorized to be involved in law and order matters, nevertheless I believe that, if required, our defense forces, assisted by ISF, may be called upon to provide additional static security and logistic support, particularly in remote areas of our country.

We will continue to welcome international observers as we have in the past. They are all welcome, from any country or institution.

All foreign media are also welcome to visit our country in 2012, to cover the elections and/or other events in our country.

I wish to make a special appeal to our very generous Prime Minister. Like me, Maun Bot Xanana was a journalist and an accomplished photographer, so I know there is a special place in his heart for our media.

In view of the financial difficulties faced by our young media, I hope that our Government and/or friendly donors provide some form of assistance to all our regular media to enable them to more thoroughly cover the historical celebrations and elections. This assistance could range from direct grants to equipment such as laptops, digital cameras, tape recorders, motorbikes, four-wheel-drive pickups, etc.

We are gathering here today in better times! It was only five years ago that our long-suffering people were shaken by a security/political crisis that first emerged within our Armed Forces, and then spilled over to the Police and into our neighborhoods.

Today our city is full of life; our people are enjoying the fruits of freedom, living in peace and security.

The economy continues to show visible signs of growth and our people's lives are clearly improving.

Nevertheless, we must acknowledge, with sorrow and honesty, that the improvements in the lives of the wretched of this Earth are happening far too slowly.

We must renew our commitment to free the poor from the clutches of perennial poverty.

We must redouble efforts to fast-track policies and implement initiatives to assist the least fortunate and most vulnerable in our society.

A year can go by very quickly. So let us not waste time; let's seize on these momentous times of challenges and opportunities to further advance our young democracy and State institutions, consolidate peace, security, and national unity. I wouldn't say all eyes of the world will turn on Timor-Leste in 2012. This would be too presumptuous, as there are many greater countries and challenges around the world requiring international attention and assistance.

But we can anticipate that the eyes of our ASEAN friends and partners will be turned on us. Others in the Asia region and friends from around the world will certainly follow the events here, as they always do, for they care about the well-being of our people.

For the sake of our own people and our national interests, in honor of those who gave their lives for us to live in freedom and peace, let us all pledge once again to actively participate in the democratic elections and contribute towards the cleanest, most transparent, and peaceful elections ever, of which we can all be proud.

Maybe God the Almighty and the Merciful continue to bless us as He always has done over times immemorial.

Elections to be Proud Of

International Herald Tribune, 17 April 2012

The real question is whether Timor-Leste will be able to emerge fully from a past filled with violence and oppression, and whether it will be able to enjoy a peaceful transition of power.

Four weeks ago, the citizens of Timor-Leste, known in many parts of the world as East Timor, went to the polls to elect a president. We were 12 men and women competing for the largely ceremonial but potentially influential office. On Monday, the voters returned to choose between the two top vote getters.

After the first round, political commentators did a simplistic analysis of the elections and how I "lost". They missed the point.

A little over a decade ago, our small island was still occupied by the Indonesian military. Hundreds of thousands of our citizens perished under the occupation, either by execution, lack of the most basic medical care or starvation by forced relocations. With a small rag-tag group of dedicated independence fighters, we faced a massive army equipped and trained by the United States. We were a forgotten people.

When we achieved independence in 1999 through a UN-sponsored referendum, our island was devastated by militia backed by the Indonesian military. Eighty-five percent of our buildings were burned to the ground, and more than 300,000 people were forcibly removed to Indonesia.

In 2006 and 2007, Timor-Leste again exploded into violence, this time in civil conflict. It was the type of upheaval that is not unusual, historically, for a new democracy, but one that caused many to fear that the country was racing towards the edge of a cliff.

I am proud and honored to have served Timor-Leste, first in exile during the occupation and then as Foreign Minister, Prime Minister and President of the world's youngest democracy. I am proud that during my presidency we achieved, for the first time in more than 35 years, a stable peace, which has allowed for new levels of development.

But having served as Prime Minister and President, I hesitated to run again for the presidency this year. At the signed request of more than 100,000 Timorese citizens, I did enter the race. I stated, however, that I would not campaign, as I had too much respect for at least two of the 11 other candidates.

In the few occasions when I did make public statements I reassured the voters about the other two leading candidates, who are indeed national heroes. One, Taur Matan Ruak, was a commander of Timor-Leste's resistance forces during the 24-year occupation and after independence commanded our defense forces. The other, Francisco Guterres, popularly known as Lú-Olo, was also a leader of the resistance and has served as President of Parliament and President of the largest and oldest political party.

I cannot compare myself with them. While we fought the same battle to free our country from occupation during a dark 24 years, we fought in different trenches. I was in the diplomatic trench, one more visible internationally. But this is not to be equated with the daily challenges and dangers of the armed resistance or political underground network, whose losses were in thousands of lives. They have earned the right to lead as much as I.

During the last weeks of the first round of the campaign, I watched a vibrant democracy at work. The capital city, Díli, plastered with posters of smiling candidates, was loud with parades and rallies.

Naturally there were tensions, and fears spread among people traumatized by past violence. But the violence did not happen.

Last week I invited the two candidates for a heart-to-heart talk and pleaded with them to tone down their language, soften their campaign rhetoric, show tolerance and moderation. They agreed. They even appeared together before the media. Tensions were lowered. The political atmosphere has been much calmer since.

Which of our two candidates will win on Monday is the lesser question. The real question is whether Timor-Leste will be able to emerge fully from a past filled with violence and oppression, and whether it will be able to enjoy a peaceful transition of power. In other words, have we learned to take our battles to the polls instead of the streets?

So far the answer is yes. We are halfway through – after the runoff presidential vote, we have parliamentary elections in July. But it appears that our democracy is emerging from the process stronger – still imperfect, but on its feet and functioning.

Timor-Leste is a different country today than it was 10 years ago or even five years ago. Its double-digit growth for four straight years has made it one of the strongest economies in Asia. Unemployment has plummeted, and we are on track for 100% adult literacy by 2015. By the end of 2012 the entire country will have 24-hour electrical power for the first time, and in few years we should have twenty-first century connectivity.

There are still many challenges ahead. Timor-Leste has not yet conquered problems of corruption and waste. The number of people living in extreme poverty is down, but not far enough.

But back in 1999, Díli was devastated. Today it is rebuilt and buzzing with a new generation of young people on cars and motorbikes, all going to work.

I view the fact that our elections are competitive with a sense of contentment. They are a sign that the country is maturing. New candidates are enjoying a well-earned moment in the sun, and a younger generation is coming up behind them. Before long, new, young leaders will emerge, eager and ready to take the reins of the country from the hands of this year's victors. This is the surest sign that our country has closed a very difficult chapter in its history, and that a new chapter has begun.

The violence of the past has been replaced by motorcycle parades and political rallies. None of us who fought for the freedom to hold these elections, who saw so many of our brothers and sisters give their lives for this day, can feel a loss at watching it occur.

It is my hope that we have sent a message to others emerging from conflict that it can be done.

A Farewell and Handover to the New President, Taur Matan Ruak

Díli, 19 May 2012

I have often said, and I repeat again tonight, there is no greater justice than freedom, and in 1999, Indonesia and the international community sanctioned the freedom for which we Timorese fought and died. This greater justice, our freedom and dignity, should prevail over the justice of the victors over the vanquished.

This is my last speech as President of this sacred land of a brave people. But it is not a goodbye speech. I am not going away for another 24 years as when I left our beloved country on 4 December 1975.

I never thought then – neither did you – that it would take almost a quarter of a century for us to regain our land and freedom before I would return home.

We walked the long walk in the wilderness of international indifference and abandonment, we crossed the desert of oppression and fear.

We climbed the mountains, crossed the ravines, valleys, forests, rivers, of this majestic island given to us by the Almighty and legated by our ancestors who first settled here 40,000 years ago.

Ramelau, Matebian, and Kablaki[91] are silent witnesses to all that happened here over hundreds of years, the good and the bad, the beautiful and the ugly.

We rose from the dead, survived our wars, and paid for our sins. But many, too many, are gone forever, human beings killed by human beings, brothers killed by brothers.

---

91 Timor-Leste's three highest mountains, among the highest in Southeast Asia, have deep symbolic meanings in the Timorese culture.

Many of our brave and beloved ones are gone. They are in another world. And in that other world, led by Nicolau Lobato, Francisco Xavier Amaral (Avo Xavi), Vicente Sahe, Mau Lear, Nino Konis Santana, João Carrascalão, they are looking down and after us, caring for our well-being and safety.

God created Man and gave us the ability to adapt and evolve over thousands of years; we mutated from the savages of the caves into intelligent beings possessing ever-increasing knowledge and feelings. Yet human beings have shown to be capable of doing harm with extraordinary savagery to other human beings, animals, and nature.

In this country we are an example of the all too common human frailty and evil.

In 2006 our country was engulfed in anarchy; law and order had dissipated as our police and defense forces imploded.

More than 150,000 people had been displaced. Our people were dispirited, having lost respect and faith in the State and leaders.

The Catholic Church was shelter and savior, providing relative safety to tens of thousands of women and children who fled their homes, shared with them their roof and meager food.

But the last 10 years have not only been years of conflicts. We can be proud of our achievements in many areas, namely in education and health sectors. Today, our country is at peace; our people have renewed hopes, their lives improving.

Among our many achievements, one of great value is the reconciliation among the divided Timorese family. Our Maun Bot Xanana, who led us to freedom when all seemed lost, has led this unique reconciliation process with courage, determination, and compassion. I am proud of being part of a society that has shown a great heart in resisting the temptation to exercise revenge in the name of justice.

In victory be magnanimous; never seek to humiliate the adversary; if he is on his knees, hold his hands and plead with him to rise up, embrace him; walk halfway and meet the vanquished ones, embrace them, invite them to join in a new enterprise of peace, a new future for all. This has been my belief, and in many ways this has been our practice since independence.

I am saddened that we have not passed an Amnesty Law that would have enabled the too many brothers and sisters still abroad to return home. I am also unhappy that we did not follow up on the Truth and Friendship Commission with a law that would have taken off the List of Indicted persons those Timorese and Indonesian citizens accused by the UN Serious Crimes Panel set up in Timor-Leste by the UN Transition Administration in 2000.

I have often said, and I repeat again tonight, there is no greater justice than freedom, and in 1999, Indonesia and the international community sanctioned the freedom for which we fought and died. This greater justice, our freedom and dignity, should prevail over the justice of the victors over the vanquished.

We have built a unique relationship with Indonesia and Portugal, as well as with others who at one time in recent history were on the other side. To our friends, the Presidents of Indonesia and Portugal, Excellencies Dr Susilo Bambang Yudhoyno and Professor Anibal Cavaco Silva, I extend on behalf of all of us our enduring gratitude and friendship.

To all our neighbors and friends from:
- the solidarity movement who were with us in our darkest years
- the Association of Southeast Asian Nations (ASEAN), represented here by His Excellency the President of Indonesia
- Australia, New Zealand, and the Pacific, represented here by the President of Tuvalu and Governors-General of Australia and New Zealand
- Northeast Asia, China, Korea, Japan
- Africa, represented here by the Foreign Minister of South Africa
- Europe, represented here by the President of Portugal and the EU Commissioner for Development
- the US
- Brazil and others from Latin America
- and the United Nations, represented here by the Under-Secretary-General for Peace-Keeping and our sister Ameerah Haq, who soon will be leaving us for even greater missions

To all go our deepest respect and gratitude for being with us for the last 10 years and for being here tonight.

But tonight, as we celebrate this great day in our history, we cannot forget a lost friend, Sérgio Vieira De Mello, killed by extremists in Iraq. Sérgio was here, his fiancée/partner, Carolina Larriera, was here with him, with us, this evening 10 years ago. Under the leadership of Secretary-General Kofi Annan, Sérgio worked with us from the end of 1999 till 19 May 2002 in trying to put together a minimally functioning State. Carolina flew in from Buenos Aires to be here tonight. She survived the Baghdad terrorist bombing in 2003. Here, tonight, I bow to Sérgio's memory and will award him posthumously the Order of Timor-Leste. His loving mother, Dona Gilda De Mello, now over 90 years of age, lives still in Rio, and will receive the award in Sérgio's name.

Last, but not least, Maun Bot President Taur Matan Ruak. You were born in Mount Matebian and lived on the edges of extreme poverty, and between life and death. Your beloved mother died in 1987 and her body and soul still wander in those majestic and magic mountains. Your father was beaten to death in 1997, just a few months before justice and freedom arrived.

Mount Matebian, where tens of thousands of souls are living, gave you the inner strength that sustained you through poverty and war. The same wisdom and strength of our ancestors and heroes will inspire and sustain you in the days and years to come as you guide this nation into the future that begins in a few minutes.

For five years you were my loyal Army General Chief of Staff, standing behind the Supreme Commander in good and bad times.

At the stroke of midnight, as you are sworn in as our duly elected President, I will stand behind you, never too far away – and with God's blessing, your term of office will always be good times, as the bad times should never return to this land and our people's homes. Together with Maun Bot Xanana, Lasama, Cláudio Ximenes, Lú-Olo, Alkatiri, Lere, Lugo, Rogério, Abílio, we will guide our people into greater achievements. To your wife Isabel, your beautiful children, Lola, Quesa, and Tamarisa, sisters and brothers, I say thank you for letting your husband, father, and brother serve the people.

Over the ages, God the Almighty and the Merciful tested our faith and made us endure our own Stations of the Cross. And time and again, at each station and fall, we rose up, stronger and with deeper faith.

God the Almighty and the Merciful will bless us tonight for the years to come, and bless our kind friends who crossed lands, oceans, and heavens to be with us.

Articles &
Press Releases

Democracy's Hero

International Republican Institute

30 July 2012

He is an inspiration to those struggling for democracy worldwide. For his tireless pursuit of self-determination, peace and democratic development, José Ramos-Horta truly is Democracy's Hero.

Few individuals embody the spirit of democracy more than José Ramos-Horta. A founding father of Timor-Leste, Ramos-Horta has selflessly dedicated his life to fighting for freedom and independence for his fellow Timorese and for the cause of human rights worldwide. Throughout Timor-Leste's tumultuous history, from Portuguese colonial rule through Indonesia's brutal occupation and finally a decade of independence marked by internal upheaval, Ramos-Horta has been steadfast in his leadership of Timor-Leste's pursuit of self-determination, peace and democracy.

Ramos-Horta's political involvement began in earnest at the age of 18, when he was exiled from Timor-Leste to Mozambique for criticizing the ruling Portuguese colonial government. When Portugal withdrew from Timor-Leste in 1975, Timor-Leste declared its independence on 28 November. Aged 25 at the time, Ramos-Horta was appointed the Minister of External Affairs and deployed abroad to seek support from the international community. Three days following his departure (and only nine days after the country declared independence), Indonesia invaded Timor-Leste in what became Indonesia's largest-ever military operation.

Ramos-Horta spent the next 24 years in exile, exposing the injustices of the Indonesian occupation and rallying the international community to support Timor-Leste's struggle for freedom. He became the youngest person to address the United Nations Security Council in late 1975 when he successfully convinced the council to pass a resolution demanding

Indonesia's withdrawal from Timor-Leste. Ramos-Horta traveled frequently from one world capital to the next, keeping the plight of Timor-Leste's suffering population on the agenda of international leaders. In 1996, Ramos-Horta was awarded the Nobel Peace Prize with his compatriot Bishop Carlos Filipe Ximenes Belo for "their work towards a just and peaceful solution to the conflict in East Timor."

In 1999, Ramos-Horta returned home for the first time in nearly a quarter century. The devastation caused by the Indonesian military was horrific; the government of Timor-Leste estimates nearly a third of the country's population perished during the Indonesian occupation due to killings and starvation. Three of Ramos-Horta's 11 brothers and sisters were killed by the Indonesian military and a fourth died from a lack of proper medical care. Instead of vengeance, Ramos-Horta adopted a philosophy of nonviolence, stating, "Never, ever surrender to hatred. Never allow yourself to be a hostage of violence."

Indonesia's military withdrew from Timor-Leste in 1999 following a referendum that overwhelmingly favored independence. In the aftermath of the vote, pro-Indonesia militias joined Indonesian soldiers in a retaliatory scorched earth campaign, massacring nearly 1400 people and forcefully displacing as many as 300,000 others.

In the precarious years that followed, Ramos-Horta was a leading figure negotiating Timor-Leste's status with the United Nations, first as a provisional administration and then finally as an internationally recognized independent state. When Timor-Leste officially joined the United Nations in June 2002, Ramos-Horta became the new nation's first Foreign Minister. He added the posts of Defense Minister and Prime Minister to his portfolio in the subsequent six years. When a crisis in 2006 nearly unraveled the political fabric of the nation, Ramos-Horta deftly secured the intervention of a foreign peacekeeping force to stabilize the situation.

In May 2007, Ramos-Horta was elected President of the Republic of Timor-Leste, earning 69% of the vote in a decisive run-off poll. His presidency suffered a shock when an assassin involved in a mutinous plot shot the newly elected President twice in February 2008. Though critically injured, Ramos-Horta made a full recovery and returned to office only months after the attack. Ramos-Horta ran for reelection in March 2012, finishing third in the poll, disqualifying him from the second round run-off. Gracious in defeat, Ramos-Horta demonstrated to both his supporters and opponents that peaceful relinquishment and transfer of power is crucial to democratic advancement.

Ramos-Horta is an inspiration to those struggling for democracy worldwide. For his tireless pursuit of self-determination, peace and democratic development, José Ramos-Horta truly is Democracy's Hero.

Nobel Peace Laureate Joins Honorary Council

Harvard Law School

6 December 2012

The Institute for Global Law and Policy (IGLP) at Harvard Law School recently welcomed Nobel Peace Prize laureate and former President of the Democratic Republic of Timor-Leste José Manuel Ramos-Horta to the IGLP Honorary Council.

As a member of the Honorary Council, Mr Ramos-Horta will advise the IGLP, strengthen its ability to mentor young scholars, and join in discussions with doctoral and graduate students working in the fields of economic development, social justice and global political economy.

Said Harvard Law School Professor and IGLP Faculty Director David Kennedy: "Ramos-Horta's appointment is representative of the Institute's strong commitment to engage leading public officials and policy practitioners thinking about global governance, social justice and economic policy in new ways. His expertise in the areas of diplomacy, democracy, human rights, mediation, and peace initiatives will enhance the Institute's research into the ways in which injustice can be reproduced and what can be done in response. We are honored to have such a prominent and distinguished individual join our Honorary Council."

Ramos-Horta, who served as the President of the Democratic Republic of Timor-Leste from 2007 to 2012, is the country's fourth President since its unilateral proclamation of independence from Portugal in 1975 and the second since its restoration of independence from Indonesia in 2002, after 24 years of occupation from 1975 to 1999. He was also the country's former Prime Minister and a founder and former member of the Revolutionary Front for an independent East Timor. He jointly received the 1996 Nobel Peace Prize with Bishop Ximenes Belo for his efforts to lead Timor-Leste toward freedom.

During his years in exile, Ramos-Horta studied public international law at The Hague Academy of International Law and at Antioch University, where he received an MA in peace studies. He was trained in human rights law at the International Institute of Human Rights in Strasbourg, France, and has received numerous honorary doctorate degrees from universities in Brazil, the United States, Australia, Portugal and Timor-Leste. He is also a founding member of the Asian Peace and Reconciliation Council.

IGLP is a collaborative faculty effort to nurture innovative approaches to global political economy, governance and policy. Founded in 2009, the institute is dedicated to bringing new voices into the discussion of global regulation and policy, recognizing that legal and institutional architectures remain manifestly ill-equipped to address the most urgent global challenges. Its signature initiatives are intensive 10-day workshops for young scholars and policy professionals from around the world that meet each June at Harvard and each January in Doha.

Former Timorese President José Ramos-Horta Appointed UN Envoy to Guinea-Bissau

United Nations Headquarters

2 January 2013

Secretary-General Ban Ki-moon has appointed former Timorese President and Nobel Peace Prize laureate José Ramos-Horta as the new United Nations envoy to Guinea-Bissau.

Mr Ramos-Horta succeeds Joséph Mutaboba of Rwanda as the Secretary-General's Special Representative and Head of the UN Integrated Peacebuilding Office in Guinea-Bissau (UNIOGBIS). Mr Mutaboba completes his assignment at the end of this month.

"The Secretary-General is grateful for his leadership of UNIOGBIS for the past four years, often under difficult political and security conditions, and for his tireless efforts to ensure international attention to the challenges of Guinea-Bissau and for working on practical solutions to address them," said a statement issued by Mr Ban's office.

Mr Ramos-Horta brings with him more than three decades of a diplomatic and political career in the service of peace and stability in Timor-Leste and beyond. Working closely with the UN Transitional Administration in East Timor (UNTAET), he helped to bring about the peaceful elections of the country's Parliament and President in 2001 and 2002, respectively.

As the President of Timor-Leste, most recently from 2007 to 2012, Mr Ramos-Horta contributed to "heal the wounds and stabilize the situation in the country following the crisis in 2006," the statement noted. He has also served as his country's Foreign Minister and as Prime Minister.

UNIOGBIS was established by the Security Council in 2009 and tasked with promoting stability in the West African nation, which has been beset by coups and political instability since it became independent in the early 1970s.

Most recently, rogue soldiers seized power in a military take-over on 12 April 2012 – just days ahead of the presidential run-off election – prompting calls from the international community for the return to civilian rule and the restoration of constitutional order. Recent incidents include an attack on a military base in October, which reportedly resulted in numerous deaths.

Abbreviations and Acronyms

ACP – African, Caribbean, and Pacific states

AMP – aid management platform

AMP– Alliance of Parliament (*Alianca de Maioria Parlamentar*), Timor-Leste

APEC – Asia-Pacific Economic Cooperation

ASEAN – Association of Southeast Asian Nations

CAR – Central African Republic

CBMs – confidence building measures

CEDEAU – (I can find a reference to this online but no mention of what alliance it is or what the letters stand for)

CIA – U.S. Central Intelligence Agency

CNE – National Electoral Commission

CNRM (National Council of Maubere Resistance, or *Conselho Nacional da Resistência Maubere)*

CNRT – National Congress for Timorese Reconstruction (*Congresso Nacional da Reconstrução Timorense*)

CPLP – Community of Portuguese Speaking Countries (Comunidade dos Paises de Lingua Oficial Portuguesa)

DPA – Department of Political Affairs

DPKO – Department of Peacekeeping Operations

ECOSC – Environment and Communities Scrutiny Committee

ECOWAS – Economic Community of Western African States

EITI – Extractive Industries Transparency Initiative

F-FDTL – Timor-Leste Defence Force (*Falintil-Forças de Defesa de Timor Leste*)

FAO – Food and Agriculture Organization (of the United Nations)

FRETILIN – Revolutionary Front for an Independent Timor-Leste (*Frente Revolucionária do Timor-Leste Independente*)

GNR – National Republican Guard (*Guarda Nacional Republicana*)

HDI – Human Development Index

HIPPO – High-Level Independent Panel on UN Peace Operations

ICJ – International Court of Justice

IDP – internally displaced person
IGLP – Institute for Global Law and Policy, Harvard University
IMF – International Monetary Fund
ISF – International Stabilisation Force
ISS – Institute for Security Studies
KOTA – Association of Timorese Heroes (Klibur Oan Timor Asuwain)
LNG – liquefied natural gas
MDGs – Millennium Development Goals
MINUSMA – United Nations Multidimensional Integrated Stabilization
    Mission in Mali
MONUSCO – United Nations Organization Stabilization Mission in the
    Democratic Republic of the Congo
MSS – Mother's Service Society
MUNJ – Movement for National Unity and Justice
NAPA – National Adaptation Plan of Action (for climate change)
NBSAP – National Biodiversity Strategy and Action Plan
NGO – Non-Government Organization
NUPA – Norwegian Institute of International Affairs
ODA – Official Development Assistance
OECD – Organisation for Economic Cooperation and Development
OSCE – Organization for Security and Co-operation in Europe
PAIGC – African Party for the Independence of Guinea and Cape Verde
    (Partido Africano da Independência da Guiné e Cabo Verde)
PCCs – police-contributing countries (to UN Peace Operations)
PDI – Indonesian Democratic Party of Struggle (*Partai Demokrasi
    Indonesia*)
PNTL – National Police of Timor-Leste (*Polícia Nacional de Timor-Leste*)
POC – Protection of Civilians
POLRI – Indonesian National Police
PPT – People's Party of Timor
PRD – People's Democratic Party (of Indonesia) (*Partai Rakyat
    Demokratik*)
SCR – Security Council resolution
SG – [United Nations] Secretary-General
SLM – Sustainable Land Management
SLORC – Burma's State Law and Order Restoration Council, replaced in
    1997 by the SPCD

SPCD – Burma's State Peace and Development Council (formerly SLORC, the State Law and Order Restoration Council)

SPM – special political mission

SRSGs – Special and Personal Representatives and Envoys of the Secretary-General

STAE – State Agency for the Administration of the Elections

TCC – troop-contributing country (to UN peace operations)

UN – United Nations

UNCBD – United Nations Convention on Biological Diversity

UNCCD – United Nations Convention to Combat Desertification

UNCLOS – United Nations Convention on the Law of the Sea

UNDERTIM – National Unity of Timorese Resistance (União Nacional Democrática de Resistência Timorense)

UNDP – United Nations Development Program

UNFCCC – United Nations Framework Convention on Climate Change

UNHCR – United Nations High Commissioner for Refugees

UNICEF – United Nations Children's Fund

UNICEF-WWF – UNICEF and World Wide Fund for Nature (joint venture)

UNIOGBIS – UN Integrated Peacebuilding Office in Guinea-Bissau

UNMISET – UN Mission of Support for East Timor

UNMIT – United Nations Mission in Timor-Leste

UNOAU – United Nations Office to the African Union

UNOWA – United Nations Office for West Africa

UNPO – Unrepresented Nations and Peoples Organisation

UNPOL – United Nations Police Force

UNSC – United Nations Security Council

UNTAET – UN Transitional Administration in East Timor

UNTL – National University of Timor-Leste

USSR – Union of Soviet Socialist Republics

WFP – World Food Program

WHO – World Health Organization